PETER LANE

STUDIO PORCELAIN

Contemporary design and techniques

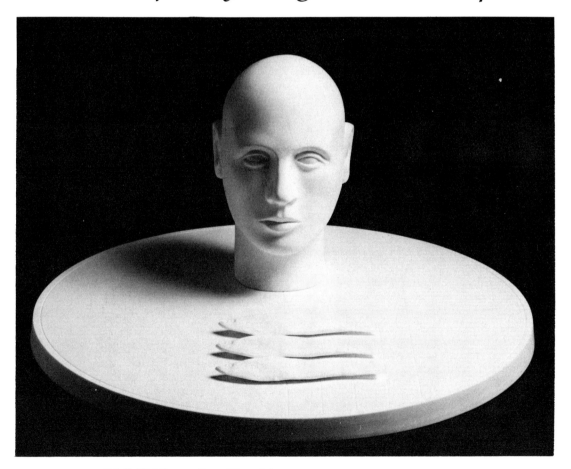

FOREWORD BY DAVID LEACH

CHILTON BOOK COMPANY · RADNOR, PENNSYLVANIA

For Jean, Jenny and Emma.

Originally published by Pitman House Limited, 39 Parker Street, London WC2B 5PB, England.

Published in Radnor, Pennsylvania, by Chilton Book Company and simultaneously in Don Mills, Ontario, Canada, by Thomas Nelson & Sons, Ltd.

Library of Congress Catalog Card No. 80-50884

ISBN 0-8019-7001-6

Text set in Palatino by Inforum Ltd, Portsmouth, England, and printed and bound in Great Britain by Fakenham Press Limited, Fakenham, Norfolk.

Previous page: *'First Transition Piece'. Slip-cast bone china, unglazed and polished. Disc, 14¾ in. (37.5) cm. Oxidised to 1240°C. By Glenys Barton, 1976.*

CONTENTS

ACKNOWLEDGEMENTS

A book of this nature is dependent upon the goodwill and cooperation of many people. In this respect I wish to express my gratitude and appreciation to all those potters who gave so freely of their time, expertise and hospitality, and to the Craftsmen Potters' Association. I am also indebted to Cathy Gosling, my editor, Fred Price, my designer, and Geoffrey Barton, my production manager, for their enthusiasm, encouragement and help at all times; to Irene Staff, one of my final year students, for throwing all the little cups and mixing up the basic glazes used for the line blend tests on page 182; Jean Monard for typing most of the manuscript; to those potters, collectors, gallery owners and individuals who may not be mentioned in the book but who have contributed in their various ways.

I would also like to thank the following photographers, organizations, museums and individuals who have kindly granted permission for their photographs to be reproduced: Peter Adams (p.52 above left, p.115 below left and below right, p.116 above); Peter Aldridge (p.23); Ashmolean Museum, Oxford (p.12, p.15); Hugo Barclay (p.164, p. 212); Val Barry (p.106); Glenys Barton (p.128); Peter Beard (p.45 above left); Ian Bennett (p.21, p.132, p.133, photographs by Michael Fear); Bill Brown (p.35 above right; p.152 below left); Jes Buusmann (p.130 above); Ian Cameron (p.24); Ceramic Review (p.30; p.40, photograph by Walter Gardiner; p.48 below right; p.58 above; p.82 below, photograph by Eileen Lewenstein; p.97 below; p.98, photograph by The Council of Industrial Design; p.121 below, photograph by Zdenek Lhoták; p.180 above); Peter Chadwick (p.129, p.153 above, p.194); Gerhard Cohn (p.216 above); the Collection of Lesley Coulson (p.215); Crafts Council (p.19 below; p.22, photograph by Richard Davies); Crafts Magazine (p.57, photograph by David Cripps); Dresden Museum (p.17, photograph loaned by Hamlyn Books); Elsam, Mann & Cooper Ltd. (p.58 below); Walter Gardiner (p.179 right); Bernard P. Göbbels (p.101 above); William Hall (p.33 below); Roelf Kauffmann (p.196 above); Mary Keepax (p.41); Gert-Jan Koster (p.205 left); Dr. Paul Köster (p.38 below, p.137, p.216 below); Jean Lane (p.70, p.75, p.140). Eileen Lewenstein (p.68); Eric Long (p.61 above); Denis Moore (p.28 left, p.42, p.83, p.89 below, p.114 below, p.151, p.158 below, p.167 above, p.199, p.206, p.207 above, p.208); Nicholas Gossip Ltd. (p.46); Julian Nieman (p.63 below); Hilding Ohlson (p.198 left, p.204); Percival David Foundation (p.13); Ian Pirie (p.35 above left, p.150 above, p.163 below); Thomas Plowman (p.203 above); Sally Bowen Prange (p.36 below, p.150 left); Quay Gallery, San Francisco (p.131); Elsa Rady (p.38 above, p71, p.179 left, p186); Gareth Redstone (p.28 right, p.31, p.51 above, p.88, p.89 above, p.96 below, p.122 below, p.142 below, p.144 above, p.147 above and below, p.155, p.156, p.159 above, p.195 above, p.211); Jacek Samotus (p.66 below); Jochen Schade, Frankfurt (p.33 above, p.44 above and below, p.76 above and below, p.80 below, p.82 above left, p.111 above, p.118, p.149 below left and below right, p.170 above and below, p.183 left and right); Schoppelin Studio, San Francisco (p.37); David Scott (p.116 below); Geoffrey Swindell (p.35 below, p.78, p.100 above and below, p.108 below, p.122 above right); M.D. Trace (p.138); Bill Thomas (p.119 below and above right); Thomas-Photos (p.107, p.125 above left); Victoria and Albert Museum (p.10, p.14 left, p.16 left and right, p.18, p.19 above left and above right, p.20); Josiah Wedgwood and Sons (title page); Cor van Weele (p.201 above); Derek Witty (p.114 above); Dick Wolters (p.181); George Woodman (p.39 below right and p.152); Ian Yeomans (p.163 above).

POTTERS FEATURED

UK

Maggie Andrews
Oldrich Asenbryl
Paul Astbury
Gordon Baldwin
Ruth and Alan
  Barratt-Danes
Val Barry
Glenys Barton
Peter Beard
Audrey Blackman
Bill Brown
Deirdre Burnett
Michael Casson
Sheila Casson
Joanna Constantinidis
Gordon Cooke
Delan Cookson
Emmanuel Cooper
Derek Davis
Virginia Doloughan
Geoffrey Eastop
David Eeles
Derek Emms
Dorothy Feibelman
Tina Forrester
Sheila Fournier
William Hall
Jane Hamlyn
Joan Hepworth
Nicholas Homoky
Agnete Hoy
Glyn Hugo
Anne James
Mary Keepax

Peter Lane
David Leach
Eileen Lewenstein
Victor Margrie
William Mehornay
Eileen Nisbet
Jane Osborne-Smith
Colin Pearson
Ian Pirie
Thomas Plowman
Jacqueline Poncelet
Mary Rich
Christine-Ann Richards
Lucie Rie
Bob Rogers
Mary Rogers
Ray Silverman
Peter Simpson
Irene Sims
Gillian Still
Geoffrey Swindell
Marianne de Trey
Alan Whittaker
Mary White
David Winkley
Nigel Wood
Anndelphine Wornell-Brown
Gary Wornell-Brown
Rosemary Wren
Peter Wright
Caroline Whyman
Andrew and Joanna Young

AUSTRIA

Gerda Spurey
Kurt Spurey

BELGIUM

Antoine de Vinck

CANADA

Randy Anderson
Keith Campbell
Diane Creber
Robin Hopper
Sylva Leser
Ann Mortimer

CZECHOSLOVAKIA

Sarka Radova

DENMARK

Anne Marie Trolle

FRANCE

René Ben-Lisa
Jacques Bucholtz
Pierre Capperon
Robert Deblander
Jean Girel
Nicole Giroud
Agathe Larpent-Ruffe
Michel Morichon

WEST GERMANY

Christa Gebhardt
Johannes Gebhardt
Beate Kuhn
Karl Scheid
Ursula Scheid
Margarete Schott

Bernhard Vogler
Gerald Weigel
Gotlind Weigel

HOLLAND

Iet Cool-Schoorl
Beate Nieuwenburg
Johan Van Loon
Hein Severijns
Marianna Franken
Petra van Heesbeen

POLAND

Anna Zamorska

SWEDEN

Stig Lindberg
Carl-Harry Stålhane

USA

Jan Axel
Victoria Dark
Harris Deller
Ruth Duckworth
Coille Hooven
Sylvia Hyman
David Keator
Marjorie Levy
Warren MacKenzie
Joe Molinaro
Sally Bowen Prange
Elsa Rady
Richard Shaw
Betty Woodman

FOREWORD

Porcelain (*porcellana*). Have you ever looked closely at a cowrie shell? Have you broken it and noticed the vitreous fracture, the fineness of grain and white translucency; the ingrained beautifully coloured decorative surface, glazed to hardness and perfection by an age-old process of nature, unsurpassed by man? It is little wonder that the potter, mastering techniques over the centuries, has said to himself time and again, 'If only I could achieve something of the qualities of that cowrie shell in the fire of my kiln!'

This thought has always been a spur to potters and few have failed to acknowledge the attractions of porcelain. Peter Lane and I are among a growing number who are addicted to the qualities of porcelain. Having known each other for some years, the writing of this book on studio porcelain has thrown us together in discussion on many technical and aesthetic points.

STUDIO PORCELAIN is the first comprehensive book on modern porcelain and comes at a very timely moment in the development of porcelain by the studio potter. It could hardly have been written earlier because it is only in recent years that the field has 'ripened unto harvest' and this has now become evident all over the world, as you will see from the wide variety of examples illustrated in the pages that follow.

Those potters who choose the medium of porcelain do so because their very natures dictate it. They lean towards a slowly and meticulously achieved perfection, in contrast to potters whose natures demand robustness, vigour and immediacy. In my opinion it is not surprising that in the pursuit of exquisite delicacy women are among the leaders. I am glad to see that the author has given prominence in this book to such potters as Lucie Rie, Mary Rogers, Jacqueline Poncelet, Karl and Ursula Scheid, Johannes and Christa Gebhardt, the excellence of whose work has brought them all to a point of universal recognition.

Potters working in porcelain can be accused of over-precision at the expense of spontaneity. The road is hedged about by technical difficulties demanding patience and respect for the imposed limitations of the material and there is little leeway for the spontaneous approach. If a degree of translucency is to be achieved, the wall thickness of any porcelain object or vessel must be made as thin as possible. Porcelain is difficult to dry and a long acquaintance is needed before the potter is confident of how it will behave in the kiln without distortion at temperatures around 1300°C.

In making this selection of porcelain potters, Peter Lane has exercised a catholic choice, not so much of his personal likes and dislikes, but of the range of work that exists today in England, Europe, America and Canada. He employs an unerring sensitivity to the qualities he sees in each potter's work and is refreshingly explicit about inspirational sources, and the mental and technical processes by which they materialize into final form. Yet the technical back-up is very informative without being intrusive.

Some 117 potters are represented in this book and much of their work is beautifully illustrated by more than 300 good colour and black-and-white photographs of pots and processes.

I am one of many who will be deeply grateful to Peter Lane in what he has given us here in this carefully compiled book, which has succeeded in revealing what porcelain potters working by hand methods are doing in the world today. I am sure it will have a broad appeal to students, teachers, potters and collectors alike.

David Leach, 1980

INTRODUCTION

The last thirty years or so has witnessed a vigorous growth of interest in the crafts generally and ceramics in particular. For many people, working with clay has become a kind of therapy, a safety valve, a way to rediscover some of the basic qualities of life otherwise submerged in the dehumanised, technological scramble of a machine-dominated age. Part-time pottery classes are oversubscribed. Many seek apprenticeship in pottery workshops with a view to setting up on their own in due course, while a growing number a craftsmen support themselves entirely by the sale of their work.

We can hardly claim all this to be a modern phenomenon because its origins can clearly be traced to the middle of the last century, to the works and teaching of John Ruskin and William Morris, and the growth of the Arts and Crafts movement. Today's craft revival has developed out of the basic desire to find ourselves, and through our natural creative urge to express feelings and responses to the world around us. Never before have we been so conscious of our environment, or so concerned with the way in which we live and use (or abuse) our natural resources.

The great social changes of the twentieth century have been reflected in the visual arts, and the field of ceramics is one in which a considerable liberation has taken place. Today, the swift dissemination of ideas from countless sources, through books, magazines, newspapers, films, television, craft societies and commercial enterprises, encourages us to try things for ourselves.

Yet we must beware of superficiality for, as Bernard Leach wrote, "only the artist or craftsman of unusual perception and strength of character stands a chance of selecting what is best from the welter of ideas which rolls in on him today".[1]*

*The superior figures refer to the Notes on page 221 at the end of the book.

How have today's craftsmen come to terms with their ideas and materials? This book attempts to assess something of the current situation and takes account of the motivations, methods and techniques of some leading studio potters working almost exclusively in porcelain. The work is considered in relation to those delightful qualities of translucency, purity, delicacy, strength and tactile appeal which have made fine porcelain ceramics so highly prized by emperors, princes and commoners alike for hundreds of years.

In practical terms the coarser clays used in earthenware and stoneware have long proved reliable and suitable for most purposes, and appropriate also for domestic ware as an alternative to the factory-made product. Much of the success enjoyed by studio pottery today is due to acknowledgement of the humanistic element lacking in its mass-reproduced counterpart. These clays have always been relatively easy to find and prepare, but if one does not have the time or the inclination to dig one's own claypit then materials can be obtained, neatly packaged, from specialist firms together with comprehensive advice on their use.

Porcelain, however, has never been so straightforward, and until fairly recently only a small number of studio potters attempted to use it seriously. Few reliable commercially-prepared bodies were available for studio use. Much experiment and testing with combinations of raw materials was therefore necessary for anyone wishing to explore its potential. Although offering an interesting challenge, this was time-consuming and uneconomic. The ever-increasing demand for all kinds of ceramic materials over the last twenty years or so eventually persuaded commercial suppliers to include a plastic porcelain body in their sales catalogue. Many of those potters who felt the need to make finer and more delicate forms turned to porcelain, secure in the knowledge that regular supplies of sound, and reasonably consistent, prepared material were available.

Each porcelain body, like all other clays, has its own characteristics, and it is wise to explore several in order to find the one which best suits the purpose and method of working. It is essential to become familiar with every aspect of the making process and to respect the very nature of this most demanding of ceramic mediums. William Morris once wrote: "Never forget the material you are working with, and try to use it for doing what it can do best: if you feel yourself hampered by the material in which you are working, instead of being helped by it, you have so far not learned your business. . . . The special limitations of the material should be a pleasure to you, not a hindrance . . . it is the pleasure of understanding the capabilities of the special material, and using them for suggesting (not imitating) natural beauty and incident, that gives the 'raison d'être' for decorative art".[2]

It is difficult to stand far enough apart from the events and works of one's own time in order to make anything more, perhaps, than a somewhat emotional or subjective appraisal of contemporary work. How much of that which now seems fresh and exciting will stand the test of time?

Bernard Leach reminds us that "there are two parts to each of us: the surface man who is concerned with pose and position, who thinks what he has been taught to think; and the real man who responds to nature and seeks life in his work". He talks of sincerity, of being 'true to oneself' and urges us to search for that quality of simplicity possessed by great works of art.[3]

Of course, making a piece in porcelain in no way guarantees that it will inherit any kind of aesthetic presence. Indeed, the recognition of excellence depends entirely upon personal response and sensitivity. It must, inevitably, be subjective. We learn to 'know' through our senses, particularly those of sight and touch, and that 'inner feeling' of composite experience. We change from day to day. We are affected by a multitude of external factors, by the influences of fashion and the opinions of others.

But who can fail to respond to porcelain, this most exalted of mediums? It has been described as 'Hell to make and Heaven to hold'. The difficulties are somewhat over-emphasised in this analogy because most potters find the material enjoyable and seductive to handle. Certainly, most people will agree that they experience considerable pleasure in holding a 'perfect' piece of porcelain. I am inclined, therefore, towards a more rational view of the problems (both real and imagined) generally associated with the making of porcelain. There can be no doubt that the very nature of the material itself provides the studio potter with opportunities for expression that no other can offer. In return it demands a special kind of respect, patience and understanding at all stages of manufacture.

In researching this book I have visited mainly British and German potters, since I am familiar with their work. In addition, I have included the work of as many other porcelain potters as I could, especially those working in the USA, Canada and the rest of Europe. There are, however, fine porcelain potters throughout the world whose work has not been featured due to shortage of space, and this I regret. My hope is that this book will help to stimulate a greater interest and awareness in modern studio porcelain.

I have deliberately covered a fairly broad spectrum of work and examined a wide variety of approaches and techniques. In this I have tried to be as objective as possible and hope to have provided an indication of the marvellous diversity of ideas to be found in contemporary studio porcelain. On page 5 there is a list of all craftsmen featured in the book and for ease of reference potters' names appear in bold type throughout the text.

The body and glaze recipes in this book have been contributed by the individual potters who use them. They are included in good faith but neither myself nor the publishers can be held responsible for their performance. I have not had an opportunity to test them all and recommend that sample trials should be carried out before any large scale batches are made up.

In examining the personal working methods of potters who are experienced in the field of porcelain, I have covered the main formative stages from the preparation of porcelain bodies through to the final firing. Information is given on most aspects of porcelain making for those who wish to undertake their own practical work in the medium. At the same time the descriptions are not overburdened with technical matter more appropriately obtained elsewhere. Much of the basic chemistry and technology is common also to stoneware, about which a great deal has now been written.

By concentrating more upon the response, attitude and personal approach of the individual potter I hope to stimulate the senses of the reader and deepen his or her appreciation of the fascinating world of porcelain.

Opposite: 'Porcelain, Stoneware and Wood'. Height 15 in. (38.1 cm), width 10 in. (25.4 cm). Reduction fired to Orton cone 10. By Sylvia Hyman (USA).

Peter Lane   *Norwich, 1979*

ONE
HISTORICAL BACKGROUND

It is not difficult to imagine the enormous impact created by the introduction of porcelain to Europe in the sixteenth century when much of the pottery in general use was coarse and often crudely functional. The rich favoured vessels of silver, gold and pewter, while common folk had nothing better than wooden platters, drinking horns, leather jugs and rough earthenwares. It is hardly surprising that porcelain, this clear, smooth substance formed into objects of refinement and elegance, came to be admired almost to the point of worship. How could such exquisite things be made merely of earth? They were extremely hard, often translucent, and of a purity so suggestive of mystical powers it was widely believed that some porcelains would shatter or change colour in contact with poison.

Not until 1295, when the Venetian merchant-traveller Marco Polo returned from China with stories of the great wealth and invention he had found at the court of Kublai Khan, did Europe begin to be more aware of an Oriental ceramic tradition far in advance of anything hitherto seen in the West. But, although intermittent trading contacts had been established as far back as Greek and Roman times, most of Europe was to remain in comparative ignorance of Chinese porcelain until the sixteenth century when the Portuguese East India Company began to open up the trade routes by sea.

The Portuguese had first rounded the Cape of Good Hope in 1497, yet long before this, the hazardous journey overland through Persia had been accomplished by the caravans of the Arab merchants who traded for fine silks and incomparable pottery in stoneware and porcelain. One Arab traveller, Sulieman, recorded in 851 that the Chinese were

fashioning 'drinking vessels as fine as glass' out of clay, and that the contents could be seen through the walls of these pieces. Indeed, fragments of a translucent ware from the T'ang Dynasty (A.D. 618–906), excavated on the site of a short-lived pleasure resort called Samarra some sixty miles from Baghdad, could not have been made later than A.D. 883. Despite some controversy surrounding the site 'the Chinese white ware certainly belongs to the ninth or early tenth century'.[4]

The earliest true, or 'hard-paste' porcelain, was invented and developed by the Chinese during the T'ang period. However, a hard, fine-grained, semi-porcellanous ware, often referred to as proto-porcelain, was being produced several centuries before this, during the later Han Dynasty (A.D. 25–220) and this was gradually refined over many years into true porcelain.

The material the early Chinese used for making porcelain was composed of kaolin (China clay), an extremely pure aluminium silicate, and 'petuntse', a feldspathic mineral similar in some ways to Cornish stone. Recent research suggests that the decomposition of potash feldspar deposits in China led to the formation of a mixture of ultra-fine potash mica and quartz which contributed to the considerable plasticity of Chinese porcelain bodies.[5] Petuntse was a material which evaded Western potters for centuries and its eventual substitute, feldspar and quartz, lacked this natural plasticity. Many authorities give the proportions of kaolin and petuntse used in Chinese porcelain as being equal. But this seems open to doubt. Nigel Wood who has made a thorough investigation into the technological aspects of Chinese ceramics states that 'Chinese porcelain is made from at least three parts of petuntse to two of kaolin'.

Père d'Entrecolles, who lived in China from 1698 until his death in 1741, wrote in one of his famous letters in 1712 describing the manufacture of Chinese

Opposite: *Covered vase, porcelain with celadon glaze, height 9⁷/₈ in. (25 cm). Lung-Ch'üan ware, Chinese Sung Dynasty, 12—13th century.*

porcelain that: "For fine porcelains the same quantity of kaolin as of petuntse is taken: for the medium quality four parts of kaolin are used to six of petuntse. The smallest part that can be taken is one part of kaolin to three of petuntse."[6]

The Chinese potters, constantly seeking to improve the whiteness of their pottery bodies, had discovered a white refractory clay, kaolin, named after the hills near Ching-tê-Chên, the great pottery town, where it was found. In order to lower the temperature at which it would fuse and vitrify another material was required to mix with it. Petuntse (pai-tun-tz'ǔ = little white bricks) suited this purpose admirably.

The Chinese term for porcelain is 'tz'ǔ', meaning a substance which emits a ringing note when lightly struck, hardness and resonance being to the Chinese of prime significance. Marco Polo is thought to have introduced the term 'pourcelaine' by comparing the ware with the smooth, glossy sea-shells of the genus 'porcellana', a univalve shaped rather like a pig's back. Although there seems to have been no direct concern at that time in emphasising translucency, the subsequent mass importation of Ming Dynasty porcelain (1368–1644), possessing both translucency and whiteness, ensured that these twin qualities came to be highly regarded in the West.

The first wares generally recognised as porcelain appear to have been made in the southern Chinese province of Kiangsi. Supplies of the essential China stone or petuntse were abundantly available in the region and there seems little doubt that porcelain originated there during the T'ang period. However, the exact location, like the precise body and glaze composition, remains open to question.

Quite noticeable differences occur between porcelain made from materials extracted from one source and others taken from elsewhere, although fundamentally they may be of the same composition. This is due to variable impurities often present in unknown amounts. It is difficult therefore to reproduce exactly the character of these old porcelains, (but it is an area of practical study currently being pursued by **Nigel Wood** in England).

Although the potters of the northern provinces were more adventurous and expressive in their use of material, geographic, geological and economic factors were such that manufacture became concentrated in the south. Nevertheless, continued wealthy patronage ensured that wares of the highest quality still came from the northern kilns. The ivory white Ting wares in particular are notable for their carved and incised decoration. One innovation in the early part of the twelfth century was the use of richly-ornamental moulds made from a compact stoneware clay. Wads or slabs of clay were beaten over these carved hump moulds so that identical patterns could be produced on the inner faces of bowls and dishes. This method also demanded less skill than throwing and carving directly, and it helped to speed production.

Ting ware enjoyed court patronage and many delicate and beautiful pieces were made. They were usually thinly potted and were often fired upside-down on their rims in an attempt to prevent warping. This meant that the rims had to be left unglazed to avoid the piece sticking to the kiln shelf and a band of metal was added later to hide the rim. Metal was sometimes also used on pieces which were fully glazed.

Quite early on in the T'ang period there is a literary reference to 'false jade', describing what are known as celadon wares, so called because a particular type of glaze, which resembles jade in colour, was used to cover high-fired stoneware and porcellanous bodies.

Stoneware mould with decoration carved intaglio, diameter 8⅝ in. (22 cm). Dated on the back to 1184.

Opposite: *Te-hua figure of seated Kuan-Yin (Goddess of Mercy) in blanc-de-chine porcelain, height 8⅛ in. (20.6 cm). Chinese, Ming Ware, 13th—16th century.*

Bottle in porcellanous stoneware with the decoration incised under a celadon glaze, height 9½ in. (24.1 cm). Chinese, 12—13th century.

Above right: Tall vase with crackle glaze by Agnete Hoy, 1950. Thrown and turned in one piece from Bullers' insulator porcelain body, height 18 in. (45.6 cm). No additions were made to produce the celadon colour which comes from faint traces of iron present in the body itself during reduction firing.

Similar glazes remain popular among studio potters today. There is considerable uncertainty over the term, 'celadon', the most commonly held belief being that it is derived from the name of a character wearing a grey-green costume in a French play 'L'Astrée', written by Honoré d'Urfe in the seventeenth century at a time when quantities of Chinese celadons were arriving in Europe. Another widely held view, strongly supported by George Savage in his book *Porcelain through the Ages*,[7] and others, is that the name is probably a corruption of Saladin, Sultan of Egypt, who sent forty pieces of this ware to Nur-ed-din,

Sultan of Damascus, in 1171. G.St.G.M. Gompertz gives a third alternative, quoted from the Thai Celadan Company's brochure, which suggests that the Sanskrit words meaning 'stone' and 'the act of wearing', together making a composite word translated as 'sheathed in stone', may be the proper root.

Celadons vary in colour from bluish-green through grey-green to olive and dove-grey. The Chinese use the term 'Ch'ing tz'ŭ', meaning green or blue porcelain, to describe all the various shades for, as Gompertz writes in *Celadon Wares*, 'there is wisdom in the Oriental view that it is a mistake to attempt precise differentiation of a range of tones which, experience tells us, are not always seen in the same way by different people'.[8] The soft colour, luminosity and texture of Chinese celadons comes from countless undissolved particles and tiny bubbles held in suspension, frozen, as it were, within the glaze. The scattering of light so caused produces a jade-like appearance and, since the Chinese revered jade as the most precious of all materials, the 'false-jade' was

Large dish with flattened rim and underglaze blue decoration of Chi'i-lin (mythical beast) in landscape, 18 in. (45.6 cm) diameter. Chinese, mid-14th century.

itself held in high esteem. Colour variations arise from differing amounts of iron in the glaze and from the reduction atmosphere in the kiln during firing.

The Chinese closely guarded the secrets of their high-fired wares and although outstanding work was also produced in Korea and Siam it was not until the tenth century that these countries developed porcelains, and not until the beginning of the sixteenth century that Japanese potters gained knowledge of its special manufacture.

Although the influence of China can clearly be seen in the work of these other Asiatic countries, they did manage to retain their own identities. Korean potters in particular produced fresh, lively pieces executed with incredible freedom and confidence. The Japanese conquered Korea in the sixteenth century and absorbed more cultural ideas from the Koreans than they did from China. Consequently, Japanese porcelains closely followed the patterns of the Korean Yi Dynasty at first, but later the predominant inspiration was provided by the enamelled Ming Dynasty porcelains from China. At this time, during

the Edo period (1615–1868), Arita became the centre of porcelain manufacture and the Japanese equivalent of Ching-tê-Chên. The Japanese blue and white porcelains were technically similar to the Ming wares but were painted in quite a different style.

The advent of Oriental porcelains arriving in quantity at European ports in the sixteenth century heralded a major artistic revolution and stimulated the search for recipes and ingredients which was to continue for over two hundred years before success was achieved. There were, of course, many imitations, and claims and counter-claims abounded. The Dutch East India Company, founded in 1609, imported vast amounts of celadons and blue and white Chinese porcelain (Ming period). The Delft potters, using a finely-prepared earthenware clay covered with a white tin-glaze, were inspired to produce designs and

Wig-stand in tin-glazed earthenware painted in Chinese style with cobalt and manganese pigments, height 7¼ in. (18.4 cm). Delft ware, about 1675.

Above right: *Porcelain bottle and stopper, height 8⅝ in. (21.9 cm). German (Meissen) 1715–1720.*

patterns which closely resembled the Chinese styles. Brushwork in cobalt blue was painted on to their wares. Later, in trying to reproduce a glossy surface akin to porcelain, some of the pieces were given an additional coat of a clear lead glaze, called 'Kwaart', making a more satisfactory imitation. Despite their undoubted economic and artistic success, especially during the years immediately following the downfall of the Ming Dynasty and the subsequent disruption of trade with China, the Delft potters never attempted to make porcelain but offered similar designs in earthenware.

Early European experiments in making porcelain centred around various mixtures of glass and earthy materials fused together. 'Lattimo' or milk glass had been made since Roman times. The Venetians produced 'porcellana contrefatta' (counterfeit porcelain), a white glass opacified by the addition of tin oxide, while a kind of soft-paste porcelain was made in Florence under the patronage of the Medici family from sand, rock-crystal and white clay in the latter part of the sixteenth century. These glassy materials enabled the mixture or 'paste' to melt and fuse at a considerably lower temperature than was required for the true or 'hard-paste' porcelain of the Orient.

Periods of relative international stability and the resumption of the Chinese trade from about 1670 prompted a new wave of Oriental influence while the growing popularity of 'Chinoiseries' coincided with increased economic prosperity. The search for the elusive porcelain ingredients intensified, although most were concerned with alchemy rather than chemistry, and many erroneous statements were made. Some European writers even claimed that the special material was formed from a concoction of egg- and seashells that had remained buried in the ground for a hundred years before use! Nevertheless, it was eventually an alchemist who, unsuccessful in his quest for gold from base metals, achieved the important breakthrough.

J.F. Böttger is usually credited with the discovery of the secret of porcelain while he was in the service of Augustus II, Elector of Saxony, but much was owed to the initial researches of Ehrenfried von Tschirnhausen, a nobleman and scientist. The latter had spent several years experimenting with the fusion of various minerals by harnessing the heat of the sun which was concentrated by mirrors and glasses. Extremely high temperatures can be obtained in a sun furnace. About 1705 Böttger, whose alchemy had failed, joined Tschirnhausen in the search for porcelain, an experimental project sponsored by the King. They first produced a kind of porcelain from a red clay which became vitrified and retained its shape at high temperatures. It was proved to be an attractive, hard and dense material capable of being polished to make artificial gems, tiles and pottery. This was well received but the search for a suitable white material continued. Tschirnhausen died a few months before success was finally achieved. Some accounts indicate that a white clay was found at Colditz and that lime was used as a flux in the first experiments. Facts have probably become distorted into legends but a rather charming story gives credit to a German blacksmith, Johann Schnorr, for first discovering deposits of a white clay quite by chance when his horse's hooves sank deep into the dust at Aue near Schneeburg. Initially, it is said, he marketed large quantities of the white dust as a dressing for gentlemen's wigs and, in due course, some of the powder reached Böttger. Realising that he had stumbled upon the missing piece of the puzzle, he triumphantly produced his first sample of white porcelain in 1708. Augustus II, anxious to reap the economic harvest of the discovery, soon established the Royal Saxon Porcelain Manufactory at Meissen, about twelve miles from Dresden, with Böttger as manager.

Despite extreme measures being taken to keep the porcelain composition and other technical information secret, within a few years details of the manufacturing process had leaked out. Rival concerns had been set up in Vienna and Venice by 1720 and soon a chain of porcelain factories were following the Meissen formula. Meanwhile poor Böttger had been deposed as manager at Meissen and spent the rest of his life virtually a prisoner. He died on 13th March 1719 at the early age of thirty-nine.

Elsewhere in Europe the manufacture of porcelain continued to be supported by kings and princes. The French had been making a soft-paste (pâte-tendre) or

Bouquet of 480 naturalistic flowers made in soft-paste porcelain. Vincennes 1749.

artificial porcelain at St. Cloud before 1700, using a less than plastic body compounded of sand, gypsum and soda fused together, ground to powder and mixed with chalk and clay. These wares remained popular for some time after the true porcelain began to be made. But the true hard-paste (pâte-dure) was not developed in France until 1768 when the discovery of kaolin near Alençon and Limoges stimulated the French industry into rapid growth. There followed an era of rococo flamboyance. Interesting innovations were the porcelain flowers and unglazed figures first introduced at Vincennes before the factory moved to Sèvres in 1756. The 'flowers' were mounted on wire stems with metal leaves, and Madame Pompadour, the mistress of Louis XV, who exerted considerable influence at court during her patronage of this factory,

Milk jug in white porcelain with pierced decoration, imitating Chinese work, height 4⁷/₈ in. (12.3 cm). Sèvres 1874.

was said to have created a mid-winter garden for the king full of spring and summer flowers, every one made entirely of porcelain and displayed as convincingly as if they had grown there naturally. Elaborate and intricate table decorations were made in porcelain and these soon replaced the equally extravagant centre pieces previously made in sugar confectionery.

W.B. Honey in *the Art of the Potter*[9] refers to the novelty of the exciting 'new' material and the esteem in which it was held in the first half of the eighteenth century. The very nature of porcelain made it more suitable for the creation of small objects which could be "handled and toyed with" and "treasured". Porcelain was "precious in the dictionary sense of something costly, rare, . . . deserving of the most fastidious delicacy and care in workmanship. It is all, of course, in a sense trivial – made for the amusement of a leisured class. But I would say that significance in a work of art may be reached through triviality as well as through earnestness. What matters is something I

might call artistic sincerity – the passionate care of a craftsman for his material."

English potters had also been pursuing the elusive ingredients of porcelain and it was probably John Dwight at Fulham Pottery, granted a patent in 1671 to make 'transparent earthenware commonly known by the name of porcelain or China and Persian Ware', who came closest to success. But, despite his ability to obtain and control the necessary high temperatures, he was ultimately defeated by his ignorance of the essential 'petuntse'.

Potters in England were not accorded the privilege and support of royal patronage enjoyed by many continental factories even though soft-paste porcelains were being manufactured from as early as 1745. A Plymouth man, William Cookworthy, finally discovered large deposits of excellent quality China clay (kaolin) and Cornish stone (substitute for petuntse) in Cornwall and it was he who produced the first true porcelain in England in 1768, sixty years after Böttger's initial success.

Chinese kaolins had proved to be perfectly satisfactory in the natural state but the English equivalent, with its larger particle size, was highly refractory and lacked the plasticity of those traditionally used in the East. In order to make a good workable body, certain other materials had to be added to the composition. Today, small amounts of bentonite (an extremely plastic clay due to its small particle size), or ball clay (a secondary clay which is also very plastic but has a tendency to discolour the body with its iron content) help to make the 'paste' or body more workable. Extra silica in the form of flint or quartz must also be included to ensure compatibility between body and glaze. French kaolins are in the main rather more plastic than those from Cornwall, but they still fall short of the super plasticity of those found in China.

The major innovation so far as the English pottery industry was concerned was the development of a kind of hybrid porcelain by Josiah Spode towards the end of the eighteenth century. He added bone ash (calcium phosphate) made by calcining cattle bones, to the essential hard-paste ingredients, thus providing a much more manageable composition well-suited to factory production. This material became known as 'bone china' and it possessed those desirable and sought after qualities of whiteness and translucency. Bone ash acts as a powerful flux with clay and up to 50 per cent may be present in a typical bone china body. There can be problems in the kiln, however, due to the high shrinkage rate and also to the fairly limited firing range. Its manufacture was confined almost

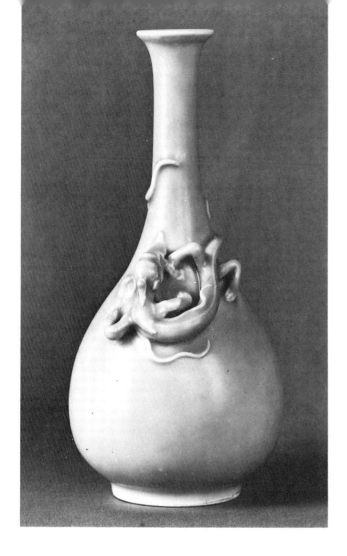

exclusively to England and up to the present day the Staffordshire potteries have supplied a world-wide market. Bone china is a difficult medium rarely handled by studio potters today, although a few, notably **Glenys Barton** and **Jacqueline Poncelet**, have worked it with imagination and originality, using industrial processes such as casting, grinding and screen printing.

The Oriental influences continued to be felt and European potters copied the shapes and decoration of Chinese wares even though these were often alien to Western art. "Nothing could illustrate more clearly the working of the potter's mind" writes Arthur Lane, "he is absorbed first and foremost with the technical mysteries of his craft, and is prepared to accept as incidentals whatever forms and decorations are proposed by his teacher, who may be at the opposite end of the world. The novelty of the new technique must wear off before he can regard it simply as a means for expressing the artistic ideas of his own society".[10]

Unfortunately more and more emphasis was placed on decoration, as technical facility increased, until forms became submerged under a mass of over-elaborate pattern and detail. The nature of the

Left: *Porcelain bottle with modelled lizard in lavender blue, height 9⅝ in. (24.4 cm). Chinese, Yung Cheng ware, 1723–35.*

Above: *White porcelain vase with pear-shaped body, height 8¾ in. (22.2 cm). Sèvres, 1875.*

Below: *Slip-cast bone china bowl with carved rim, 6 in. (15.2 cm) diameter. Oxidised to 1240°C. By Jacqueline Poncelet.*

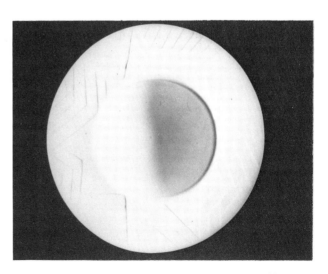

19

material encouraged European factories to display their skills with precision and exuberance through many changing fashions, reaching their greatest excesses, perhaps, during the nineteenth century. Later Chinese wares were similarly afflicted by a rash of over-decoration, partly as a result of the commitment to the export market in a period of cultural decline at home. The concentrated application of industrial techniques in China and Japan led inevitably to a decline in quality of the finished objects supplied to the Western markets.

The story of porcelain has many facets and the different styles and fashions are far too numerous to consider in detail here. Further reading of a more specialised historical nature can be profitably undertaken by anyone wishing to investigate particular developments and a list of recommended titles is given in the Bibliography on page 222.

In all the complex history of pottery, the period which has gained the deepest respect of most modern

Porcelain vase by Bernard Moore, 1903, height 7⅞ in. (20 cm). Glazed in crimson, streaked with brown and purple. Rich glaze effects created most of the interest in work of this period.

studio potters is that of the Chinese Sung Dynasty (A.D. 960–1279). Sung pottery was made with great vigour, spontaneity, sensitivity and eloquence, and, although some classes of wares were decorated, it was in the main monochromatic. The pots generally possessed a quiet, restrained dignity and beauty which has never been surpassed. Although Ming porcelain is whiter, more thinly potted, more translucent, more smoothly glazed and probably more widely known than the work of the Sung period, it rarely captures that subtlety of shape, proportion, colour and glaze which has so fascinated and influenced many twentieth century potters. "Creative art invariably expresses the spirit of its age" writes Bernard Leach in *A Potter's Book* "and ours is one which, despite its indecision, is feeling towards a human synthesis. We are being forced both individually and nationally to review the past and select from it the best. If we lay great stress upon the Sung pottery it is not because we shall be content merely to imitate it, but because it offers the highest and most universal standard with which to vitalise the technical achievements of the West".[11]

It is useful to place current developments in individual studio pottery within this vast historical framework of ceramic tradition, and the relationship to artist-potters of the late nineteenth century and early twentieth century must be acknowledged. Potters such as the four Martin brothers of Southall, famous for their lively salt-glazed stonewares and grotesquely styled animals; William de Morgan with his revival of the art of decorative, lustre ware; and the small or more adventurous commercial potteries in Britain, notably Doulton, Ruskin, Ault, Elton, Bernard Moore and Pilkington all contributed towards the momentum of the Arts and Crafts Movement which set the scene for the creative craftsmen of today. Attempts were made to capture some of the Oriental glaze effects and Bernard Moore produced decorative 'flambe' wares in porcelain (copper oxide under reducing conditions in the kiln gives brilliant reds).

But France can claim to have had artist-potters before any appeared in England. Charles Avisseau was making faïence at Tours in 1829 and Theodore Deck had a pottery studio in Paris from 1856. "French precedents were important to the Martin brothers when they set up on their own in 1877, and as late as 1894 a writer in *The Studio* magazine was recommending the practice of French artist-potters such as Delaherche and Bigot, and regretting that it was hardly known in England".[12]

'The Magazine of Art' published an article on the Martin brothers and Charles Brannam of Barnstaple in 1882 in which their ceramics were described as not

having "the transparency of porcelain nor the elaborately and costly ornamentation of Sèvres" but both sets of work was "pure and honest". Most of the work of these 'Art Potteries' was executed in earthenware or stoneware, the former offering a much wider palette for experiment in the richly-coloured, variegated glazes often used to complement wheel-thrown forms devoid of other decoration. Nevertheless, the practice continued whereby the manufacturing process remained divided so that no one individual craftsman was able to conceive, make and complete any single piece. Makers were usually quite separate from decorators. Later when Bernard Leach established his studio pottery (in which the potter dealt with the whole process from beginning to end) at St. Ives, Cornwall, on his return from Japan in 1920, the pattern became clear for others to follow. The influence of Leach through his writing and teaching at home and abroad has been enormous, and continues just as strongly today despite changing attitudes. William Staite Murray, whose approach differed from Leach, is another who must also be acknowledged for his contribution in treating pottery as an art form in its own right.

The well-known Staffordshire company of Bullers, which specialised in the manufacture of porcelain insulators for the electrical industry, had been adventurous enough to establish a small art studio in 1934. They had had no previous experience in producing either ornamental or tablewares but the advanced kiln technology necessary to make their

Porcelain bowl with pale celadon glaze, diameter 9 in (22.9 cm), by Bernard Leach, 1950. The fluted decoration is done freehand with a strap-iron tool. A similar piece is illustrated in A Potter's Work *(Jupiter Books) and Leach's caption explains that he believed the shape to be one of the best he produced in porcelain as it is 'true' to the nature of the material.*

insulators in "true oriental hard-paste porcelain . . . a rare commodity in Britain"[13] provided an unprecedented opportunity for experiment. The studio operated quite successfully, despite marketing problems, for eighteen years under the guidance initially of Gordon Forsyth (Principal of Burslem School of Art 1919–1944) and his close friend Guy Harris, the company chemist. Students of the School of Art were able to use the hard-paste material during the 1930s as a result of the Principal's association with Bullers.

In 1940 a Danish designer, **Agnete Hoy**, took charge of the studio in partnership with Guy Harris, who developed his glazes to a high level of consistency. The studio gained considerable respect during this period but was suddenly closed on 11 April 1952 and an interesting but economically disappointing experiment was over.

Individual studio potters have often been critical of what they see as a rather remote approach to pottery design for factory production. Pieces conceived on a

'Time at Yagul' by Glenys Barton, 1976. The base is cast-pressed in bone china. The figure and three upright slabs are cast in bone china, unglazed and hand polished. The slabs have been partially glazed where photolithographic ceramic transfers (clouds) have been applied. Height 6¾ in. (17.1 cm). Made in a limited edition of four during the period when the artist was resident at Wedgwood.

drawing board and modelled from lathe-turned plaster often lack the warmth of those which are worked directly in plastic clay by hand. Commercial considerations have rarely favoured a close association or even a sympathetic dialogue between the two approaches. Occasionally, independent craftsmen have been called in as consultants, and some firms, particularly in Scandinavia, retain potters, with established reputations in their own right, to work in factory studios. In 1976, at the invitation of Wedgwood, **Glenys Barton** was able to use the full resources of industry to work at Barlaston "with a completely open brief". John Mallet, Keeper of Ceramics at the Victoria and Albert Museum, wrote that "in backing Glenys Barton for a year Sir Arthur Bryan and Wedgwood took a generous and courageous gamble, and the gamble has paid off. . . . One hopes that Wedgwood, having tasted the nectar of creative patronage, will not let the matter rest at

that". Certainly, some fine pieces of bone china sculpture were produced during this period and following the exchange of ideas an innovation emerged "which combined two processes — slip-casting and hand-pressing— to achieve (the) precise dimensions and finish"[14] of some of the elements.

In 1948 Harry and May Davis, continuing the Leach tradition, made some fine celadon table wares at the Crowan Pottery which they started in Cornwall. At least ten per cent of the output was in porcelain and the German potters who worked at the Crowan Pottery in the 1950s told me that Harry Davis seemed able to breathe life into each piece, often as many as four hundred salt and pepper pots being thrown in a morning. The celadon glazes were green, and a strong blue-green. **Lucie Rie**, whose finely-thrown, well-proportioned pots and bowls are much admired, began producing a range of oxidised porcelain domestic ware as well as her distinctive individual pieces, with emphasis on the purity and simplicity of shape and form.

In contrast to the lively experiment and vigorous creative approach demonstrated in earthenware and stoneware during the 1950s and early 1960s in Britain, porcelain was still only being tentatively explored by studio potters. The preference for reduction-fired stoneware, enhanced by those extra surface qualities created in the firing of iron-bearing bodies, was

Slip-cast bone china bowls, height 8 in. (20.3 cm). Carved and pierced when dry. Fired in oxidation to 1240°C. By Jacqueline Poncelet, 1973.

evident in the dominance of mottled creams, ochres, browns and blacks in the many craft shops which appeared almost overnight, following increased public awareness and the new-found respectability of the crafts. The 1970s have witnessed a plethora of anonymous wares claiming quality under a 'hand-made' label and these far outnumber those of any real significance.

Much of the credit is due to the art schools for stimulating a more adventurous spirit in ceramic expression. Modern studio potters are freer than ever before to develop their own styles, techniques and imagery, and this freedom has led to the enormous diversity of contemporary ceramics, functional, decorative and sculptural. **Bob Rogers**, writing in *Ceramic Review*[15] explains this succinctly when he says that the modern studio potter "has to establish his own boundaries and impose his own disciplines. Every aspect of his work, from the most trivial to the most fundamental, is open to choice and is a matter of personal responsibility. Whether the decisions are hard or easy, or consciously taken or slipped into by degrees, they have to be made. Only the most extroverted, single-minded and deeply convinced, or else hopelessly blinkered, potters can keep pressing on cheerfully down one road without ever looking back. Often the most mature and apparently assured and successful potters suffer from bouts of self-questioning reappraisal, and wondering whether they have taken the right road".

The range of imagery now open to potters is limitless, encouraged by the cross-fertilisation of ideas, culture, ethics and standards of the most cosmopolitan kind. It is, therefore disappointing to find that some potters still value domestic functionalism in pottery above all else and view anything outside this definition with resentful suspicion. Opportunities abound for all who have the courage to take them and, if they remain honest to themselves and respectful of their chosen material, they will find that porcelain has provided the means of escape from the predominant earthiness of stoneware. But it demands a new freshness and vitality of expression, and a sensitively disciplined approach in the making. The past decade has seen many potters accept the challenge of porcelain in exciting and original ways, and some of these will be examined more thoroughly in the following chapters.

"Pottery reached the summit of its main technical evolution when the Chinese found out how to make porcelain. Infinite variety will be provided by fresh creative impulse, synthesis and invention, but beyond non-porosity, whiteness and translucence, there is no further stage". **Bernard Leach.**[16]

TWO

APPROACH TO DESIGN

All clays offer their own rich qualities and strengths to the artist-craftsman with sufficient skill and imagination to exploit them. Stoneware can satisfy the needs of many potters for it is a medium that invites a direct, vigorous approach, at the same time demanding a sensitivity to its particular characteristics similar to that required in the handling of porcelain bodies. But for porcelain, this sensitivity, this awareness, is of a different order, and the inherent difficulties generally associated with this clay may induce, at first, an unnecessarily inhibited and hesitant approach.

Although problems are encountered in the making of porcelain, experience and growing familiarity with its working will lead to a deeper appreciation of its special nature. Awareness and respect for the nature of porcelain can only develop through constant use of the material, and will eventually help to lessen those difficulties which, at the outset, seem poised to defeat genuine creativity.

Potters usually choose to work in porcelain in preference to other clays because they wish to make use of one, or more of those special properties that are not to be found in other materials. The value of making a piece in porcelain in such a way that it disguises its 'true' nature may be questioned. For example, if a dark, opaque glaze completely hides the whiteness of the body and denies translucency. But, generally potters do agree that glazes which may appear drab on stoneware, acquire a brilliance and depth when applied to porcelain. There are also occasions when certain forms require especially delicate modelling, where translucency and whiteness are of no significance. But if neither quality is evident then it might be claimed by some that the artefact has been deprived of much of its appeal, at least to Western sensibilities. This suggests that its purpose could, perhaps, have been achieved through other means. It must be conceded, however, that ceramic history provides us with an abundance of eloquent precedents in the use of strongly-coloured and opaque glazes in porcelain, and the clarity of form and treatment in the best of these more than vindicates the choice of body. Its dense vitrification also contributes to uniquely impeccable qualities in terms of surface, colour and glaze.

Many potters acknowledge the sheer physical pleasure they experience in handling smooth porcelain clay. Crisp, clean profiles seem natural to the material. Some people believe that while throwing rings can add character and life to a stoneware form, they are more likely to be an obtrusive element in porcelain. The controlled refinement of a form thrown with the aid of ribs, or in turning later at the leather-hard stage, can often be taken further in porcelain than would be wise, for aesthetic reasons, in stoneware. In fact, porcelain shaves away so cleanly during the process of turning that it is not difficult to become seduced by the technique, to the detriment of the form.

Most of the constructional methods employed in working other clays can be adapted, with care and certain modifications in handling and approach, to hand-building in porcelain. It should not be regarded as so 'precious' a medium that its only worthwhile application must be aimed at emulating the styles of the past, however much these may be revered. Almost any piece displayed behind glass in a well-lit museum case seems to acquire an aura of preciousness, of remoteness and untouchability. In this way it becomes utterly divorced from its original function, whether for household or ritual use, which satisfied the requirements of a particular community at a given time.

Opposite: *Group of wood structures (made by Steve Grant) containing tiny ceramic forms by Geoffrey Swindell. Overall height 8 in. (20.3 cm).*

25

Thrown and carved porcelain, 5⁷/₈ × 3 in. (12.3 × 7.6 cm). Such complex fluting takes at least one full day to complete. By Karl Scheid (West Germany), 1975.

Modern potters are also called upon to meet the needs of society but the emphasis has shifted from the utilitarian to the decorative. Pieces made by hand seem to possess a kind of spiritual advantage over machine-made items, but with such wealth of tradition and achievement behind them we might almost expect contemporary potters to be overawed and even inhibited, rather than stimulated, in their work. We still marvel at the great skill in design and in the control of materials and fire of potters in the Orient, long before the technological processes had been fully analysed and more widely understood. When so much has already been accomplished aesthetically and ceramically, what is there left to say or do that is not mere repetition or pale imitation?

The world-wide ceramic industry of today has accumulated a vast range of highly-developed technology exercising precise control over the blending of materials and their subsequent conversion into objects for a multitude of purposes and applications, from teacups to high-voltage insulators, and from dental fillings to rocketry components used in the exploration of space. But those earlier potters had no pyrometers and no pyrometric cones to warn them when the heat had completed its work in maturing clay and glaze. They learned how to read the colour in the firing chamber, to judge fuel, flame and atmosphere and patiently waited for the glazes to melt on their test rings. Such knowledge, gained through trial and error, was handed on from generation to generation with each succeeding line of craftsmen refining materials and colours even further as dictated by social or economic needs or by their own curiosity in experiment.

Fortunately, the sources of stimulus and inspiration for the potters of today are as widely varied as there are individuals. Inevitably, there are paths which cross and influences that overlap, but the personal response to experience and the handling of ideas arising therefrom is often extremely complex. The word 'design' itself implies organisation as opposed to pure accident and must take full account of materials, methods and techniques in realising those ideas. Technical facilities now at our disposal, and the general reliability of materials available today, free us to concentrate upon those design aspects more provocative of imagination and ideas. But true invention often comes from heightened sensitivity and awareness, followed by deep thought applied to a particular problem, for imagination has been so well described as a "muscle which thrives on exercise". Techniques are, after all, only the means by which we express ideas, not an end in themselves.

The nature of porcelain as a material seems to suit the perfectionist approach. Many of the potters who work with porcelain do so with an exactness which is part of their natural make-up. This is a general statement, of course, which invites exceptions, but if one examines the work illustrated in this book it will be seen that there is, in the main, a kind of synthesis of character between maker and material. This is clearer, perhaps, in the work of those for whom throwing and turning is the formative technique. There is often a brighter clarity of form in porcelain, a sharpness of contour and a feeling for precision which, if executed in stoneware, would appear tight and self-conscious. Fired in a reducing atmosphere, the impurities present in the majority of stoneware bodies will enrich the surface of a piece in a casual way, emphasising its earthy origins. But, having been evolved by man, porcelain does not so easily betray the common ancestry of its composition. It still possesses those qualities which set it apart from all other ceramics from the beginning. Fashioning porcelain *roughly* with conscious disregard for its properties and character

*Thrown and turned translucent porcelain bowl, 10 in. (25.4 cm)
diameter with carved and incised trees and hills. Three glazes
sprayed and shaded. Colours obtained from copper, cobalt and iron
oxides. Fired in an electric kiln to 1280°C. By Peter Lane, 1978.*

*Below: 'Metchosin Mists.' Porcelain slab-built dish 16 × 16 in.
(40.6 × 40.6 cm). Multiple overlaid glazes, glaze trailing and wax
resist. By Robin Hopper (Canada).*

goes beyond the desecration of tradition, and is almost
certain to be a pointless exercise. It is not a medium
which satisfies every potter, therefore, and many find
greater stimulus for expression in other clays.

Sources of Stimulus

No one can ignore a ceramic heritage bequeathed
through thousands of years and, in taking whatever is
necessary from this bank of tradition, potters learn to
stretch their materials and their expertise to the limits.
Many do, indeed, find great refreshment and discover
new directions by studying the ceramics of other times
or different cultures, but attempting merely to

Thrown porcelain bowl with fluted decoration, 6 in. (15.2 cm) diameter, fired to 1280°C. By Marianne de Trey, 1979.

Above right: Porcelain teapot, height 7 in. (17.8 cm). By William Mehornay, 1979.

reproduce pottery of earlier periods would be to deny the presence of the twentieth century. Creative thought usually develops through a process of assimilation, through the merging of feelings, images and experiences, and from things seen and heard and touched. It may be difficult to pinpoint exactly the origin of a specific idea pursued in clay, not only because the material itself will condition expression to some extent, but because the boundary between conscious and unconscious response is often blurred.

Most of us feel secure in the familiar and may well require something, perhaps an event or happening, to trigger our awareness. The varied pressures of life do not permit us to exist constantly in a 'switched-on' state. The extremes are certainly more obvious. A blazing sunset, a snowfall or a road accident will probably shake our consciousness while the subtleties around us are seldom noticed.

I remember, as a boy, cycling many miles in search of the ideal composition for a watercolour painting. I never found it because it does not exist. However, I did discover that if I made myself stop and really *look*, superficiality began to disperse revealing so much more than I had ever imagined to find in a simple subject. The subtle relationships of colour, tone, texture, line and form were waiting to be explored all around me but I had to bring them into focus by conscious effort, through concentrated looking and drawing, before I could even begin to understand anything about the subject or of my response to it.

Visual awareness need not always be directed towards a specific end. Students (and in a sense we all remain students throughout our lives) sometimes make the mistake of searching for design elements for direct translation into ceramic terms. Often the most eloquent and sensitive work grows out of an

Three porcelain vases, height 8 in. (20.3 cm). By Christine-Ann Richards, 1979.

accumulation of many things closely observed, digested and stored away in the subconscious. Whether the initial stimulus comes from studying natural design, the wider field of the visual arts or the work of other potters, these experiences are never wasted. They will re-emerge as ideas related to form, texture, pattern and colour when the time is right.

In Britain, where the influence and philosophy of **Bernard Leach** remain strong, many potters continue to look to the classical shapes and glazes of the Chinese for inspiration and example. This will be readily understood by anyone who has admired the serenity and perfection of these porcelains. **David Leach** is stimulated in particular by Korean celadons and by the Sung celadons and Ting wares of the Chinese. **Marianne de Trey** tries to translate the form, patterns and colours of natural objects into clay and glaze but feels that visiting a good museum "proves that the Chinese, Japanese and Koreans were all so much better at it" and their work is often the best possible stimulus for her.

Christine-Ann Richards and **William Mehornay** (an American working in England) are two more potters whose forms and glazes seem to owe a great deal to the classic simplicity of Chinese porcelain. It seems perfectly natural to William Mehornay that the purity of the material has led him to develop "very simple shapes and glazes." He believes that porcelain "demands a kind of perfection which involves a clearing-up and sorting-out process both in one's studio and in one's self. The clearer one becomes, the more that clarity is reflected in the work".

Translucency of Porcelain

When researching this book I was surprised to find that a comparatively small number of contemporary potters had any special regard for translucency in their porcelain, greater significance and importance being attached to the whiteness of the body for its reflective properties and as a vehicle for colour. However, translucency remains an important element for **David Leach** who feels that too many potters produce sets of textured stonewares "thick like brick". He likes to make cups and saucers, among other things, which are delicate and translucent and "suitable for special teas for people of more elegant tastes". For me also, the pleasure of handling is greatly enhanced by translucency, especially when the weight and proportions of the piece are in harmony with the form. Undoubtedly, the quality of translucency, where appropriate to the idea, increases the visual and tactile appeal in a way that transcends function.

Mary Rogers exploits this particular property to great effect in her 'poppy flower' bowls where the overlapping layers within the wall permit the passage of light to varying degrees according to thickness. She began working in porcelain in 1968, although she admits that it was to be another three years before she really "fell in love with the material." A visit to an exhibition of Scandinavian glass made her realise that, in some ways, glass seemed to have the edge over ceramics because the whole bulk and substance of the piece could be seen at once— not just the back or the front. She had previously tried to reveal inner surfaces of closed, hollow forms in stoneware by piercing and carving the walls, until her exploration of porcelain enabled her to manipulate the soft milkiness of light passing through thinly-potted pieces.

"I feel that ideally the whole pot should seem to have evolved naturally, with the decorative surface qualities as part of the structure, like the whorls of a shell. In attempting to maintain this organic inevitability and completeness, I find that to study natural objects and to make sketches and notes frequently is a necessary part of my working cycle. Often these sketches are forgotten, emerging later as form-realisations without conscious reference. Or else, in a patch of creative dullness, I sort through and reshuffle the sketches bringing together different

Hand-built porcelain bowl suggested by the translucent overlapping petals of a poppy flower, 5 in. (12.7 cm) diameter. Oxidised to 1300°C. By Mary Rogers, 1979.

ideas. I find, anyway, that there is a greater depth and interest when a form combines qualities taken from a number of sources to create a visual metaphor. But the thought and analysis happen during the looking, drawing and note-taking, and not during the making; this progresses at its own pace intuitively, directly in the clay. When analysis and questioning creep in at the forming stage I find that the work becomes hard and contrived."[17]

Translucency is exquisitely demonstrated in the work of **Irene Sims** where it complements and contributes to the delicate fragility of finely-carved and pierced sections. The basic forms are cast in porcelain or bone-china from slips prepared for industrial manufacture, so the wall thickness can be carefully monitored and controlled. The fired strength of her porcelain is considerable in relation to its thickness yet the extra quality of translucency makes it appear even more precious through the gentleness which its handling seems to demand.

Opposite: Fluted teacups and teapot, celadon glazed porcelain. By David Leach, 1977.

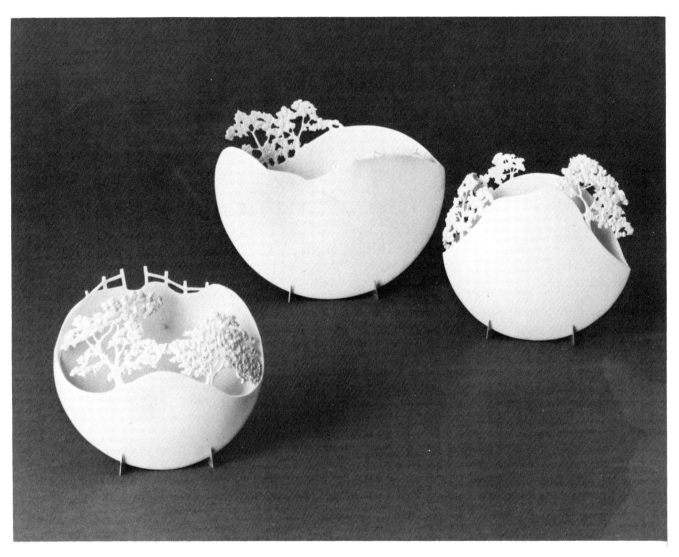

Three slip-cast, hand-carved porcelain forms 3½–4 in. (8.8–10.2 cm) diameter. Oxidised. By Irene Sims.

Her source material comes mainly from photographs of and visits to the countryside. Certain features within landscapes are particularly meaningful to her for their beauty, simplicity or power of image and these occur repeatedly in her work. For **Irene Sims**, the challenge of actually working an uncompromising material like porcelain, with so many inherent problems, provides her with the motivation to overcome the difficulties, and the desire to produce something of beauty without flaws becomes almost obsessive.

Karl Scheid, a leading West German potter, renowned for his crisply refined forms and for the attention paid to detail and finish, enjoys ornamenting some of his pieces by meticulous carving. On thinly potted open forms (as in the bowl illustrated on page 83) the depth of carving orchestrates the light passing through in a delightful way. Karl and his wife, **Ursula Scheid**, are constantly searching to capture that more elusive quality of dynamic tension which, in an indefinable way, can make a particular piece stand out among others of apparent similarity: where the contour of the form seems barely sufficient to contain its volume; "as if one puff of air into it could cause it to burst."

Translucency for **William Hall** offers not so much the facility of 'seeing through' as 'looking into'. Porcelain, he feels is more than a *surface* material for it seems to possess additional depth. His approach is mainly in a two-dimensional slab form or in very low

The different levels of carving orchestrate the light passing through this translucent thrown porcelain bowl, height 3½ in. (8.7 cm). Celadon glaze fired to 1360°C in reduction. By Karl Scheid (West Germany), 1975.

relief. Texture, colour and line interest him and it is with these elements that he investigates space, depth and layering in his ceramic paintings and drawings.

One theme running through his work over the past four or five years has been a concern with the balance of order and disorder. For example, he may adopt the grid as a symbol of order and, by building up layers of contrary images, arrive at a visual statement. Calligraphic work, Kufic script, illuminated manuscripts, musical notation and computer print-outs all fascinate him. He is conscious of communication as the tool of civilisation but beyond this he is intrigued by those messages and records whose meanings are now lost. The marks, indecipherable in themselves, take on a fresh abstract form. He finds that a more immediately available and dispensable material such as paper is an ideal vehicle for exercises working towards eventual ceramic expression and it encourages spontaneity. He believes that far too much of modern ceramics is tight and inhibited.

Rolled porcelain panel, painted and inlaid with green, red and black oxides, 8¾ × 4½ in. (22.2 × 11.4 cm). By William Hall, 1978.

33

Two pierced unglazed porcelain vases height 7 in. (17.7 cm) slip-cast, carved and sand-blasted. Oxidised to 1240°C. By Alan Whittaker.

'Pierced Terrain.' Slip-cast and sand-blasted sphere in unglazed porcelain. Oxidised to 1280°C. By Ann Mortimer (Canada), 1977.

Two potters, who use sand-blasting techniques to texture, cut into and even pierce right through porcelain forms, **Ann Mortimer** of Canada and **Alan Whittaker** in England, also value translucency. Considerable variation can be achieved by this method and translucency becomes an integral part of the whole concept. The main source of Alan Whittaker's inspiration derives from the sea and its surroundings. He is especially attracted to sand patterns left by the tide, by rock strata and by the effects of erosion.

Environmental Influences

Landscape and the forms of nature have certainly provided the major stimuli for many potters working in Britain in the 1970s and, of course, this is neither new nor unusual, but it may have been encouraged by the attention focused upon threatened environments, the need for conservation, and ecological problems of all kinds. Potters have been able to exercise their whims and fantasies, translating their responses to nature into evocative imagery, supported by an indulgent, buying public eagerly consuming countless miniature worlds fashioned from clay and glaze. Among other potters who draw inspiration from landscape we must include **Ian Pirie** whose confidently airbrushed pictorial plates are gently suggestive of trees, hills and sun, as if viewed through a soft-focus lens. **Bill Brown** brings an heraldic style to similar subject matter, making decorative use of repeated shapes of leaves and flowers on his lidded boxes and dishes. **Maggie Andrews** also formalises elements of landscape into box vases, carving the horizon line of rims, impressing leaves and inlaying colour stains and oxides for trees and foliage; while **Jane Hamlyn** employs paper resists to illustrate trees in silhouette on her salt-glazed wares. Hills and trees frequently occur as decorative elements in my own work which could be traced back to my childhood close to the Berkshire Downs.

The environmental influences in the United States, on the other hand, have often tended to be those of a more materialistic kind, particularly on the West coast. Television, advertisement hoardings, neon signs, surrealism, pop culture and all the clutter of a throwaway, plastic, pre-packaged society has provided unlimited material of considerable interest to many potters and ceramic sculptors.

Elaine Levin, organizer of an exhibition of avant-garde ceramics in California, described the

Above: *Thrown porcelain plate with landscape design 12 in. (30.4 cm) diameter. Incised and airbrushed with oxides over paper resists with pale celadon glaze. By Ian Pirie, 1979.*

Above right: *Porcelain plate with design cut through coloured slip under a celadon glaze, 12¾ in. (32.4 cm) diameter. By Bill Brown, 1979.*

Below: *Slab-built porcelain vase, 5 in. (12.7 cm) high, carved and impressed, on a landscape theme. Oxides stain the impressions for greater emphasis. By Maggie Andrews, 1979.*

work in an article in *Ceramic Review* saying that, "these works add the viewer's feelings of anxiety to the intensity of each piece . . . by making the familiar strange, by combining related objects to bring out their differences or unrelated objects to show their similarities, by deceiving the eye the artist challenges the spectator to see a slightly different perspective, to be pulled away from apathy and indifference, to feel a presence in these objects."[18]

The American ceramic sculptor, **Richard Shaw**, combines his own very personal cast work with a complex process of silk-screening in presenting "fragments of objects in an overcrowded world". A high degree of technical skill is required to produce these pieces yet some traditionalists question the use of ceramic material to achieve such images because its character is completely disguised. American potters often give verbal clues to aid the spectator by titling their work. Since, in such cases, the message is more important than the object itself, the nuances of glaze, texture, 'depth', and those subtle relationships of contour and form so revered in Europe become superfluous. In considering the work of most British

Above: 'Edge-scape Vessel'. Thrown and cut porcelain bowl, height 9½ in. (24.1 cm). 'The vessel is trimmed at the base and the clay findings are applied to the top edge while still plastic.' High zinc and rutile glaze with some barium to create crystalline matt surface. By Sally Bowen Prange (USA), 1979.

Below: Thrown and re-shaped porcelain vase. By Gotlind Weigel (West Germany). (In the collection of Dr Karl-Joseph Simons).

and German potters, for example, one notices fewer titles and pieces are usually left to stand or fall by virtue of their own existence and by those recognised ceramic qualities previously mentioned.

Ruth Duckworth now working and teaching in Chicago, USA (since 1964) can also claim to have roots in Germany and Britain. Writing about her in *Ceramic Review*, Emmanuel Cooper entitled his article. "Ruth Duckworth: A Great Original" which is how she was once described. Her fertile imagination and versatile approach to ceramics in general has influenced many potters. Few people can handle soft slabs of clay with such fluency and directness, and her pieces often seem as if they have grown organically.

There are clear organic influences in the work of **Sally Bowen Prange** (North Carolina, USA) who, like several other potters, delights in cutting, piercing or re-shaping and adding to the rims of open thrown forms. She describes these pieces variously as 'edge-scaped vessels' and 're-edged vessels'. She first

Opposite: 'Walking Figure Jar', 18½ × 10¾ × 9 in. (46.9 × 27.3 × 22.9 cm). Glazed porcelain with overglaze transfers. By Richard Shaw (USA), 1979.

Cut-edged porcelain bowl, 9 × 5½ in. (22.9 × 13.9 cm). By Elsa Rady (USA), 1979.

Hand-built oval porcelain bowl with impressed texture, 6 in. (15.2 cm) high. By Ruth Duckworth (USA), 1973.

began working with porcelain in 1968 and soon became addicted to it. Since 1973 she has worked exclusively with porcelain using two bodies fired to Orton Cone 11. She loves "porcelain for its whiteness, softness and sensuousness in throwing, and for its aristocratic heritage'. At first she felt in awe of the material and only used colour in brushwork, but now she does not hesitate to use any glazes, colours or surface treatments which she feels are right for the forms she makes. The whiteness of the body may be completely hidden but its strong reflective qualities contributes to some striking effects even with a matt black glaze.

Elsa Rady (California, USA) also cuts away the edges of bowls creating, sometimes, an almost metallic appearance. Her more conventional thrown pieces possess an equally sharp clarity of contour, and are executed with the degree of precision only possible in porcelain. The apparently functional vessels of **Betty Woodman** (Colorado, USA) are quite different

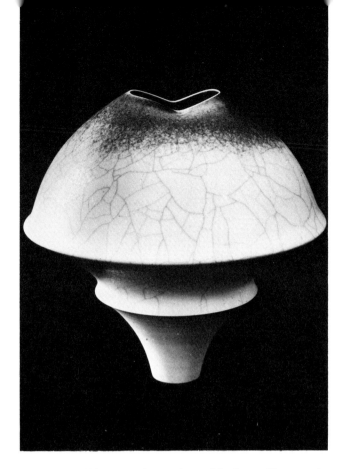

Narrow-based thrown and turned porcelain form with sprayed oxides on rim, height 4 in. (10.2 cm). Crackle glaze. By Geoffrey Swindell, 1978.

in character and scale. They retain clear evidence of their free and vigorous manufacture. She enjoys making pots "whose relation to function is metaphorical, symbolic or transformed; pottery the content of which is pots, not sculpture". She is concerned with the *idea* of function and attempts to produce pots "that make significant reference to the vernacular of pottery".

Reference has already been made to the reaction generated by an overwhelming abundance of domestic stonewares, often clichéd, heavy and subdued in colour and wit. The transition to porcelain made by many potters has therefore been a natural and relatively painless process. Here was a material remaining white or off-white when fired; which would accept colour to a predictable level through staining, or painting directly on to the body in a variety of ways; that possessed reflective properties to heighten the brilliance of colour within the glaze or applied upon it; having a strength, hardness and durability no naturally-occurring white-burning clays can match; fine-grained enough to accommodate the most detailed carving or modelling; and with the added attraction of working so thinly and delicately that it could barely resist the passage of light.

The fresh appeal of individual porcelain work which began to appear in Britain during the 1960s, and the

extra sensitivity which the making demanded, were quickly recognised by discerning collectors. Of course, the material itself was not the prime interest, but attention focused upon the objects and forms which porcelain's very nature had stimulated potters to make. The increasing involvement of British potters like **Mary Rogers**, **Deirdre Burnett**, **Colin Pearson**, **Peter Simpson**, **Geoffrey Swindell** and **Mary White**, encouraged by gallery owners like Pan Henry (Casson, London), Henry Rothschild (Primavera, Cambridge), Joan Crossley-Holland (Oxford) and Peter Dingley (Stratford) in England, and Dr. Paul Köster (Mönchengladbach) in Germany, 'gained ever-widening publicity and interest which *Ceramic Review*, *Ceramics Monthly* and other magazines continued to stimulate. More potters were soon encouraged to venture into porcelain. Meanwhile ceramic departments in Colleges, constantly

Saltglazed porcelain floor vase, height 18 in. (45.7 cm). Fired to 1200°C. By Betty Woodman (USA).

Group of porcelain pots. By Derek Davis.

searching for new opportunities for expression, found that growing numbers of students were drawn towards porcelain and bone china. Not surprisingly, the Royal College of Art in England launched several of the leading young potters now specialising in porcelain and evidence of their influence through teaching can be seen in art schools around Britain. Their work often exploits industrial processes and materials.

Any approach to design must recognise and allow for the constraints of the material if failure rates are not to reach unacceptable levels and one restriction accepted by most potters is that of size. In general terms the working of porcelain and its fired qualities seem to favour a fairly small scale. Tactile appeal is bound up to some extent with the ability to hold a piece of porcelain rather than just to touch it and

smallness in this respect is often an advantage. In the kiln small pieces make convenient 'fillers' to fit into spaces left between larger stoneware pots. Alternatively, quite small kilns can accommodate a good number of pieces with cheaper fuel costs and a quicker firing and cooling cycle. It is quite possible to make porcelain commercially with only a couple of electric kilns each having chambers offering a mere 15 inch cube of space.

Gordon Cooke, for example, finds that two kilns of similar capacity are economical to run and adequate for the small scale slabwork he does. When the need arises, kilns of this size can be fired one day and unpacked the next. This would be difficult to manage safely with a larger kiln. His work, which is described more fully on page 110 includes delicate textural treatments suggested by his study of natural objects.

From fairly tentative beginnings, and spurred on by

'Out of Chaos'. Set of five hand-modelled porcelain panels, each 12½ in. square (31.8 cm). By Mary Keepax, 1979.

the work of their contemporaries in the early 1970s, potters began handling porcelain with an adventurous confidence and fluency. The excellence and rather remote preciousness of museum collections and the high technology of industrial wares had seemed to place porcelain manufacture beyond the scope and expertise of most studio potters and, prior to the late 1960s, the market remained somewhat indifferent to porcelain wares produced by hand. Stonewares and earthenwares for domestic use had become fashionable, as they still are at the time of writing, and they exemplified the hand-made, back to nature image which forms a large part of their popular appeal.

Glyn Hugo began making porcelain in 1962 but abandoned it soon after discovering that shops and galleries were not interested. Perhaps the time was not yet right but it does raise the question of supply and demand and the emphasis given to each.

I am reminded of an occasion in 1962 when my wife wanted to buy an armless but reasonably comfortable chair for nursing our first-born daughter, Jenny. We soon discovered that few styles and even fewer colours were available in the shops. A particularly unappealing shade of cherry red seemed to predominate and upon enquiring the reason we were assured by the furniture salesman of one emporium that he sold more chairs of that colour than of all the others together. It appears logical that he *would* do since it covered about 80% of his stock! In a way he expected us to conform to the 'popular', fashionable taste. It seems to me that that kind of narrow attitude regarding stock, whatever the commercial reasons, had fostered, dictated and perpetuated a 'taste' and style merely by limiting choice. Perhaps the majority of his customers judged the basic function of an object above all other considerations.

There still seems to be little demand for purely domestic hand-made ware in porcelain. This may be due, in part, to the greater cost of production which is reflected in prices. If studio potters are to continue serving the needs of society, the one-off or individual treatment of pieces appears to be what is required of porcelain at the present time. This is not to say that

Porcelain pot, 6 in. (15.2 cm) high, with indented rim and brushed iron oxide bands. By Ray Silverman, 1979.

with a young family, without any loss of quality. The successful female porcelain potters in Britain certainly outnumber the men, most of whom prefer to alternate their individual porcelain work with a 'bread and butter' line in other clays.

Indeed, some people attribute 'feminine' characteristics to porcelain and refer to stoneware as a 'masculine' material. **Ray Silverman** subscribes to this view declaring that "stoneware is masculine. It is domineering in character when you work with it. Yet it is soft enough to wind around your little finger. Porcelain is without doubt a tactile material. You have to touch, feel and not just look at it. Porcelain is feminine, delicate and has a will of its own. It requires firmness but at the same time you must be gentle. It must never feel that you are handling it with force, needing subtlety in approach and finesse to win over, because you can rarely make good any mistakes."[19]

This analogy is too simple for me and may seem chauvinistic to some because, although this description of the character facets of porcelain holds true in essence, it can be argued that these are by no means the prerogative of females!

Improved porcelain bodies with better plasticity became available from a number of firms and this contributed towards the growing confidence with which potters were working by about 1975. Much larger pieces could be thrown on the wheel, dispersing myth, mystique and inhibitions. **David Leach** told me of the enormous pleasure it gave him to see the wide variety of approaches employed by his co-exhibitors, using the porcelain body designed by him, on show at the Casson Gallery, London in 1974.

Scale has been less of a problem to potters to whom translucency is of no concern. **David Eeles** and **David Lloyd-Jones** are two English potters well-known for their vigorous, thrown wares who treat plastic porcelain bodies with the fluency and apparent ease of control normally reserved for stoneware clays. Both potters, not concerned with translucency, make large pieces in porcelain using the whiteness and reflective quality of the body for colour and glaze decoration. On the other hand **Michael Casson**, himself a strong thrower, says that porcelain is the only clay which makes him want to make small pots.

Margarete Schott (West Germany) uses the whiteness to display an exciting diversity of coloured glazes, and the rich copper-red reduction glazes beloved by **Derek Davis** need the 'clean' background to develop their intensity and depth. The purity of the material is an essential ingredient of the sculptural panels of **Mary Keepax**, who enjoys the "silence of whiteness." Porcelain enables her to preserve

ideas may not be repeated, developed or expanded. It does seem unlikely, at the moment, that repetition porcelain tableware from studio potters will ever find and establish the kind of popularity now enjoyed by the equivalent in stoneware.

Lucie Rie, **Harry Davis**, **David Leach** and a handful of others had previously succeeded in making acceptable porcelain tableware in Britain, but it was to be the fresh, sculptural and sometimes whimsical pieces which were to catch the public eye and the interest of students and collectors.

Limited plasticity caused problems in throwing unless a fairly small scale was attempted and hand-building for a while became the norm. **Mary Rogers** found that pinch-building could be done at odd moments between preparing meals and coping

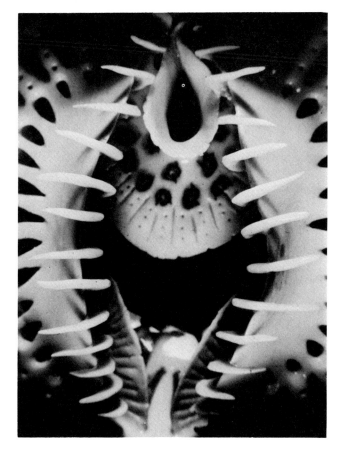

Above: *Pinched and inlaid porcelain, boxed, 3 in. (7.6 cm) diameter. By Dorothy Feibelman.*

Above right: *Detail of the porcelain.*

Right: *Two thrown cylindrical porcelain vases with celadon glazes, 6 in. (15.2 cm) high. By Michael Casson.*

extremely fine detail under matt off-white glazes. Her work is a deeply personal, philosophical statement executed with great care and precision. Sometimes thousands of individual pieces make up the final image.

Beate Kuhn in West Germany also builds her sculptural forms from many small units but the pieces or sections are all cut from thrown forms. She is particularly fond of animals and in clay she endows them with lively vitality and a generous helping of her own wit and good humour.

Peter Beard is another potter who uses multiple shapes closely grouped to create a strong visual image. The delicacy and organic quality of his porcelain 'fungi' appears fresh and growing against the heavy, unglazed, black architectural forms from which they emerge.

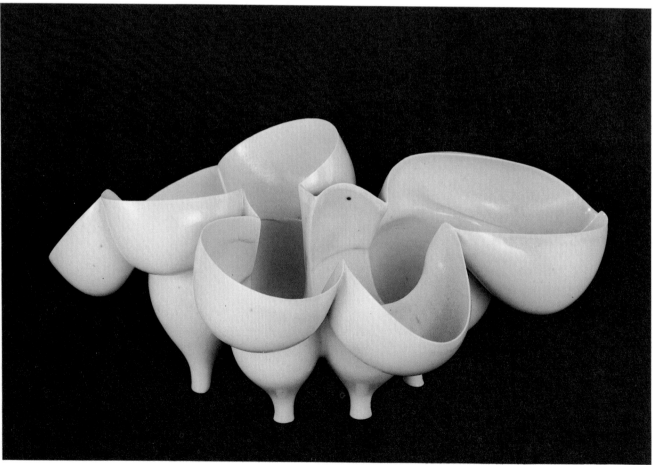

The property of 'anonymity' which allows a variety of surface treatments and colours is sought by **Peter Simpson**. For him the white, hard surface of porcelain does not intrude in the way that stoneware does. His early work was strongly influenced by natural forms. Fungoid shapes, spheres and bowls packed with paper-thin sheets, rolled or pinched, and his mesh extruded filaments sandwiched within flanged bottles, gained wide acclaim and many imitators. However, his recent work owes more to cycladic dolls, neolithic fertility figures, furniture hand-tools, ethnic objects, archaeological fragments and decomposing matter. Brancusi and Arp are also influences which he acknowledges. "I find it increasingly difficult to separate and indeed to identify areas of my influences: and also to separate those influences from working methods and techniques. One's pattern of work must in some way 'edit' one's ideas and by doing so become influential . . . Other influences were not seen; rather they have been suggested and felt — some only half remembered."[20]

Opp. above: *Double-walled porcelain pot with richly-coloured, iron-bearing glaze, height 4 in. (10 cm). Reduction fired to 1360°C. By Margarete Schott (West Germany), 1978.*

Opp. below: *Porcelain sculpture constructed from multiple thrown forms. $6\frac{1}{2} \times 11^{3}/_{8} \times 8^{5}/_{8}$ in. (16.5 cm × 29 cm × 22 cm). Reduction fired to 1360°C. By Beate Kuhn (West Germany).*

Above left: *Pyramids of slab-built stoneware with porcelain 'fungi', height 9 in. (22.9 cm). By Peter Beard.*

Above: *Split sphere porcelain form, height $4\frac{1}{2}$ in. (11.4 cm). By Peter Simpson, 1976.*

Paul Astbury finds the whiteness of porcelain necessary to give the glaze colours added brilliance, while the smooth surface retains essential detail and receives drawn line sympathetically. He experiments with broken and re-assembled images using all kinds of adhesives and even paper in the joining of fired sections. He takes "moulds ranging from construction kits, textured meat packs and hand-grips from pistols to rubber washing-up gloves. All synthetic textures are important for inclusion in my work. They are a language in themselves and the moulds become the books from which paragraphs are taken out and transplanted into the basic structure of the work."[21]

If he feels that the quality is not 'right' when a piece is taken out of the kiln, he will break and reassemble it to create "a totally new personality or rearrangement of data, or lack of it, depending on which fragments are chosen and which are discarded."

Separately-fired shapes are also assembled into powerful visual statements by **Eileen Nisbet**. To fully appreciate the beautifully related elements within the final pieces they should be viewed with strong backlighting. This reveals the scraped-down edges

45

with their translucency outlining the individual layers.

Eileen Nisbet "pushes" the clay as far as she can and understands its limitations. Ideally she would like to make very large pieces because she feels that her work is sometimes "like little toys" and not at all what she really wants. But large pieces composed of smaller units would not satisfy her because she wishes to make visual statements which demonstrate simplicity, not complexity. This may lead her towards the use of other materials in conjunction with porcelain. Although trained as a potter who can throw well, her interest is much more in painting and sculpture and she prefers to regard clay simply as a material for expressing ideas.

Exploring a Theme

Combining other materials with ceramics is not uncommon and **Dorothy Feibelman** has often made pieces which have included non-ceramic 'inlays' of tiny feathers or minute tapestries, designed to be fixed in place after the final firing. The colour and pattern of these and the porcelain agate designs are chosen to echo and complement each other in a small bowl form, which performs a purely decorative function and provides a visual and tactile adventure for its owner. She occasionally embellishes pieces in similar fashion with silver and precious stones, rather as a jeweller might. Few of her bowls do, in fact, claim any

Spinner form in porcelain, height 7 in. (17.7 cm). Nepheline syenite and barium glaze. By Peter Simpson, 1976.

domestic function and the fragility is sometimes emphasised by pierced and carved holes making a delicate tracery in parts of the form.

The ceramic sculptor **Glenys Barton** has always worked with white-firing bodies and her screen-printed, slip-cast bone-china cubes won a top award in the International Academy of Ceramics exhibition at the Victoria and Albert Museum (London) in 1972. Being a "totally urban person", city architecture made a great impression upon her, particularly the way in which the sky was "captured and defined in reflective tower blocks". Calmness and order was achieved through the use of crisp geometry in line and shape. Later, Stanley Kubrick's film *2001—A Space Odyssey* and the books of J.G. Ballard (*Terminal Beach* and *Concrete Island* in particular) combined with her love of modern dance, prompted the introduction of human figures into her geometric landscapes and the realisation of a new, evocative symbolism.

Time and space have proved a major interest for **Glenys Barton** but she "senses the dilemma of scale against the technical practicalities". She would like to "conceive a cathedral but cannot forsake the timeless, almost precious quality of pure ceramic materials. Plastics, metal and glass do not have the emotive power of high alumina bodies and porcelains. They can live at temperatures and in environments where most other media would be destroyed. They are the jewels to survive the holocaust".[22] Recently, however, she has been experimenting with a white earthenware body for slip-casting and firing to vitrification (about 1260°C). She describes this as a kind of semi-porcelain. The whiteness makes an important contribution to the form and modelling of the over life-size heads illustrated on page 129.

Although **Colin Pearson** considers himself to be primarily a stoneware potter some of his finest and most memorable pieces have been executed in porcelain. The latter presents more of a challenge to him because he finds it difficult to work with . . . "not always enjoyable in the making but giving immense satisfaction in the final result." He feels that thin glazes over porcelain bodies reveal the subtlety of form better than stoneware and that the colour, textural and surface possibilities offered are important elements for him. While working on his individual pieces he often tries to create conditions in which 'accidents' can occur. For example he usually throws porcelain slowly, using ribs, and he stops immediately the 'right' sort of form and texture has appeared. Generally, his methods of working tend to favour asymmetry which he prefers anyway because he

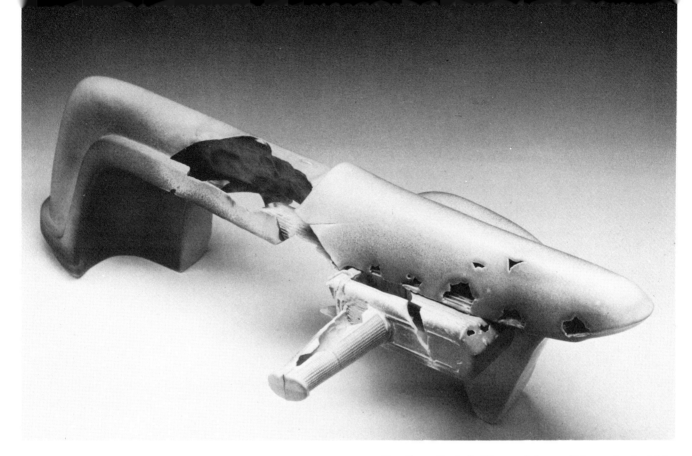

Slip-cast and assembled porcelain sculpture, length 18 in. (45.1 cm). By Paul Astbury.

seldom throws or hand-builds with precision, finding that kind of approach rather dull.

Colin Pearson's well-known winged forms demonstrate his fertile imagination through an enormous variety of 'answers' within a single theme. Their origin is not consciously due to any particular source although "he has been delighted to recognise in jade ware, with its elegant, long-necked winged vases, an historical precedent for his work".[23] Similar ideas can also be seen in Chinese porcelain bottles and vases.

A high degree of precision, attention to detail and creative thought in thematic exploration can be seen in the work of **Geoffrey Swindell**. He was born and brought up in the pottery town of Stoke-on-Trent and feels that he owes much to his background and to the English pottery tradition. The best products of this have had a greater influence upon him than those of other cultures. Inspiration for his work has come from his various collections of sea-shells and sea creatures; tin-plate toys; illustrations of science fiction landscapes, space hardware and natural forms; and moulded plastic artefacts. He can see no sense in attempting to compete with the products of industry and has never been interested in making (or using) any of the rough stoneware pots more commonly seen in craft shops. He believes that the most useful social role to be played by studio potters is in the creation of objects to stimulate the senses.

Geoffrey Swindell's work is small in scale, but his precisely-engineered and crisply-defined, well-finished pieces are rich in visual interest. Many of his forms stand on impossibly narrow bases rising upward and swelling like a flower bud about to burst. Clean, hard profiles, positive curves and sharp flanges combine to make a strong personal statement which can be traced back to elements found among his collection of toys and other objects. The size of the pieces, coupled with their comparative instability, makes them objects to be cossetted and enjoyed visually rather more than in the tactile sense. Porcelain provides him with the white ground ("rather like a painter's canvas") he requires for the range of very pure colours he likes to use in the form of on-glaze lustres.

This quality of whiteness and dense purity is equally essential for **Nick Homoky** to whom decoration is always rewarding "since porcelain enhances rather than breaks up the design as with gritty clays." He is not interested in the pot as a container but as a vehicle for exploring both visual and tactile elements. He uses very little glaze, preferring to inlay fine linear designs with black-stained porcelain slip contrasting with the body and attempting to achieve a balance between form and decoration.

He smoothes and polishes the vitrified ware with fine grades of 'wet and dry' carborundum paper. His ideas "move between the intuitive and the intellectual and a great deal through drawing. Source material comes by chance: a thing found, a mental image of a ceramic form." He feels that he is as much a

47

Above: 'Graphic Permutations 1' Slip-cast bone china cubes oxidised to 1240°C and then precision ground. Screen-printed graphics. By Glenys Barton 1970. (Now in the permanent collection of Stoke-on-Trent Museum.)

Left: Stemmed pot with combed rim, height 8 in (20.3 cm). Copper red reduction glaze. By Colin Pearson, 1979.

Below: Porcelain bowl, 6 in. (15.2 cm) diameter. Reduction fired. By Colin Pearson, 1979.

'Horizontal Flower'. Porcelain sculpture, 12 in. (30.4 cm) long, assembled from rolled slabs. Oxidised in an electric kiln to 1240°C. By Eileen Nisbet, 1979.

draughtsman as a potter since he reads the profile of a form in line and volume. Further stimulus comes from forms such as bones, shells and fossils.

The linear decoration of **Joan Hepworth** contains more easily recognised motifs derived from architectural and other sources using under-glaze crayons to draw directly on to the bisque-fired piece prior to spraying a thin, transparent glaze.

A number of potters have successfully revived neglected or forgotten techniques which in themselves provide a particular kind of impetus to their work. **Dorothy Feibelman's** beautifully controlled marqueterie or neriage pieces immediately come to mind. Her methods are explained more fully in Chapter 3 but it is a technique which originally achieved only limited commercial success (Doulton made an earthenware version between 1886 — 1906) in factory production due to the inherent difficulties encountered during manufacture.

Robin Hopper, an English potter who emigrated to Canada in 1968, uses a technique called mocha diffusion in which oxides and weak acids are dropped into coloured liquid clay or slip to create feathery and flowing decoration reminiscent of ferns or trees. This method was quite common in Europe and North America for a period around 1800 but has not appeared much since that time. He also employs the neriage technique but in rather bolder style than **Dorothy Feibelman**. Agate ware is another traditional process with layers of differently stained clay and **Robin Hopper** uses this or layered glazes to suggest the patterns and moods of landscape.

Inspiration, encouragement and support can also come from working with a sympathetic partner and the medium of ceramics has produced a number of successful husband and wife teams. **Karl and Ursula Scheid** share the same concern for purity of form and high quality craftsmanship. Since they also share a workshop they try to co-ordinate their working so that they are both throwing, turning or glazing at the same time, although remaining quite separate. They never throw more pots than can be easily turned before drying out too much. They began working in porcelain because the glaze colours seemed brighter and they also liked the way in which the thinner glaze on rims revealed the whiteness of the body.

Thrown, turned, inlaid and polished porcelain. Footed cylinder 6 × 4 in. (15.2 × 10.2 cm). Handled bowl 5½ in. (13.9 cm) wide. By Nick Homoky.

Karl Scheid is one of three West German potters who spent a year working at the Crowan Pottery in Cornwall with **Harry Davis**. The others are **Margarete Schott** and **Bernhard Vogler**. Much of Karl Scheid's philosophy, technical exactitude and concern for materials can be attributed to this experience. In talking with all three of these potters one becomes aware of their great respect and warmth of affection for **Harry Davis** (a former colleague of **Bernard Leach**). His influence remains strong more than twenty-six years later, and, although his subsequent travels have taken him around the world (setting up workshops in most difficult situations as far apart as Peru and New Zealand) these potters still try to maintain contact with him.

As elsewhere in Europe, German potters have been searching for originality and individual identity in their work. They do not enjoy the same kind of support given to potters in Britain. There is no national organisation to speak on their behalf although they do have the major Westerwald competition and

exhibition to aim for every two years. Where groups of craftsmen have formed co-operatives of one sort or another there have been communal benefits, and the 'London Group' as they have become known (following an exhibition in London at the Primavera Gallery in 1969) made up of **Karl and Ursula Scheid**, **Beate Kuhn**, **Margarete Schott** and **Gerald and Gotlind Weigel**, have gained considerably from their friendly association with each other. Similar groups have been formed in Germany from time to time, following their pattern and example, but few have survived more than two years, possibly because they have lacked the sense of common purpose, lasting friendship and deep respect for each other's work that has contributed so much to the harmony and success of the 'London Group'. This group, both individually and collectively, has managed to set and maintain the highest standards in design and craftsmanship from the very beginning and each new exhibition is eagerly awaited by collectors (one of whom has over two hundred pieces of the **Scheids'** work alone).

Gotlind and Gerald Weigel also share a workshop but Gotlind, a strong, fluent thrower with thirty years experience, produces individual wheel thrown forms (sometimes modelled further by hand-building) and makes a range of domestic tableware. Her husband,

Marqueterie porcelain bowl in blue and white, 3 in (7.6 cm) diameter. By Dorothy Feibelman, 1979.

Right: *Porcelain agate shang vase, height 6 in. (15.2 cm). By Robin Hopper (Canada).*

Gerald deals with all the necessary glazing and makes slab-built sculptural pieces in stoneware or porcelain.

Christa and Johannes Gebhardt both use similar techniques for cutting and texturing clay but maintain their own individual imagery. They share the 'London Group's' dedication to the production of high quality one-off pieces.

Johannes Gebhardt is a Professor in Ceramics at Kiel where he has taught for many years. He conducted a series of experiments on porcelain bodies in the middle 1960s but did not begin working seriously in the medium until 1973. The first pieces were exhibited in 1975 in which year he won a special award at the 'Deutsch Keramik 1975', the biennial Westerwald competition in Höhr-Grenzhausen.

His wife, Christa, trained as a graphic artist and successfully practised this profession for a number of years until "the ceramic studio began to exert its ancient fascination as an alchemists' kitchen and it drew her more and more under its spell . . . The

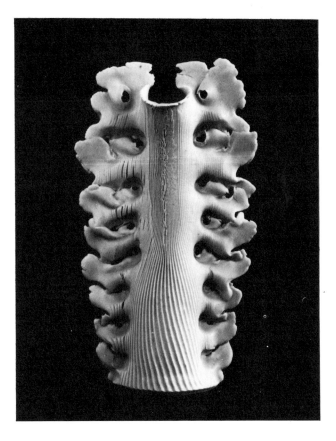

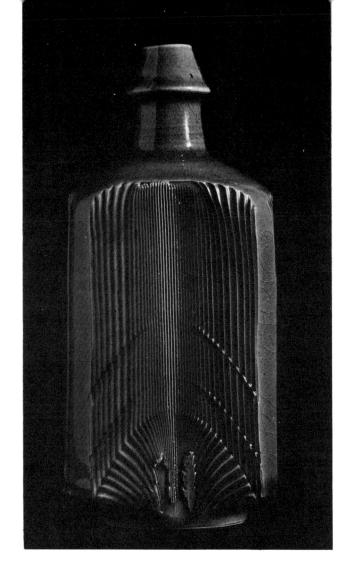

Above left: *Rolled and pinched porcelain form with celadon glaze, height 7 in. (17.7 cm). By Christa Gebhardt (West Germany), 1979.*

Above: *Rectangular porcelain bottle with relief decoration under a celadon glaze, height 7¹/₈ in. (18 cm). By Christa and Johannes Gebhardt (West Germany), 1979.*

Left: *Christa and Johannes Gebhardt working on the cut-sided porcelain bottle above.*

maintenance of one and the same principle of shape, that of imperfect symmetry, which she had used in graphic design and which she now continued with cut and double-sided porcelain reliefs, guaranteed continuity and independence of artistic conception"[24]. Both Johannes and Christa draw their inspiration from intensive studies of nature: the shapes and surfaces of plants, trees and their fruits, growth and decay, landscape formations and the effects of erosion.

Christa explains that the "slightly imperfect symmetry" which she finds in "the flight of birds; butterflies; and shapes of leaves and the human face" continues to fascinate her. "In all these examples symmetry is only superficially perfect. In reality it is

often only a delicate nuance of colour or a slight deviation in line which produces the imperfection. It is these minimal differences that I find exciting.''

Like other married couples equally engaged in ceramics yet independent in their work Johannes and Christa Gebhardt through discussion, criticism and encouragement are able to support and enrich each other.

Ruth and Alan Barratt-Danes collaborate more closely still in the modelling of extremely personal narrative works. They both ''readily acknowledge the influence of Bosch, Richard Dadd, Dürer and Blake both for inspiration and reference.'' Fungoid environments with frogs, toads, slugs, snails and snakes; lidded boxes in the tight clasp of frogs; anguished figures trapped in ceramic cushions or struggling to escape the voracious grip of armchairs present disturbing images of surrealism and fantasy. Alan makes the thrown boxes enveloped by Ruth's frogs. Their fascination for fungi shared by many

'Figure trapped in armchair'. Porcelain sculpture. This piece has been partly modelled by soaking textile fabric in porcelain slip and the additional texture has come from sprayed porcelain slip. The fabric structure or core is burnt away during firing. By Ruth and Alan Barratt-Danes.

potters of the 1970s, began one day when out with their children they discovered toadstools growing in long grass on a hill near Cardiff.

Whereas, **Michael and Sheila Casson** work independently within their shared workshop space with Sheila producing most of the porcelain.

Whether working in close liaison with another potter or quite alone, similar influences and experiences have provoked widely varying responses to the medium of porcelain in terms of the imagery produced. The problems encountered in the making are also dealt with in a variety of ways which will be more thoroughly examined in the following chapters.

THREE
WORKING WITH PORCELAIN

Porcelain Bodies

Remarkably few of the potters whom I consulted have any real interest in, or deep knowledge of, the chemistry of clays and glazes beyond the basic essentials for the successful practice of their craft. Many told me that they had no time to spare for what, for them, would be an unnecessary labour. That is not to say that no experiments are carried out, but each potter has come to know and understand his particular choice of materials so well, through trial and error, that any adjustment to recipes which may be required to suit any special purpose is done empirically, by instinct. If a body 'works' for one's purposes consistently enough why tamper with its composition'? If ready-prepared materials are available why waste time and energy on such non-creative aspects? Disinterest in the chemistry does not hold true for everyone, of course, but without doubt the emphasis is firmly placed upon the idea and the artefact.

Porcelain is basically a combination of kaolin and feldspar together with extra silica in the form of flint or quartz fired almost to the point of melting or glassification. Theoretically, the ideal composition of a hard-paste porcelain body is given as 50% kaolin, 25% feldspar and 25% quartz, normally requiring a temperature in excess of 1350°C. At this temperature needle-shaped crystals of mullite (an alumina silica compound) are formed into a 'felted mass' which strengthens the body. In practice, adjustments are made to these proportions in order to increase plasticity or to reduce the temperature at which vitrification takes place.

Kaolins alone are highly refractory because they consist of alumina and silica, both with very high melting points, and contain only tiny percentages of

Opposite: Black porcelain vase, mocha diffusions with coloured slips and oxides. Glazed internally only. Height 6½ in. (16.5 cm). By Robin Hopper (Canada).

fluxes such as sodium, potassium, calcium or iron, much larger amounts of which are present in other clays.

In Germany all the potters I visited fire their porcelain to 1360°C and in this respect remain close to their European hard-paste traditions. **Karl and Ursula Scheid** experimented with about fifteen different China clays in many mixtures until they arrived at their present body composition. They, and **Margarete Schott** use a white secondary clay with feldspar sand, quartz and between 2% — 5% of a local bentonite.

Few of the hard-paste compositions in Europe or China indicate the use of more plastic secondary or ball clays and **Daniel Rhodes** gives the following typical recipes[25]:

Germany		France	
Clay	54	Clay	44
Feldspar	20	Feldspar	30
Flint	25	Flint	25
Whiting	1	Whiting	1

In both cases whiting serves as an auxiliary flux.

One problem experienced by several potters has been the variation in quality of some of the commercially prepared bodies, and the choice available remains narrow. Most potters state a preference for one body or another but they usually temper this with some reservations. Individual requirements vary considerably and a particular property essential to one potter is of no importance to another, yet they may favour the same body and use it to good effect.

Harry Fraser of Potclays explains that "all commercial porcelain bodies are manufactured on plant used for other clays as well; consequently porcelain production tends to be 'sandwiched' between production of other bodies. This inevitably results in a little cross-pollination with whatever was

Large fluted porcelain bowl, 12 in. (30.4 cm) diameter. By Nigel Wood, 1979.

Below: *'Pocket piece with vestigial handle'. Porcelain, height 8 in. (20.3 cm). By Marjorie Levy (USA), 1977.*

in process before and this may be significant if the production run is not sufficiently large to dissipate it. Potclays are installing a special sliphouse which will be devoted exclusively to porcelain and bone china bodies. This should enable bodies to be very true to

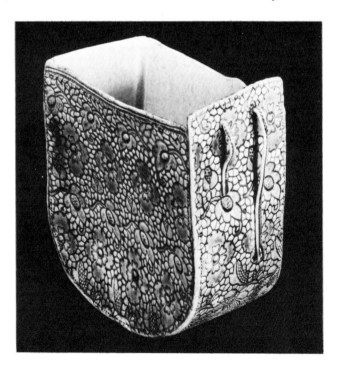

recipe and allow best possible translucency, for we find that very slight amounts of non-recipe constituents can affect translucency quite noticeably.''

Plasticity and Translucency

Almost without exception reasonable plasticity and good throwing properties are rated second only to the prime need for whiteness and purity. But plasticity is a variable commodity. Even from the same source supplies may differ in quality from batch to batch. A number of potters, therefore, prefer to purchase raw materials and to compound their own bodies in an attempt to maintain a reliable degree of consistency. Early Chinese potters prepared porcelain bodies for their children to use because 'ageing' undoubtedly improves plasticity. This process can be accelerated artificially by the addition of a small amount of vinegar during preparation.

Plasticity can also be improved by adding larger amounts of a more plastic clay but this risks losing whiteness and impedes translucency where ball clays are used, and increases the problems of drying, shrinking and cracking when a white bentonite is the plasticiser. Bentonite, despite these drawbacks, has contributed enormously to the composition of workable porcelain bodies for studio potters and it forms an important ingredient of those that have become widely used.

Bentonite is a highly plastic colloidal substance with an extremely fine grain size, and only a small percentage, (normally up to 6%) is sufficient to plasticise the kaolin, feldspar and quartz. However, increased plasticity magnifies the usual shrinkage problem and over-large amounts of bentonite can make a body unworkable. It can also impart a more thixotropic nature to the body so that seemingly stiff clay will quickly loosen up under pressure.

Bentonite bodies have been criticised for various reasons and even rejected for not conforming to the characteristics or appearance of 'true' porcelain. Richard Parkinson writing in *Ceramic Review*[26] claimed that they are no more than white porcellanous stonewares. This is a question of definition. If Chinese porcelain is taken as a guide we must bear in mind the

Opposite: *Porcelain fluted bowl with Y'Ching glaze, $6\frac{1}{4} \times 3\frac{3}{4}$ in. (15.8 × 9.5 cm). By David Leach, 1979.*

Potion bottles and boxes, height 3 in. (7.6 cm). Porcelain with matt white glaze and enamels. By Jane Osborne-Smith, 1977.

Left: *'Scrambler'. Porcelain sculpture, 10 × 11 in. (25.4 × 27.9 cm), oxidised. By Gillian Still. (In the collection of Mr and Mrs M. Bridgman).*

fact that it was fired at temperatures around or below 1300°C and not as high as the European porcelains demanded (1340°–1400°C) due to the more refractory nature of the available kaolins. Parkinson says that bentonite bodies have a "tendency to yellowness due to impurity" which "would suggest that the development of truly plastic translucent bodies . . . cannot be pursued beyond a certain point." Yet the Leach body is remarkably translucent where thinly potted. The particle size of the quartz used is also an important factor governing translucency, as is the length of the firing. Finer particles provide a greater surface area for contact with fluxes and dissolve more readily into silica glass. A fully vitrified porcelain body demands "the most intimate correlation of the various particles." **David Eeles** tries to counter some of the problems he finds in bentonite bodies by hand-building with thrown and turned forms.

The pure chemical composition of feldspar contributes to the whiteness of porcelain forms, while its high viscosity, allied to that of kaolin, is one of the contributory factors which enable them to retain their shape.

Daniel Rhodes states that for translucency to be preserved an absolute minimum of 25% feldspar is essential.

Potash feldspar is normally used but nepheline syenite can replace all or part of the feldspar, effectively lowering the maturing temperature of the body. However, it must be remembered that nepheline syenite in large amounts can also affect the ability of a body to retain shape during vitrification.

The performance of a body is affected by the different qualities of the materials used. **David Leach** believes that the ECC Standard Porcelain China Clay is marginally better (and more expensive) than Grollegg which he also recommends. Both occur in varying amounts in most of the body recipes given here.

BODY RECIPES

The following recipes are given as parts by weight but in most cases the amounts total 100 and percentage additions of colouring oxides may easily be calculated.

Randy Anderson (Canada)
(Cone 10 1300°C)

Grolleg China clay	50
Custer spar	25
Flint	25
Bentonite	4

René Ben-Lisa (France)
(1300°C)

China clay	80
Feldspar	20
Bentonite	3

Keith Campbell (Canada)
(Cone 10 1300°C)

EP kaolin	32
G20 feldspar	16
Flint (400 mesh)	20
Bell dark ball clay	8
Nepheline syenite	4

(+ $\frac{1}{2}$ gallon vinegar to 800 lbs for ageing)

Michael Casson
(Cone 9 1280°C)

ECC porcelain china clay	4	(55)
Feldspar	2	(28)
Quartz (at least 300 mesh)	1	(14)
Bentonite	3	(3–5)

Harris Deller (USA)
(1300°C)

Grolleg China clay	55
Potash feldspar	15
Flint	28
Bentonite	2

Harris Deller occasionally inlays coloured slips made by adding 3% copper carbonate to the above recipe for red; and 10–15% yellow ochre for green. Both colours are obtained in reduction.

Ruth Duckworth (USA)
(Cone 9)

Grolleg	60
FFF Feldspar	20
Flint	20
Maccalloid	2

(+ a little gum arabic for dry strength)

Johannes Gebhardt (Germany)
(Cone 9–10)

Kaolin (from Zettlitz)	15
Quartz	25
Feldspar	35
Light firing stoneware clay	25

William Gordon[27]
(All fired to 1300°C)

Feldspar	45
China clay	45
Flint	10
For slip casting	
Feldspar	20
China clay	79
Whiting	1
Casting or some throwing	
Feldspar	28
China clay	45
Quartz	27
Casting or some throwing	
China clay	20
Ball clay (white)	30
Quartz	25
Feldspar	25

Very white with reduction.
Translucent and slightly more plastic for throwing.

Robin Hopper (Canada)
(Orton cone 10)

EPK kaolin	25
Nepheline syenite	25
Bell dark ball clay	25
Flint	20
Silica sand	5
Bentonite	2

This is a very workable body – "throwing with ease to 24 in. high, or wide, but it needs to be used within two months or the nepheline syenite will deflocculate".

David Leach
(Orton cone 10 1300°C)

Grolleg ECC	52
FFF Feldspar	25
Quartz (200 mesh)	18
Special white bentonite	5

Mitchell Lyons[28]
(Cone 9)

Grolleg		32.9
EPK		27.5
Trowston	Feldspars	19.5
Buckingham		11.5
Flint		8.6

Richard Parkinson[29]
(1320–1370°C)

EEC JM China clay	51
Feldspar	18
Quartz (300 mesh)	24
EEC BB Ball Clay	7

Karl Scheid (Germany)
(Seger Cone 12)

Kaolin	34.2
Feldspar	17.4
Feldspar sand	48.4
Bentonite	2.8

Peter Simpson[29]
(Cones 8–9)

Kaolin	40
Feldspar	30
Flint	20
Bentonite	4
Kaolin	45
Nepheline syenite	30
Flint	20
Bentonite	4

Marianne de Trey
(Cone 9 1280°C)

Kaolin	48
Feldspar	28
Flint	20
Bentonite	4

David Winkley
(Cone 8–10)

Grolleg China clay	21
Feldspar	23.5
Flint	26
Hymod KC ball clay	15.5
Hyplas 71 ball clay	15.5

(+ ½ pt vinegar to 100 lbs dry weight body mixture)

"*Must be ball milled*: feldspar and flint are ground for 12–18 hours prior to mixing with clays and then ground for a further 4 hours to thoroughly mix the body. It is then dried to a plastic state and should be left as long as possible before use."

Nigel Wood
Celadon porcelain body)
(Cone 8–9)

SM ball clay	80
North Cape nepheline syenite	20
Grolleg China clay	5
Synthetic iron oxide	0.25

This body is prepared as a thick slip in the dough mixer, then de-watered on an outdoor drying trough. Fires 1240–1280°C.

Nigel Wood
Translucent porcelain body
(Cone 8–9)

Grolleg or standard porcelain clay	45
Quartz (200 mesh)	32
North Cape nepheline syenite	25
Bentonite	5

plus "plenty of vinegar in the mixing"

This body is based on Chinese porcelain, though not micaceous.

Betty Woodman (USA)
(Cone 9–10)

Grolleg ECC	110 lbs	(51.5)
Feldspar (potash or soda)	50 lbs	(23.5)
Flint	50 lbs	(23.5)
Bentonite	3	(1.5)

A number of potters suggest slight variations on the following recipe for a plastic body:

China clay	55
Feldspar	25
Quartz	15
Bentonite	3–5

Alan Whittaker omits the bentonite from Michael Casson's recipe because he wants to eliminate impurities, and extremes of plasticity are not required for his slip-cast work, so the ratio 4 : 2 : 1 gives approximately:

ECC porcelain China clay	57
Feldspar	28.6
Quartz (at least 300 mesh)	14.4

Geoffrey Eastop gives the following casting slip recipe:

China clay	90 (46.4)
Flint	30 (15.5)
Feldspar	50 (25.8)
BBV Ball clay (Watts, Blake & Bearne)	20 (10.3)
Bentonite	4 (2)

Porcelain teapot and two bowls, with copper red glaze.
Wheel-thrown, with extruded handles and legs. Height 7⅛ in.
(18 cm). Reduction fired to 1305°C. By Harris Deller (USA),
1977.

Below: Handbuilt porcelain sculpture, 4 × 9 × 4 in. (10.2 × 22.9
× 10.2 cm). By Jan Axel (USA), 1979.

Right: 'Folded Form'. Slab-built porcelain with blue slip inlaid. By
Kurt Spurey (Austria), 1978.

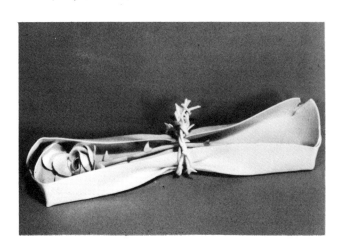

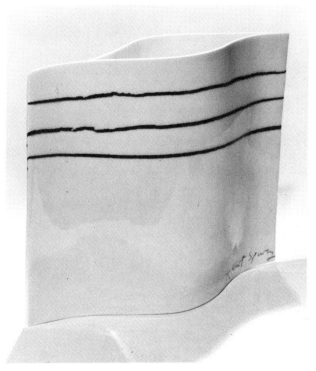

Above left: 'Pollution'. Unglazed modelled porcelain, height 9⅞ in. (25 cm). Reduction fired to 1300°C. By Pierre Capperon (France), 1979.

Above: Thrown and carved porcelain vase, height 8 in. (20.3 cm). Reduction fired to 1280°C with pink and white dolomite glaze. By Peter Lane, 1976.

Porcelain sculpture, made in Mexico, 1978. By Gerda Spurey (Austria).

The Limoges porcelain bodies are popular in France and Holland, and the David Leach body, which is now marketed in Europe, is also used by an increasing number of potters.

Iet Cool-Schoorl (Holland) throws porcelain with as little water as possible (almost dry). She started off by compounding her own body but, although this was successful, it took far too much time and energy. She used the David Leach body for a while but is now using a Limoges body which matures around 1250°C with "very satisfying results".

Porcelain wall panel, 59 × 78 in. (150 × 200 cm), fired to 1280°C. By Jacques Buchholtz (France), 1979.

Right: *Two celadon-glazed porcelain bottles with free oxide decoration, height 3½–7 in. (8.8–17.7 cm). By Tina Forrester, 1979.*

Preparing Porcelain Bodies

Porcelain bodies can be made up quite easily by hand using a minimum of equipment but mixing them mechanically in a ball mill or blunger assists in breaking down the particle size and therefore improves plasticity. Ball milling is preferable as the ingredients, especially bentonite, become more evenly dispersed. Bentonite readily absorbs water and swells into a slimy mass unless carefully mixed. It is best to add water slowly to the powdered materials, stirring until a thick slurry is formed. More water can then be added to bring it to a smooth, even consistency. China clay is usually added to the mixture later in the form of a thin creamy slip to preserve its plasticity. When thoroughly mixed

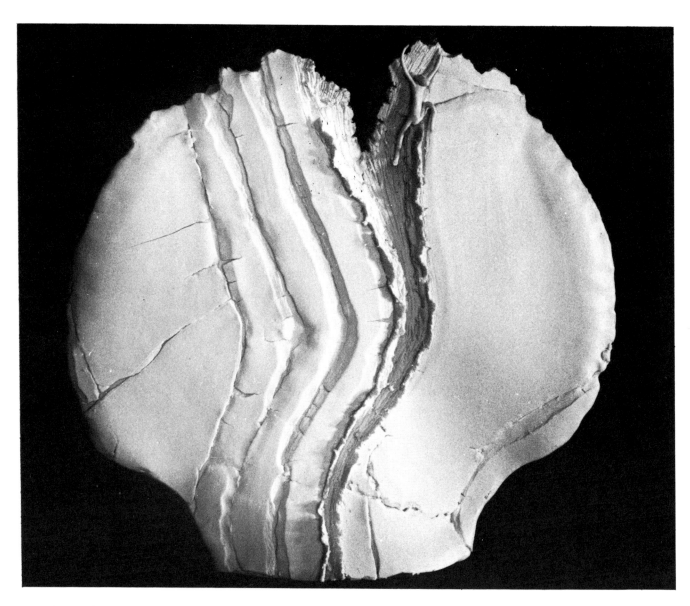

together the body should be left to soak for a few days.
Excess water is then removed and the settled material
can be put through a 100 mesh sieve and poured into
plaster containers (old moulds are ideal) lined with
canvas or nylon cloth until it has stiffened sufficiently
to handle. It is then wedged a little and stored,
wrapped in polythene, for as long as possible without
allowing it to dry out. **Michael Casson** firmly believes
in the value of ageing his porcelain body and tries not
to use it until it is at least three or four years old.
Ageing is a process in which water slowly penetrates
between the particles reducing them to smaller sizes.
The bacterial action of 'souring' also helps improve
plasticity through the creation of a colloidal gel in the

*'Rock Vase'. Unglazed modelled porcelain, height 18 in.
(45.1 cm). Reduction fired to 1300°C. By Pierre Capperon
(France), 1978.*

Opposite: *Slip-cast porcelain vases, largest 7½ in. (19 cm),
smallest 2 ⁵/₈ in. (6.6 cm), with decoration in underglaze blue.
Fired to 1420°C. By Anne Marie Trolle (Denmark).*

water and **Frank Hamer**[30] suggests that souring
should be encouraged before any attempt to de-air the
body takes place. Vinegar is often included at the
mixing stage to accelerate the souring action.

64

Thrown porcelain plate and two lidded boxes. By Christine-Ann Richards, 1979.

Left: 'The Cloud'. Part-glazed porcelain, height 39³/₈ in. (98.7 cm). Fired to 1420°C. By Anna Zamorska (Poland), 1978.

The initial cost of all prepared porcelain bodies is considerably more than similar amounts of most other clays and the risk of 'wasters' is much higher. A surprising number of potters are prepared nevertheless, to accept a wastage rate of between 25–50% which they would not tolerate in any other ceramic medium. This represents an enormous investment of time and effort and inevitably leads to the relatively greater price of the finished piece.

A high proportion of potters in Britain and Europe use the body developed by **David Leach** (P1035) and marketed by Podmore and Sons. It is popular for its translucency over a fairly wide temperature range (1240°C – 1300°C) and for its workability. Inconsistent supplies of bentonite created problems with it for a while, frustrating some who used it, but with this difficulty resolved its popularity was assured — at least until supplies of the high quality bentonite are exhausted! Further reliable properties which potters require include resistance to warping, cracking, excessive shrinkage and bloating. To a certain extent these faults are less likely to arise if meticulous care is taken at particular points during the making, drying or firing processes. Slow-drying, for example, will allow

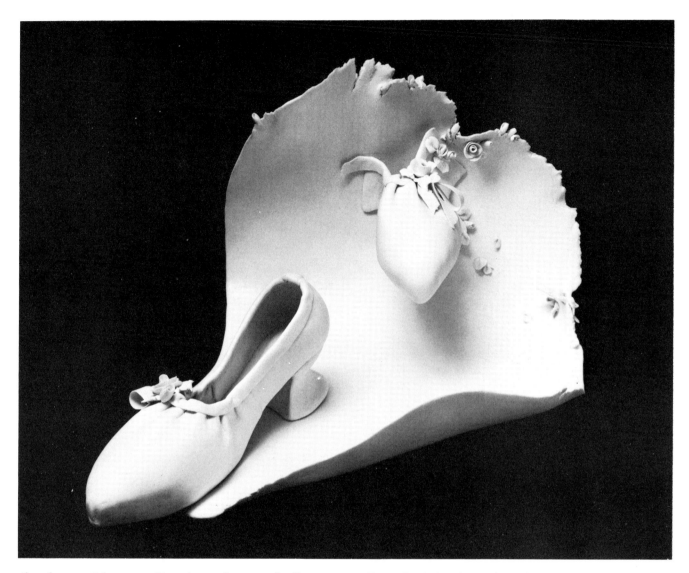

'Future Past'. Porcelain sculpture (with fibre), hand-built, 8 × 10 × 9 in. (20.3 × 25.4 × 22.9 cm). By Jan Axel (USA), 1978.

the clay particles to realign themselves gradually as the water evaporates. Porcelain, especially on thin rims and edges, dries and contracts rapidly if left exposed, causing the inevitable results of stress described above. Certainly, the invention of thin polythene sheeting has proved of immense value to potters, allowing them to dispense with the chore of covering pots with damp cloths. I have been able to store quite large thrown bowls wrapped in polythene for several weeks while away on holiday, knowing that they would be in the same leather hard condition when I returned.

Warping can be caused by any number of things. Careless handling at any stage from wet to almost dry sometimes programmes the particles to 'remember' directional pressures. Porcelain certainly seems to possess a 'memory' which must be taken into account and allowances made. **Geoffrey Swindell** greatly exaggerates the indentations which he makes in the rims of his pots knowing that the clay will remember its thrown form and return part of the way towards its previous section as it dries. Similarly, problems can develop if a pot is distorted when being cut from the wheel; uneven bats and shelves should be avoided; drying should be slow and as even as possible and the clay should be even in consistency, especially for throwing.

Throwing and Turning

Throwing

Throwing is the method of making most readily associated with pottery. The immediate, direct and fluent growth of hollow clay forms in the hands of a skilled thrower never fails to fascinate and enthral beginners and experts alike. Personality and feeling are often revealed in a way which identifies each thrower's work like a signature. The sympathetic consideration of form, the responsiveness of the clay, the techniques and sensitivity of the potter, and even the time taken over each piece in the throwing, combine to give hand-thrown pots an organic quality and a kind of personal 'presence' that no machine can reproduce or successfully imitate.

Some potters use the immediacy of the wheel to make forms which are then cut and re-shaped away from the usual circular cross-section of a thrown pot and, occasionally, there may be no evidence of the throwing process remaining in the finished piece. Some feel very strongly that to remove those pressure marks which occur naturally in the making deprives the pot of liveliness, while others regard throwing merely as a means of quickly shaping hollow sections for further manipulation towards a particular end. Occasionally, forms are more clearly assemblages of a number of thrown parts, sometimes with additions made by different techniques.

Although the principles remain the same, there are several throwing methods which may be used and potters evolve their own individual variations of these to suit themselves. Throwing is not in itself difficult but it does require a knack, rather like riding a bicycle, and has to be experienced and understood for confidence to grow to the point where technique is no longer a conscious element in the action.

Certainly with porcelain a deeper level of concentration is necessary, together with a heightened awareness, so that one feels in tune with the material; alive to its changing needs and able to smoothly adjust pressure, movement and speed.

Some potters refer to the sensual pleasure of throwing porcelain. The smooth silkiness of the material is most noticeable if one alternates a period of throwing stoneware clays with a porcelain session. Stoneware will withstand quite severe directional changes in form which would cause porcelain to collapse without warning. Although imparting a wet-strength to the clay and encouraging a more vigorous approach, the open sandy texture of the

Above: *Three porcelain vases, thrown and incised. Left to right (a) 1% copper carbonate plus 1% red iron oxide; (b) 2½% red iron oxide plus 2½% copper oxide; (c) 1½% copper carbonate. The base glaze is feldspar 4; whiting 31; flint 18; China clay 40; dolomite 7. By Eileen Lewenstein.*

Opposite: *Porcelain vase, height 5¾ in. (14.6 cm). Reduction fired to 1300°C in a wood-burning kiln. By René Ben-Lisa (France), 1979.*

Porcelain teaset. Teapot 10 in. (25.4 cm) high with silver handle. By Elsa Rady (USA), 1979.

popular stoneware bodies feels decidedly gritty after working with porcelain. For those who choose to alternate their work between stoneware and porcelain, there is the additional chore of thoroughly cleaning all working surfaces and equipment before commencing work, if the whiteness of the porcelain is not to be sullied by iron spots and blemishes which would deprive it of one of its major attractions — purity. It is wise to have a sustained period with either one or the other to avoid too much disruption in the rhythm of work.

Careful preparation will help to ensure trouble-free throwing. The clay can be taken straight from the pugmill or cut direct from the supplier's bag but many potters prefer to knead it before use. I like to knead it

Opposite: Throwing a bowl in porcelain.

spirally, as do many others, on an unvarnished wooden table. This helps to remove some of the excess moisture without de-plasticising porcelain bodies in the way that plaster does. If the body has any tendency towards thixotropy it should be kneaded shortly before throwing. Some like their porcelain to be in a slightly stiffer condition than they would wish in other bodies, because it so readily absorbs water during throwing.

Most porcelain potters feel that it is important to have a very clear idea of the form one intends to make on the wheel because tired, over-worked porcelain is too easily prone to sudden collapse. Direct, firm but gentle movements are more likely to give life and strength to the form. Undoubtedly porcelain is less tolerant of careless treatment at any stage of throwing than coarser clays. It is particularly important not to allow the hands to become too dry because, being an extremely thirsty material, it can snag and distort beyond redemption if lubrication is lost before

71

Porcelain teapot and mugs. By Diane Creber (Canada).

completing a shaping movement. It is often quite helpful to wet a small sponge and cup it in the palm of the right hand, gently squeezing it before this point is reached.

A fairly fast wheel speed is generally preferred for centring, with gradually slower speeds as the ball is opened and shaping proceeds. A smooth, positive approach is advisable throughout, for any jerkiness

will be evident in the finished piece. The centrifugal force of a spinning wheel is constantly spreading the pot outwards from the centre and the wider the rim becomes the slower the wheel should revolve. This is especially important when throwing porcelain bowls and it is wise to maintain a convex upward curve until the final moments of shaping, to safeguard against untimely collapse.

Mary White, whose work is mainly thrown, makes porcelain bowls with extremely wide-flanged rims, a form which takes the material to the very limits of its

endurance. She throws these rims as flat as possible, allowing for the further flattening that occurs in the glost firing, and experience has taught her the degree to which the thickness, the width, the weight and the angle of the flange must be related to preserve the shape. The flanges can be made surprisingly thin and they are usually translucent, although she does not consciously set out to ensure this, and she tends to regard translucency as an added bonus.

Porcelain bodies produce a good deal of slurry which may help in lubricating the fingers but it should not be allowed to build up too thickly on the pot. Slurry can obscure the form and should be removed with a throwing rib or modelling tool while the wheel is turning. Similarly, excess water must not be left too long or it will pool in the bottom and weaken the base. Where it is intended to complete a pot leaving the bottom unturned, it is necessary to apply sufficient pressure on the inside of the base to align the clay particles and prevent cracking as it dries. Running the fingers back and forth across the base as the pot rotates offers additional insurance against this problem.

The continental-type wheels used by German potters I visited do not have trays, unlike those normally produced in Britain. Without trays to contain the usual water, slurry and discarded material with which most British potters seem to surround themselves, only a meticulous approach will prevent covering the workshop in slip spray. However,

Above left and right: Porcelain bowl, 12 in. (30.4 cm) diameter. Oxidised to 1250°C. By Mary White, 1979.

Below: Lidded porcelain box, height 3½ in. (8.8 cm). Carved and incised under a celadon glaze. By Agnete Hoy.

practice allows just enough water to be used to lubricate the hands so that the absence of trays poses few problems for those who do have continental wheels. Most of these potters stand a large foam sponge against the edge of the wheelhead to collect any excess water or slip.

Ursula Scheid's workshop. Note the absence of a wheel tray.

Left: *Thrown porcelain bowl on pedestal, 5³/₈ in. (13.6 cm) diameter. By Gordon Baldwin. (In the collection of Mr and Mrs R Hyne).*

The rims of wheel-trays are often padded and can be used as a comfortable anchorage for the forearms when centring. I find this an essential part of my own throwing technique. I have an 'Alsager' electric wheel with a wide speed range which enables me to deal with every stage of throwing and turning, while its constantly variable, step-less speed control offers considerable advantages in complementing the extra sensitivity which porcelain demands.

Once the walls have been thinned under ¹/₈ in. 'collaring' or closing in becomes rather difficult unless the diameter is small. The clay particles tend to pile up on each other rather than slide across to realign themselves. This loss of plasticity results in diagonal ripples in the walls and is an indication that the clay has 'tired'.

The way in which porcelain is cut from the wheel can affect it later. A slowly revolving wheel will help to equalise the pressure of the cutting wire. Extra thin stranded wire such as 'Laystrate' slices through cleanly without creating undue stress. Some people prefer a stainless steel or nickel chrome wire, to avoid the risk of rusting.

Small bowls can be removed from the wheel by floating off with water if sufficient thickness is left in the base.

Lifting a pot clear of the wheel is another knack which has to be learned; although many potters prefer to throw on bats that can be fixed to the wheel-head in various ways, leaving the pot undisturbed until it stiffens enough to be cut free without distortion. **Emmanuel Cooper** favours a hard rubber wheel-head into which a square, bisqued tile is inserted for each thrown piece. Some use a studded wheel-head which accepts asbestos or marine-ply bats. **Christine-Ann Richards** only uses bats when throwing her flat dishes and, like so many potters, lifts all other forms directly from the wheel by hand.

Sticking a small sheet of newspaper on top of the rim prior to lifting can lessen the risk of distortion. Large, open forms like bowls are best thrown on bats, but it is possible to remove bowls if one is prepared to leave plenty of thickness in the base and lower wall to be turned away later, and this is a method I often use myself. After cutting the bowl free I sometimes insert a wooden modelling tool at the bottom edge to lift it up enough to slide my fingers underneath to transfer it on to a hardboard bat. Another method, of course, is to wet the wheel-head and use the cutting-wire to pull water under the pot to act as a lubricant. A gentle twisting pressure at the foot will then slide the pot from the wheel-head on to a watered bat or on to my spare hand.

Whichever method is used slight distortion is inevitable but its effects can be minimised if the bowl is inverted on to a flat surface as soon as the rim has stiffened enough to take the weight. This also aids drying, for if the drying is at all uneven, 'S' cracks are liable to form in the base of thrown pots. Turning undoubtedly reduces this problem but it has also proved worthwhile to place freshly thrown pots on to newspaper immediately after removal from the wheel.

Turning

When he first began working with porcelain **Nick Homoky** found that he was unable to throw tall forms without them buckling, nor was he able to throw thinly enough to get the shape he wanted unless he was prepared to do a good deal of turning. He solved the problem of weak forms by throwing thick and turning until he arrived at the appropriate shape, but once he had understood and accepted the limitations

Opp. above: Porcelain thrown form, height 2⁵/₈ in. (6.5 cm). Reduction fired to 1360°C. By Ursula Scheid (West Germany), 1975.

Opp. below: Porcelain thrown form, height 3½ in. (9 cm). Glaze includes potash feldspar, lime feldspar, petalite, China clay and zinc in both pieces. The black colour is obtained by adding a natural ore containing iron and manganese. By Ursula Scheid (West Germany), 1975.

Thrown, turned, shaped, inlaid and polished porcelain. Height of largest piece 8 in. (20.3 cm). Oxidised to 1260°C. By Nick Homoky.

of the material he began to enjoy working with it. He still turns all his pots with great thoroughness before damping them down and bending them into two, three or four-sided forms. Occasionally, he beats them with a wooden paddle and scrapes down further with metal kidneys. Sometimes he finds that the newly-formed corners will break under this treatment. Handles are thrown separately and joined when leather hard.

Geoffrey Swindell also relies heavily upon turning to realise any form which requires a narrow foot. These particular shapes would be extremely difficult to complete in one piece by throwing alone with any clay, but are quite impossible in porcelain. He uses very hard pieces of clay which, although weighing

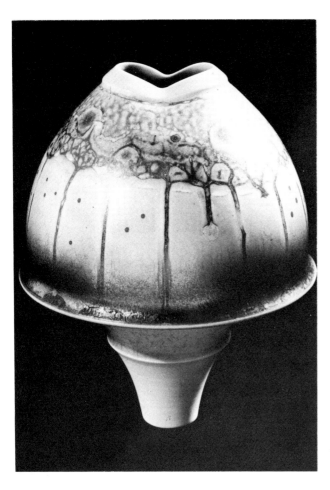

Thrown and turned porcelain with lustre glaze, height 4½ in. (11.4 cm). By Geoffrey Swindell, 1978.

bandsaw blades set into dowels. The pot is recentred and fixed to the dampened asbestos wheel bat by running a wooden tool down the lower wall and around the base to the wheelhead. Any turning necessary at the top is completed first. A wide enough opening is left at the throwing stage to enable him to insert his finger to feel and judge the form and thickness during turning. The excess material is pared away without cutting right through to the surface of the bat until the rest of the form has fully emerged. So much is turned away that the final pieces usually weigh no more than four ounces. The tops are wetted and indented at this stage.

David Leach also throws porcelain which is fairly stiff but **Mary White** prefers to throw it in a much softer condition. I have certainly found that a lump of soft porcelain is much more responsive when throwing fairly large bowls and I can leave a thick foot to support the belling form above. Soft porcelain demands a very direct approach. It will not tolerate indecision or second thoughts but if quickly and spontaneously handled it can be stretched until very thin with the aid of throwing ribs.

Peter Beard tends to throw quite thickly so that he can indulge his "greatest pleasure" in working with porcelain — turning, which is "very relaxing". On the other hand **Michael Casson** tries to avoid turning by throwing and coils feet and rims whenever he can. This requires joining the coil to the pot when it is softer than leather-hard.

All **Sheila Casson's** work is thrown, even the pieces she adds to extend the rims.

Beate Kuhn also uses the wheel exclusively. She even throws any flat shapes she may require and every single piece is turned. It usually takes her about two days to throw, turn, cut and assemble the pieces into one of her cats or other sculptures. With so many separate parts and sections to join she finds it safer to undertake the modelling directly on to a kiln bat so that it need not be moved until after the bisque firing.

Emmanuel Cooper feels that throwing-rings give the foot a growing quality and that any subsequent turning should marry in with these. "Unless precisely placed they interfere with the form." Porcelain seemed a natural progression from the range of carefully made domestic stoneware he produces. He finds it not so much "difficult" as "slow" and somewhat exhausting to work. "It is not a production material and is totally uneconomic in terms of the time

only two pounds each, usually take all his strength to centre. He has fitted an asbestos bat to his wheel-head to help the clay to stick and resist the pressure he has to apply. Stiff clay is essential to his method of working. The ball is opened and brought out rather like a bowl initially and the top is then taken back almost like a dome. Wetter clay would refuse this treatment and very quickly slump. He takes the clay direct from the supplier's bag without wedging it further but 'cones' it a lot on the wheel. He likes to make narrow-based pieces "to carry the idea above" but as so much of the clay is turned away later, he completes the inner shape and leaves plenty of thickness in the lower wall so that each pot can be safely picked off the wheel.

Turning is carried out at the leather hard stage using standard aluminium tools and flexible steel kidneys, which he has reshaped to suit his needs, and also thin

Opposite: *Turning the base of a porcelain bowl.*

78

Anne James working on porcelain 'pod' forms, thrown and modelled.

'Fan'. Porcelain sculpture composed of thrown units, height 4¾ in. (12 cm). Celadon glaze. By Beate Kuhn (West Germany).

which it is necessary to put into one piece". Its particular attraction for him is the degree of refinement that can be achieved and its colour possibilities through glazes.

Christine-Ann Richards learnt to throw using porcelain exclusively. She was attracted by the purity of the material "there's a finesse about porcelain which makes even ordinary stoneware glazes look and feel quite different". She does not normally throw with lumps much larger than 3lbs, unless it is grogged, but feels that with grog much of the quality is lost. Her work is turned very little but when she does do it she uses normal steel kidneys reshaped for her purposes with tin snips and finished on a grindstone. Working sessions of two to three months on her 'standard ware' are followed by delivery trips up and down the country.

All the work of **Joanna Constantinidis** comes from thrown forms. She often throws, pinches and remodels from a simple basic form such as a cylinder. Sometimes thrown without bases, she squeezes them into an oval section and adds the bottom when they have stiffened enough to manage. The openings of tall oval-sectioned cylinders are reduced in size by pinching the tops together at left and right. Where extra height has been gained by joining one cylinder

on top of another, the junction is sometimes disguised by texturing the lower part. One unusual variation has been to cut away alternate segments of pinched clay from the sides leading up towards the top, again reducing it to a small opening. The sinuous necks of these pieces are perfectly balanced, physically and visually, and each varies subtly in its proportions. Wide thrown cylinders opened up right down to the wheel-head are flattened to a narrow section with one side eased into vertical ripples. Joanna Constantinidis occasionally throws the rims very thinly between two ribs and does very little turning despite finding throwing-rings a distraction in porcelain.

For **Anne James** also, throwing is just the first stage of the forming process. She feels that she needs the discipline of keeping thrown forms simple. She enjoys turning as thinly as possible and often scrapes even more away by cross-hatching to break up the leather hard surface with a piece of fine-toothed hacksaw blade and smoothing down with a steel kidney. Many pieces are finished with a flexible steel razor-blade which suits the small scale of her work. Some forms, reminiscent of seed pods, are thrown with quite thick walls and turned while still fairly wet so that they can be easily reshaped. These forms are split, damped down and the tops pinched slightly. Then vertical

Three porcelain forms, height 3½ in. (8.9 cm). By Anne James.

Porcelain bowl. 5 in. (12.7 cm) diameter. Oxidised. By Emmanuel Cooper.

Thrown and re-shaped porcelain, height 5¾ in. (14.6 cm). Reduction fired to 1360°C. By Karl Scheid (West Germany), 1976.

Above right: *Thrown and re-shaped porcelain bowl. By Anne James, 1979.*

Below: *Porcelain bowl, height 4 in. (10.2 cm), with incised and applied decoration. Celadon glaze. By Michael Casson.*

indents are pushed in with modelling tools and emphasised by narrow coils stuck on and smoothed in to become integral parts of the whole. She tries to make all her forms "right before messing them about" because she has found that any piece which begins as a weak form remains so after further modelling.

She has never experienced base-cracking in her work because every piece is carefully turned, upside down, in a chuck.

Tiny flattened bottles inspired by sunflower seeds are gently beaten into shape with wooden paddles when still plastic — without cutting or removing the base. Her lidded boxes are thrown in one piece and shaped also by beating. The air sealed inside cushions the impact and keeps the profile firm.

Anne James' split-sided bowls are turned and then dampened along the line of the intended groove. This serves to replasticise the clay sufficiently for the particles to become realigned in the adjusted form. She wets both sides in a pinching action because wetting alone without the pressure will cause the clays to flop and crack.

Almost all the pots from **David Eeles'** workshop are thrown and turned on kick wheels. He has trained his sons to throw and to observe the developing form reflected in a mirror propped on the shelf beside the wheel. **Gotlind Weigel** and others use mirrors in this way also. It helps potters to avoid that awkward

Opposite: *Tall porcelain form thrown in two parts, cut, pinched and burnished, with flattened section. By Joanna Constantinidis, 1979.*

Lidded porcelain box. 6 in. (15.2 cm) diameter. By Warren Mackenzie (USA), 1979.

Lidded porcelain box thrown in one piece, 3 in. (7.6 cm) diameter. Banded lustre decoration. By Glyn Hugo, 1979.

twisted crouch dreaded by those who suffer from an aching back. David Eeles makes large pieces in porcelain, assembled from several thrown parts, which allow him plenty of scope for his distinctive painted decoration.

Lidded boxes are enjoyable to make in porcelain. They seem well-suited to the medium and are popular with many potters, the best of whom fashion precisely-fitting lids. The basic simplicity of the forms can be treated in many ways and the method used to fit the lid is often an interesting part of the design.

One of the most satisfying techniques involves throwing both box and lid in one piece. The most usual shapes and those presenting the least difficulty are based upon a straight-sided cylinder pulled up and collared until closed right over at the top. It is wise to maintain a slightly domed section when this is being done to avoid untimely collapse. The top can be flattened further when the seal is complete, or gently beaten when stiffened. A straight-sided box can be turned in the usual way and the lid cut free while at the same time making an inner rim to hold it in place. The lid drops down when finally released by a needle cut (see diagram below).

Opposite: Miniature porcelain teapot with onglaze lustre decoration, height 6 in. (15.2 cm). By Mary Rich, 1979.

Below: *One-piece box and lid.*

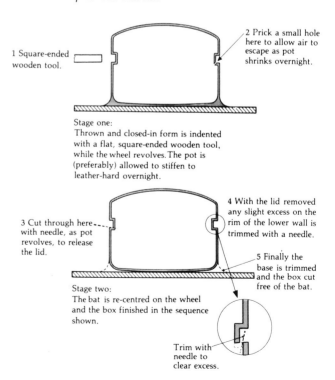

1 Square-ended wooden tool.

2 Prick a small hole here to allow air to escape as pot shrinks overnight.

Stage one:
Thrown and closed-in form is indented with a flat, square-ended wooden tool, while the wheel revolves. The pot is (preferably) allowed to stiffen to leather-hard overnight.

3 Cut through here with needle, as pot revolves, to release the lid.

4 With the lid removed any slight excess on the rim of the lower wall is trimmed with a needle.

5 Finally the base is trimmed and the box cut free of the bat.

Stage two:
The bat is re-centred on the wheel and the box finished in the sequence shown.

Trim with needle to clear excess.

'Mermaid Series II'. Porcelain teapot, height 10½ in. (26.6 cm). By Coille Hooven (USA), 1976.

Another method appropriate to straight-sided or curved forms is to cut through the wall making a clean line moving above and below the horizontal to key the two parts together, as in the boxes made by **Glyn Hugo** and **Eileen Lewenstein**.

When lids are thrown separately, in order to ensure a good fit, use two pairs of calipers, one pair for the inner and the other for the outer dimensions.

The lidded boxes by **Antoine de Vinck** (Belgium) are

Left: *Porcelain teapot. By David Winkley.*

Teapot with pulled strap handle. By Sylva Leser (Canada).

Below: *Fluted teapot. By David Leach, 1979*

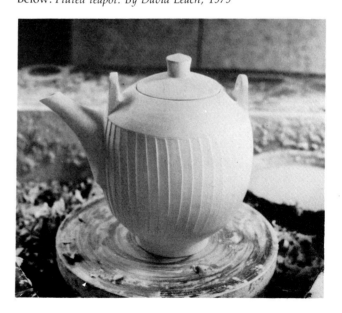

thrown with thick walls to allow facets to be cut from them. The lids are separately thrown and fit like a cap over a shallow rim (see page 152).

Teapots are usually composed of separately thrown parts and they invariably present a challenge to most potters irrespective of the material used. The relationship of spout, lid and handle to the main body must be aesthetically pleasing, physically balanced and pay proper regard to function. It is not a form many potters relish tackling in porcelain. **David Leach** is one of the few potters making them regularly. A number of people, notably **Mary Rich** and **Mary White**, have made miniature pieces as vehicles for delicate decorative treatments. **William Mehornay's** teapot is an object of classical simplicity (see page 00).

Coille Hooven's (USA) teapots parody their supposed function to become decorative, whimsical objects.

Although pulled handles are often fitted, the weight of one attached at the side can distort thin porcelain unless a small opening is left. Many potters prefer to fit a preformed cane handle to lugs or loops of clay on the shoulder. **Sylva Leser** (Canada) has fitted a strap of

Opposite: *Porcelain vases thrown in sections and joined. Height 8 in. (20.3 cm). Painted with oxides and incised. By Lucie Rie, 1979.*

Above: *Two 'Pebble pots' with brushed oxides and dolomite glaze. By Delan Cookson, 1979.*

Right: *Globular porcelain pot with crackle glaze. By Ray Silverman, 1979.*

porcelain to perform the same function to her teapot.

Bottles and other narrow-necked forms can be thrown in one piece if shaped and collared fairly quickly before too much water has been absorbed and the clay grown 'tired'. If the shoulder changes direction at all sharply towards the neck, a reasonable thickness, related to the size, should be maintained at this point in order to withstand the collaring and to support any further work to be carried out above it. **Lucie Rie's** beautiful tall-necked vases are made from thrown and joined sections. **Delan Cookson** throws his 'pebble' pots in one piece bringing them crisply in to finish with a tiny neck emphasising the taut volume of the form, and similar tension is achieved by **Ray Silverman** in his globular crackle-glazed pot.

Hand-Building

Pinching

To understand some of the problems and rewards of hand-built porcelain we can examine more closely the individual methods and approaches of artist-craftsmen concentrating their work in this direction.

In the plastic state, smooth porcelain bodies are so appealing to the tactile sense that shaping and extending the material by pinching is one of the most enjoyable, and perhaps the most natural, method of building with it. It was probably the earliest forming technique to be used in the history of pottery and it is a method employed throughout the world with many different clays. Pinch-building requires no special tools or equipment, just a pair of hands; a sympathetic feeling for the material; an awareness of the changing character as it dries, and a patient relaxed approach.

One can begin with a well-kneaded ball of clay, soft enough to retain the slightest finger impression without feeling sticky. Cradling the ball and slowly rotating it in one hand, the thumb of the other hand is gently pushed in towards the centre and the base rounded with the pad rather than the tip of the thumb. Squeezing the clay between the finger and thumb while continuing to turn the pot in step with the rhythmic finger pressure, will resolve the shaping of the base, and its ultimate thickness.

The thinning, raising and forming of the wall then follows through similar movements circling the pot, with each pinched depression slightly overlapping the one previously made.

If the aim is to make a wide-mouthed bowl it may be necessary to allow the piece to stiffen for a short while, supported by the rim of a jar or some circular container, until ready to be worked further.

Making several pieces at a time helps to preserve the rhythm of the work and allows the pinching/ stiffening/pinching cycle to be comfortably maintained. The nature of porcelain invites pinching to be continued until egg-shell thin, by which stage it will be drying rapidly.

Above left: *Stoneware dome with blue-pink porcelain fungi, height 14 in. (35.4 cm). Reduction fired. By Peter Beard.*

Left: *'Bird'. Coiled and pinched porcelain, pale blue celadon glaze, height 6 in. (15.2 cm), length 6 in. (15.2 cm). By Rosemary Wren. (In the collection of Mr and Mrs R. Hyne).*

The next six photos are all of Mary Rogers working. Opening up the ball of clay with the thumb.

The base is pinched to its necessary shape and thinness.

The walls are shaped by rhythmic circles of pinching.

The circles of pinching slightly overlap each other from the base up to the rim.

Pinching dents are gently smoothed out up the walls of the pot.

Scraping over the dry pot to refine the form and the surface.

Pinch-built porcelain bowl with painted agate design, 6 in. (15.2 cm) diameter. By Mary Rogers, 1979.

Pinched pots often have an attractive organic quality which is the natural expression of their gradual, rhythmical growth. The slight unevenness of surface and form can contribute a unique liveliness to each piece. Irrespective of the amount of final scraping and smoothing given to a porcelain pinch-built pot, its distinctive character will remain. Open forms are straightforward enough because the clay readily stretches and spreads outward, but if the pot has to swell and curve in again at the top, allowances must be made for this during the pinching process. Collaring or squeezing the pot inwards from time to time before the walls become too thin will help to counteract this spreading movement. Any creases and folds which such action produces can be pinched in and smoothed over as the work proceeds. The walls can be extended further by the addition of coils applied with a little slip and thoroughly integrated.

The rim is the final statement of any pot and the undulating line of a pinched rim can complement the form in an attractive way. As the clay dries, its tendency to crack can be used as a decorative feature and can be emphasised further by curling or rippling as it is pinched to a very fine edge. Rims can be cut

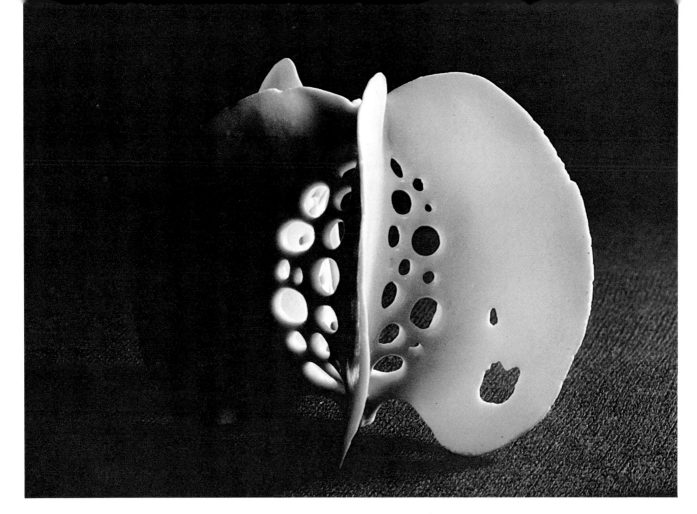

'Pierced Core'. Pinch-built porcelain. By Mary Rogers.

Right: *'Winged form', Pinch-built porcelain with painted oxides, height 7 in. (17.7 cm). By Mary Rogers, 1975.*

level, or to any other line, with a needle and smoothed off with a damp leather, or with wet fingers and the slightest of pressure.

Closed or spherical forms are more conveniently made by joining two pinched pots together, rim to rim, with slip in the usual manner, before the walls become too thin. The join is easily hidden by smoothing over and adding extra clay if necessary. When thoroughly joined the pot can can be cupped in the hands and gently inflated by blowing into a hole in the top. This will give the pot more visual tension and is a simple method which can also be used to vitalise other forms, provided that the aperture is not too large.

One of the best-known pinch-builders in Britian is **Mary Rogers**. Her work is unmistakable despite many imitations of her style (often by those who have not understood the roots of her motivation). She feels that the technqiue of pinching favours asymmetry and although some further twisting or slumping in the kiln may exaggerate this tendency, it is less likely to offend than the unintentional distortion of a thrown piece.

She makes allowances to compensate for distortion in drying and firing. Her work "is very much a personal exploration of natural forms translated into clay and glaze qualities, and the decorative aspects are an integral part of this." She finds such rich symbolism and depth in the idea of hollow container forms that this remains "a continual source of interest and challenge."

After completing the forming process and when the pot has dried out, Mary Rogers usually refines the surface by scraping (wearing a face mask to avoid inhaling the dust which this creates) with kidney steels. She feels that "porcelain is at its best when it approaches the perfection of form and surface found in smooth shells such as the cowrie." She likes to remove the finger marks in porcelain so that they do not disturb the form and distract the eye from appreciating the whole. Matt or semi-matt glazes will

'Landscape-edged canyon'. Pinch-built porcelain, 7 in. (17.7 cm) diameter. By Mary Rogers.

Opposite above: 'Fin Pot' porcelain, thrown with pinched additions, height 7 in. (17.7 cm). Celadon glaze. By Peter Lane, 1973.

Opposite below: Two porcelain bowls, thrown and pinched, with crackle glaze and brushed copper oxide on rims, height 3 in. (7.6 cm). Reduction fired to 1280°C. By Peter Lane, 1979.

more readily disguise those small indentations which cause reflections under a shiny glaze.

Work in progress is often supported by carefully placed pieces of foam sponge. Very soft, open forms unable to hold their shape when upright are draped over a child's ball which, to prevent sticking, has been covered with a piece of cloth. Once the pot has stiffened sufficiently it is removed before it shrinks too tightly on to the supporting ball.

Convoluted porcelain pot, thrown and pinched, height 3½ in.
(8.8 cm). By Deirdre Burnett. (In the collection of W. Lenzen).

Left: *Double-edged porcelain bowl, thrown, pinched and carved,*
6½ in. (16.5 cm) diameter. By Deirdre Burnett, 1979.

Footings can be made from a ring of coiled clay or from a rolled-out strip and are added with a little slurry at the leather-hard stage. Where no foot is to be added to a pinched pot a slight hollowing under the base will help it to stand better when fired. This can be done by impressing with a fingertip while still plastic or by gently scraping away a small depression in the dry state.

Deirdre Burnett has also developed the art of pinching porcelain to a high level, but in a different way. Most of her work is initially thrown and the rims are then pinched into almost impossible convolutions or flattened into thin horizontal flanges. Further interest is sometimes generated by carving and piercing through the flange or its supporting wall. Deirdre Burnett's work, like **Mary Rogers'**, possesses a strongly organic quality.

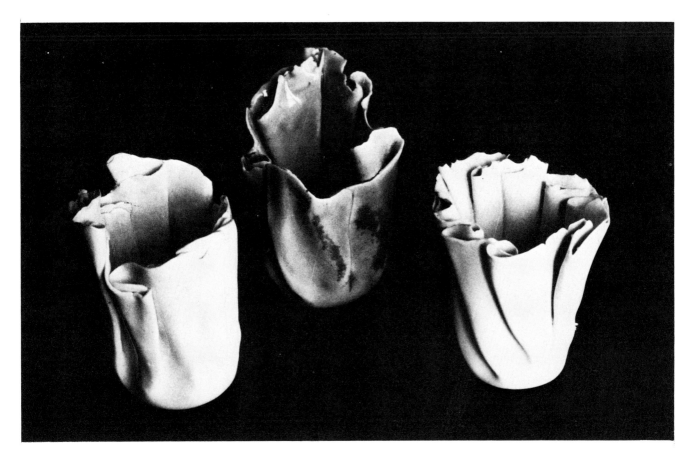

Three folded porcelain forms, moulded over the end of a wooden rolling pin. By Anna English, 1976. (Student at Keswick Hall College of Education).

Right: Porcelain form, $9\frac{1}{2} \times 9\frac{1}{2} \times 2^{3}/_{8}$ in. (24 × 24 × 6 cm). Made in Mexico. By Gerda Spurey (Austria), 1978.

Press-moulding

Press-moulding is a technique which has been used for a very long time. In the twelfth century the Chinese began using hump moulds richly ornamented with carved designs over which a sheet of porcelain was beaten and pressed into shape. Plates were made from discs of clay by 'jiggering' on to moulds fixed to a fast-turning wheel. Designs were more easily cut into solidly thrown lumps of smooth stoneware clay which were then fired to preserve the crisp design. Subsequent pressings imposed a sharp relief on the inside surface of the bowl or dish.

Hump moulds are not often used by individual

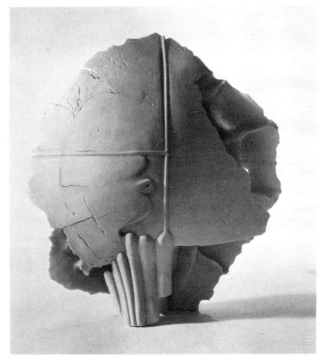

potters for this kind of decorative work today, most people preferring to carve and incise direct into each individual piece. But it remains a useful method of forming pre-decorated slabs, where the pattern is to show on the inside, and for making a variety of plain shapes. As with most other clays, porcelain sheets can be draped over temporary moulds such as inverted basins, bowls, balls, pebbles, beakers etc., provided that thin polythene, paper or cloth is used as a liner to prevent sticking. As soon as the moulded piece has stiffened sufficiently to retain its shape it should be removed or it may shrink, gripping the mould tightly until it cracks.

Recessed or hollow moulds cast in plaster seem to be

Press-moulded porcelain sphere, 24 in (60.8 cm) diameter. Made in two halves and joined. The texture was achieved by placing clay trimmings in the mould prior to pressing. Oxides were brushed in to emphasise the texture. By Mary Keepax, 1971.

Opposite: 'Water Movement'. Extruded porcelain sculpture, 36 in. (90.2 cm) long, decorated with sprayed enamels. By Oldrich Asenbryl, 1979.

more popular than hump moulds and they can continue to support the pressed sheet until dry. Alternatively, if the mould is symmetric in plan two pressings from it can be joined with slip at the rims to make a closed form. It is usual to leave the first

pressing until it has shrunk sufficiently to release from the mould without distortion. A board or tile is placed flat across the rim and the whole carefully inverted to allow the moulded form to drop and be evenly supported by the board. This can be wrapped in a sheet of thin polythene until the second pressing is made and has stiffened to the same consistency. Joining the two is straightforward and can be undertaken while still protected in the mould. Again, if the rims are designed to match, a series of shapes may be press-moulded and joined in various combinations.

If a deep-section mould is used for pressing it may be impossible to insert a sheet of porcelain in one piece without making creases and folds. These can be used as decorative features and even if pressed firmly against the mould, the outer walls of the piece are almost certain to retain the marks of creasing as fine indented lines.

Clay can be pre-shaped by pinching or throwing sufficiently to drop cleanly into a deep or narrow mould ready for final shaping and pressing to the contour required. Roughly thrown cylinders are often 'jolleyed' in moulds set in cup wheelheads when making cups or deep bowls industrially.

Geoffrey Swindell has press-moulded a series of porcelain pots composed of two joined pressings. Most of the moulds he designed were too deep to accept one sheet cleanly and the pressed shapes were made by inserting two or three strips patched and smoothed together with the fingers while in the mould. The porcelain body was prepared into a block from which even sheets were cut with fine wire and used directly, because he found that rolled sheets dried out more quickly and had less plasticity for his purpose. The scale of the pieces was small and pressings could be removed from the moulds after ten to fifteen minutes so that those which were to form the top parts could be centred, trimmed and lightly thinned on the wheel.

Emphasising the junctions with flanged or sudden directional changes of contour actually disguised them because joints are notorious for reappearing in porcelain in the glost firing, no matter how carefully they were smoothed over earlier.

Above: *Group of press-moulded porcelain forms with lustre decoration, height 4½ in. (11.4 cm). By Geoffrey Swindell, 1976.*

Left: *Porcelain pot, press-moulded in two parts and joined. Height 2½ in. (6.3 cm). By Geoffrey Swindell, 1970.*

Slab-building

Slab-building is one of the simplest methods of making pots and sculptural forms and, although this technique is most commonly used for constructing angular box-like pieces, many imaginative variations are possible once the essential stages of rolling, joining and drying have been understood.

Usually, prepared slabs of clay are allowed to stiffen to a leather-hard condition prior to joining, but they are sometimes used in a freer manner while still fairly soft. Slabs are more difficult to control in this state and a good deal of practice and experience is necessary before they can be handled fluently. There is also a greater risk of cracking later as the clay dries.

As with other clays used for slab work, a granular material is often added to porcelain to open it up and to decrease shrinkage. Molochite, ground from bricks of calcined china clay into several grades from coarse to fine, is used for this purpose and ten to thirty per cent can be wedged into the plastic porcelain body. The Molochite is sprinkled between successive layers of clay and thoroughly kneaded in, the process being repeated until the required amount is evenly distributed throughout the body.

The prepared lump of clay is then beaten approximately into shape and rolled out, rather like pastry, with a long wooden rolling pin. Two slats of wood or battens of equal thickness, spaced on each side of the slab, make useful guides for the roller and guarantee an even sheet of clay.

It is quite possible to roll out slabs successfully on a dry wooden bench or sheet of hardboard provided that the slab is gently eased clear of the surface, and reversed to prevent sticking, following each completed rolling movement. An absorbent surface is normally essential for rolling slabs or the clay can stick and tear hopelessly when lifted, but it does have the disadvantage with porcelain of removing a good deal of moisture from the body. A board covered with fine canvas also works well, although some potters prefer to leave the canvas loose so that it can be used to support the slab when moved elsewhere to stiffen. Others, however, like to roll out porcelain on polythene sheet to preserve the moisture content.

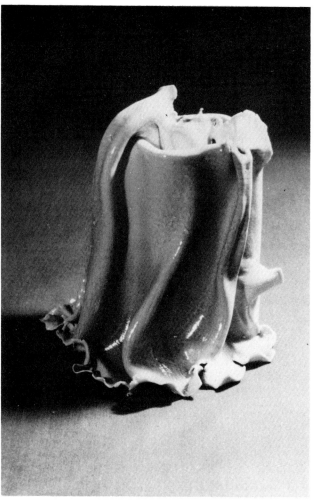

Above: *Porcelain slab-built piece, height 5¼ in. (13.3 cm). Reduction fired to 1360°C. By Gerald Weigel (West Germany), 1978.*

Right: *Porcelain folded forms, soda glazed, height 6 in. (15.2 cm). By Anndelphine Wornell-Brown, 1979.*

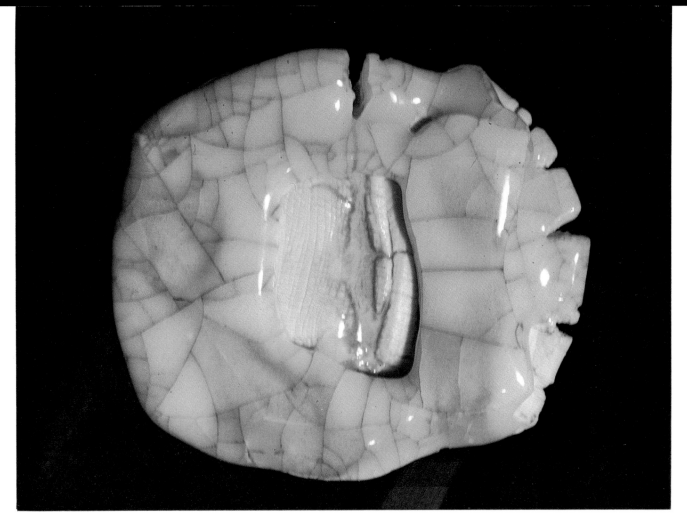

Opposite: *Porcelain slab-built 'blossom vase', height 7¾ in. (20 cm). By Johannes Gebhardt (West Germany), 1978.*

Above: *Porcelain slab, 3⁷⁄₈ × 3⁵⁄₈ in. (10 × 9 cm). By Agathe Larpent-Ruffe (France), 1979.*

Below right: *Porcelain wall construction, height 13¾ in. (34.8 cm). Celadon copper red glazes. Reduction fired to 1260°C. By Victoria Dark (USA).*

Slabs can also be cut from a block, like slices of cheese, with a fine wire. This may produce an interesting, pitted texture where particles of Molochite have been dragged across the face, but if a smooth surface is wanted it can be restored with the aid of a flexible steel scraper or rubber kidney. However, the rolling method compresses the clay better and improves its strength. Porcelain tends to dry out more quickly than other clays so the slabs must be turned over to expose the underside as soon as they are stiff enough to be handled without being deformed. This enables them to dry evenly and helps to avoid warping.

Slabs may also be draped over various formers and allowed to stiffen to the shape of a particular cross-section but it is advisable to put paper between the former and the slab in case the clay sticks as it shrinks. If formers are used for porcelain, the chosen section should be simple. If, for example, a shallow D-section is required there is the choice of employing a former, or of partly bending the slab, when almost stiff, round a tube or biscuit tin and fixing it to a base slab. When it is in the right condition the clay should not crack as it bends and it should be firm enough to hold its shape without collapsing.

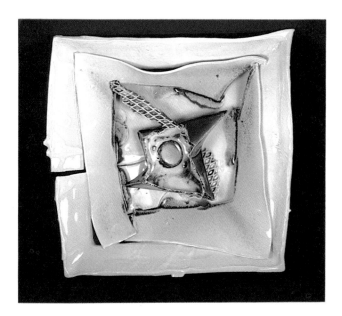

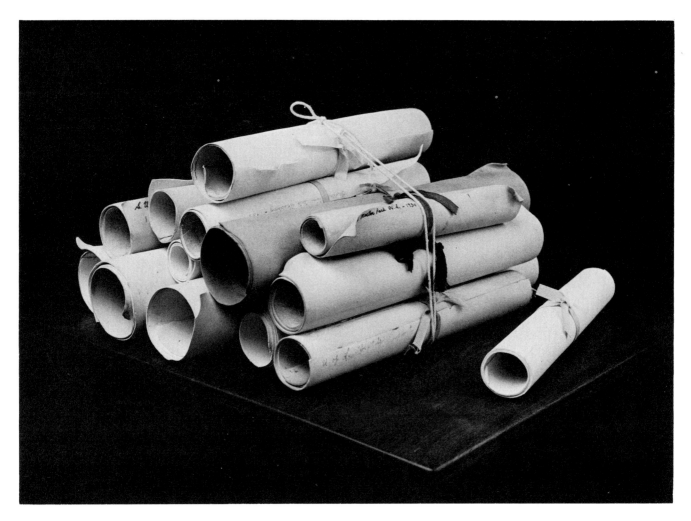

'Family Records'. Unglazed porcelain on walnut base. Rutile was wedged into the body in various amounts to produce the creamy-yellow colour of aged paper. Each roll is a slightly different off-white colour. Oxidised to Orton Cone 8. By Sylvia Hyman (USA), 1979.

Cylindrical forms can be made by bending a slab completely round a tube or tin over a layer of newspaper immediately after rolling. The strongest joint in this case is made by overlapping the ends of the slab around its support and making a diagonal cut through both layers, removing the waste clay. The bevelled edges of the cuts are cross-hatched, porcelain slip brushed on, and then pressed together to complete the joint which can be tidied up later at the leather-hard stage. It is possible to make use of the former itself as a 'rolling-pin' to seal the joint, if care is exercised, but too much pressure will thin the wall and stretch the clay so that it loses contact with its former.

The paper sheath will ease the subsequent removal of the former and this is done as soon as the clay is stiff enough to stand on its own for, if left too long, it may shrink tight and split as it dries. Blocks of wood off-cuts make good formers and hollow square, rectangular and oval cross-sections can be made by the method described above.

Card or paper templates are used as guides for the accurate cutting of the leather-hard slabs. A thin narrow-bladed knife is best for cutting cleanly without dragging, and a steel rule is to be preferred to the more easily damaged wooden type when slicing along straight edges. The knife must be kept upright for clean, right-angled cuts that will ensure good butt joints later (although some potters prefer using mitred joints). Again, all edges to be joined are scored and slipped, and gently moved up and down against each other until resistance is felt. Any slip squeezed out in the process is left to stiffen and is then smoothed over

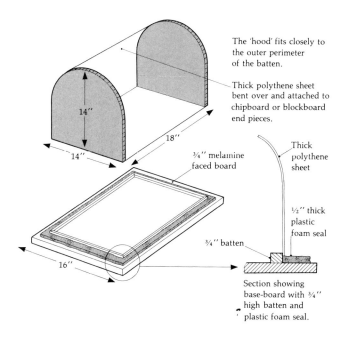

The 'hood' fits closely to the outer perimeter of the batten.

Thick polythene sheet bent over and attached to chipboard or blockboard end pieces.

14"

18"

14"

¾" melamine faced board

Thick polythene sheet

½" thick plastic foam seal

¾" batten

16"

Section showing base-board with ¾" high batten and plastic foam seal.

Damp box similar to that used by Audrey Blackman. The size can be adjusted to suit individual requirements.

to cement and conceal the joint. It is advisable to weld a thin coil of clay into the internal corners, rounding them off, so that stresses during drying and firing are not concentrated upon these, the weakest points in a slab-built form. The slabs should be joined promptly because porcelain takes up moisture very quickly and may soften under a heavy coating of slip.

When all the wall slabs have been fixed together they are joined to the base in similar fashion and if the base slab is cut fractionally larger than the bottom of the walls, the surplus can be smoothed up over the join with a wooden modelling tool.

Whenever slabs have been used, slow drying is important to equalise the stresses of shrinkage. Polythene bags make ideal covers and can be gradually loosened to let more air in as the piece hardens. **Audrey Blackman** has designed a rigidly-hooped container which she uses to protect her delicate porcelain figures. This is easily constructed and prevents contact damage.

Potters do not necessarily wish to exploit *all* the properties of porcelain at any one time in their work and, although translucency is often regarded as a desirable quality, slab-building normally requires clay sheets which are too thick to allow the passage of light. **Val Barry**, for example, declares that shape is much more important for her and that translucency is of no

interest at present. Her work is not confined solely to porcelain but she feels that it is "cleaner, smoother and nicer to handle than stoneware". She uses porcelain because she likes the glaze quality, "a kind of purity", which she gets with it. Much of her work is raw-glazed and once-fired, for which thicker walls are essential (if the piece is not to lose its shape through distortion). She also finds more adventurous shapes are possible with thicker slabs.

Some of her work has suffered from bloating when she has used commercial porcelain bodies so she prefers to make her own based upon the David Leach recipe (see page 60). Another advantage of this is that she can adjust the ingredients as needed for a particular purpose. By reducing the feldspar and increasing the flint content she can counteract the extra fluxing that seems to happen in a raw-glazed piece.

Small amounts of the powdered materials are mixed up by hand and dried to a plastic state on an 'Asbestolux' sheet, but it is not an easy method and she feels that she should leave it longer to age before using. Molochite (80s mesh) is wedged into the body which is rolled-out and allowed to stiffen to leather-hard. It is then cut to shape, slightly bent round a bucket and fixed to a base slab.

Glaze tended to distort the extreme angular forms she made so she began inlaying coloured pieces of porcelain on the outer faces of her pots, dispensing with glaze altogether. Browns, greys and blues are obtained from various metallic oxides by layering and wedging direct into the body. Val Barry has never used commercially prepared stains, nor does she grind the oxides, although to avoid heavy speckling she is careful to sieve any cobalt carbonate; cobalt is such a strong colourant that only minute amounts are added for some of the blues.

This kind of inlay can be tackled in a number of ways. The simplest method is to press soft pieces of stained, coloured porcelain into equally soft sheets of the white body by rolling. Soft clay has good adhesive properties but it helps to encourage this further by slightly dampening the surfaces to be joined. The inlaid clays will spread under pressure yet still retain well-defined shapes. Marbled patterns, similar to the popular agate wares of the eighteenth century Staffordshire potteries, are also easily obtained, but the quality is variable and is subject largely to chance. Brief spiral wedging of a block which contains alternating layers of coloured clays can give an interesting swirling pattern. Lengthy wedging, however, is likely to result in an over-complex linear arrangement of clays, if it does not so blend them

together that all pattern is eventually lost. Val Barry often rolls strips of stained porcelain into the white body so that the surface of the slab becomes marbled with broad veins and diffuse areas of colour.

Two other potters who use thinly rolled-out sheets of porcelain, but in very different ways, are **Eileen Nisbet** and **Audrey Blackman**. The work of both these artists is highly personal and of a unique character. **Audrey Blackman's** figures are brought to life by her expressive use of thin, flexible sheets with which she clothes a simple skeleton constructed from stiffer rods of clay. She always tries to display the translucency of the porcelain within areas of a figure's apparel and will often extend a shirt or cloak to achieve this. The absence of facial details adds, rather than detracts, from the communicative power of her work because the attitudes, postures and emotions of her figures are so well described through the use of beautifully-controlled clay sheets alive with movement.

As each figure takes about a week to complete, one of the major problems is keeping the piece from drying out too quickly while working on it, so Audrey Blackman blows water through a mouth-spray diffuser on to the clay to retard drying and keeps the

Above: Inlaid slab-built porcelain form height 7 in. (17.8 cm). By Val Barry, 1979. .

Opposite: 'Adagio'. Rolled porcelain figure, height 8 5/8 in. (22 cm). By Audrey Blackman.

work under a plastic cover at other times (see page 105).

There is a risk that the thin sheets of clay will crack as they shrink and this can be countered by arranging them loosely enough to allow for the inevitable movement to take place without causing undue stress. More detailed information on the making of rolled pottery figures may be obtained from Audrey Blackman's book, *Rolled Pottery Figures*.[31] **Eileen Nisbet** also uses thin sheets of porcelain clay but she is much more concerned with the hardness and very tense surface qualities which she can achieve with it. She uses flat slabs precisely shaped, and spaced vertically one behind another, like a kind of three-dimensional painting. The forms are abstract, derived from the composite experiences of a lifetime rather than from anything identifiably specific such as the ingenuities either of nature or of man. They appear organic yet almost mathematical in concept.

106

Eileen Nisbet exploits the whiteness of porcelain, the translucent edges of thin slabs, the brightness of light passing through pierced holes, and the shadows both sharp and diffused between the planes to create her own potent images.

She rolls out her clay on thin polythene so that it neither sticks nor dries too quickly in the process. It is possible to achieve quite large slabs this way. Shapes are cut from these in the leather-hard condition and

'Aeroplane'. Porcelain sculpture, 17 × 6 in. (43.2 × 15.2 cm). Slip inlaid and painted with enamel. Oxidised to 1240°C. By Eileen Nisbet, 1979.

Below left: *Carved and impressed porcelain slab vase, height 5 in. (12.7 cm). By Maggie Andrews, 1979.*

Opposite: *'Folded Form'. Slab-built porcelain. The thin slabs were pinched in the centre after joining while still soft. By Kurt Spurey (Austria), 1979.*

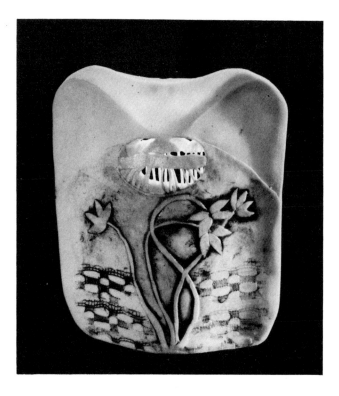

then scraped to give sharp edges, any incising is done at this stage. Coloured porcelain slip is 'blobbed' into the incised lines and any excess scraped away later. Body stains are sometimes painted directly on to the clay, occasionally mixed with oxides for variety. All her energy is directed towards the relationships of shapes and the slabs have to be counter-balanced physically, as well as aesthetically.

Despite the size and thinness of the slabs there is little evidence of warping in the finished pieces. This is because the slabs are dried with great care, constantly checked, and very slowly fired as individual sheets to 1240°C prior to assembly into the final form. The finished slabs are joined and spaced by short tubes of porcelain fired to the same temperature and then glued into position.

Maggie Andrews uses a forming device which allows thin sheets of clay to dry to the particular form she requires before constructing her 'landscape' slabbed pieces. The clay is rolled into thin sheets and impressed with a variety of natural and man-made materials. Occasionally pellets, strips and coils of clay are also applied and rolled in. Fascinating textures suggesting fragments of landscape are produced in this way. The treated slabs are then draped over

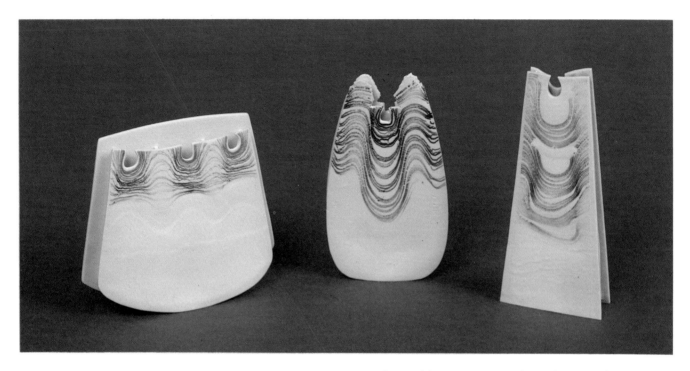

Three porcelain slab pots with decorative textures from rolled oxides, height 5 in. (12.7 cm). By Gordon Cooke, 1979.

corrugated plaster formers and allowed to stiffen for about an hour, when they are joined together in the usual manner with slip, and a base is added. Oxides and stains are brushed into the textures when the pot has dried out. The only cracking problem she has experienced has been caused by unequal stress when the piece has been glazed too thickly inside while the outer surface remains as bisque. A very thin skin of glaze, however, is normally satisfactory.

Gordon Cooke's work has developed into a highly personal idiom. The patterns of landscape and textures of natural objects have prompted him to explore similar textural rhythms in his finely made slabbed pieces. The purity and whiteness of porcelain are of "paramount importance" for him to display the delicate linear patterns he achieves with applied oxides and stains. This clarity of surface together with its dense hardness are essential because he leaves most of the work unglazed. He finds that the high shrinkage rate and its tendency to warp are the most taxing problems in working with porcelain. Most of Gordon Cooke's slabbed vases have very thin walls so he often braces them internally with equally thin strips, to prevent undue distortion.

One particular technique, which he has developed with notable success, involves the use of coloured stains applied to one side of a very thick wad of the plastic (David Leach) body. The stains are mixed with water and a small amount of the powdered body before application by brush in broad bands. When the moisture shine has dulled, the wad is inverted on to a plaster slab to accelerate the drying of the painted surface. Timing is quite critical if the process is to succeed but this can soon be judged with practice. Gordon Cooke usually finds other things to do while waiting for the wad to be ready for the next stage. This requires rolling the wad into a slab, using wooden guides for even thickness, with the stained surface uppermost. He alternates one wooden roller with another so that neither becomes so damp that the surface is marred through sticking. The stained surface is broken and stretched into linear patterns by this method and can be controlled to the fine degree demonstrated in his work. Sometimes he places coils of clay underneath the slab in order to push the pattern in particular directions as he rolls it. On other occasions he will cut and reassemble slabs, rejoining them with a coil rolled vertically at the central junction to create a chevron design. There are many further decorative possibilities for any who care to experiment.

There are a number of other methods by which slabs can be prepared for building in porcelain. One fairly obvious one is to throw cylinders which are then cut

Thrown and re-shaped porcelain form, $4\frac{3}{4} \times 7\frac{1}{2}$ in. (12 × 19 cm). By Gotlind Weigel (West Germany), 1976.

Right: *Porcelain vase assembled from thrown pieces, height $5\frac{1}{2}$ in. (13.9 cm). Reduction fired to 1360°C. By Gotlind Weigel (West Germany), 1978.*

and unrolled into ready-made sheets. **Gotlind Weigel** emphasises the flowing plastic nature of the material using this method, sometimes as a free-standing, convoluted, sheet sculpture or by attaching an extra sheet to an oval, thrown form, she creates the impression of a peeling outer layer.

Slabs can also be cast to different thicknesses and shapes. **Kurt Spurey** (Austria) uses a factory-prepared slip to make thin slabs in this way and which he then assembles into 'envelopes' or rectangular forms bent and folded "interfering with light and space".

Another variation with slip is to pour or trail it on to a plaster slab to form particular shapes. The plaster face can be angled to allow the slip to run down the slope a little before it stiffens. Rich textural effects have been achieved by **Gerda Spurey** (Austria) with leaves of droplet-edged slip mounted successively in the form of wall panels.

Very thin sheets of porcelain lend themselves most readily to bending, folding and pinching together into forms reminiscent of organic growth. Sheets can easily be cut directly from a block of plastic clay or even thinly shaved off with a taut fine wire, thus ensuring

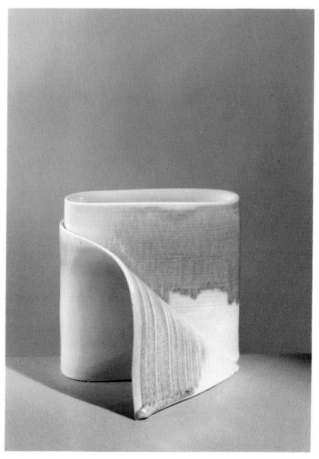

Three porcelain forms, wheel-thrown and modelled, height 6–8 in. (15.2–20.3 cm). Reduction fired to Orton Cone 10. By Sylvia Hyman (USA), 1979.

translucency. **Sylvia Hyman** (USA) offsets this delicate organic quality in gathered layers of thin sheet porcelain against the heavy permanence of a wood or refractory firebrick base upon which they are mounted. Such pieces appear visually mobile, like waving plant fronds growing upwards and outwards from the static base.

Peter Simpson explored the potential of organic forms in ceramic terms through the medium of porcelain perhaps more than any other potter during the 1970s. Spherical forms whose outer casings were split to reveal interiors tightly packed with paper-thin sheets of porcelain or cupped fungoid forms displaying radial gills of the same fine material attracted many admirers and became the forerunners

of a plethora of ceramic 'fungi' all over Britain, although few potters came anywhere near to the sensitivity or control of Peter Simpson. Extra-fine sheets were prepared by rolling the porcelain out on polythene until quite thin and, using the polythene as a support, they were transferred to a piece of newspaper for further rolling. Cardboard templates helped in gauging the size and shape for each sheet to be added to build up layers or 'gills'. They were shaped and allowed to stiffen (even to become quite dry) before slotting into place and joined with a little brushed slip. Bisque firing was taken as high as 1240°C to overcome the problem of fragility and this created further difficulties in the subsequent glazing. Peter Simpson found that the only way that he could apply sufficient glaze to these pieces was to heat them up and spray several layers over a period of time. Adding gum to the glaze caused difficulties with the spray gun so he did not persevere with the use of additives.

Much of his work has moved away from this

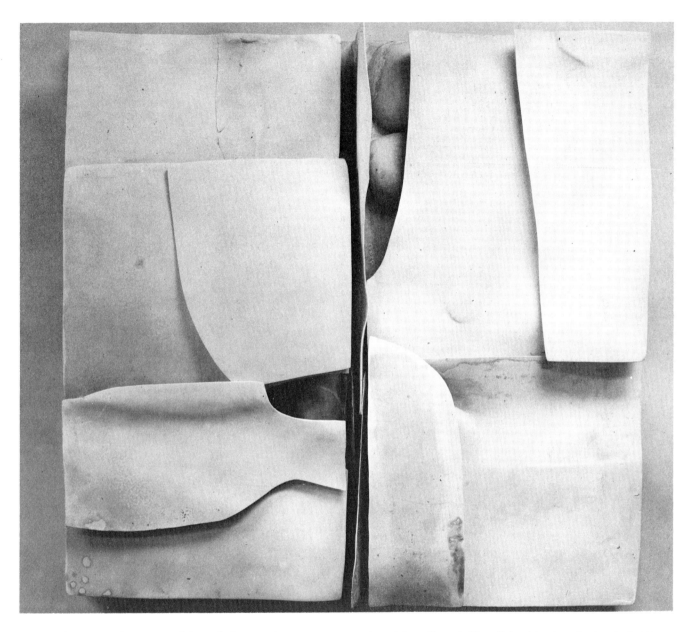

Porcelain wall panel. 42 × 42 in. (105.4 × 105.4 cm). Oxidised. By Ruth Duckworth (USA), 1979.

particular area of interest although he continues to slab-build but in a rather freer, more consciously sculptural, way and in much larger scale. His most recent work consists of very large slab-built sections made from Potclays' porcelain body fired to about 1240°C. The sculptures are assembled from several parts after the final firing, using resin adhesives and fixing pins.

One of the most expressive potters using soft clay slabs to build up forms that seem almost to have created themselves is **Ruth Duckworth** (USA). She has used a variety of building methods with

considerable ingenuity, including casting thin porcelain slabs on plaster bats in a similar manner to that already mentioned on page 111. Her work is remarkable also for the richness and diversity of its textural treatment. She likes to work large even in porcelain and one of her major problems is that all the large and complex pieces have to have special supports made for firing them. Her studio is filled with innumerable supporting pieces!

*Three porcelain fungoid forms, height of largest 7 in. (17.7 cm).
Oxidised to 1260°C. By Peter Simpson.*

*'Melon slice'. Porcelain form, 5 in. (12.7 cm) long. Oxidised to
1260°C. By Peter Simpson.*

The stresses set up in making and firing large slabs
or sheets of porcelain is considerable and one must be
tolerant of a certain amount of warping and the
occasional shrinkage crack. There is no limit to the
scale of wall tiling or relief panels if they are made in
small separate sections or units to be mounted later
when fired. Ruth Duckworth's fireplace-wall mural is
made in several parts which combine together to give a
total area of 8 ft × 1 ft 6 in. It would be much more
straightforward to work on this scale in stoneware
clays but it would lack the particular communicative
power of porcelain.

Christa and Johannes Gebhardt have developed the
textured cutting of slabs into a fine art form. Strong
linear patterns are cut into the surface of slabs
followed by pinching at the edges and further
manipulation to make them stand as organic free
forms. Christa uses a similar surface treatment, yet
more crisply defined in her framed panels. A block of
clay can be cut into slices using an expanded wire
spiral to create textural effects not too far removed in
character from this, but the Gebhardts' sensitive
control of their personal techniques and their
sympathetic understanding of the nature of porcelain
has enabled them to produce individual pieces of
outstanding quality.

Porcelain wall panel, height 18 in. (45.7 cm), width 8 ft. (2 m 44 cm). Sprayed feldspathic glaze. Fired to 1280°C. By Ruth Duckworth (USA), 1979.

Below: 'Meditation Piece'. Porcelain relief 11 × 11 in. (28 × 28 cm). With black metallic glaze, mounted in black stoneware frame. By Christa Gebhardt (West Germany), 1977.

Right: 'Little Vessel with Ears'. Porcelain with celadon glaze, height 3½ in. (9 cm). By Christa Gebhardt (West Germany), 1979.

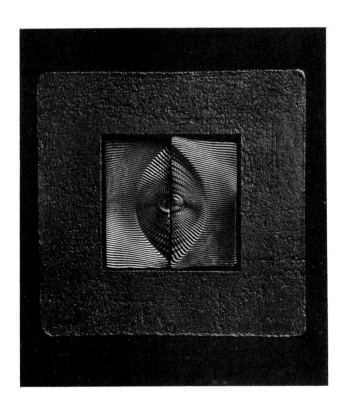

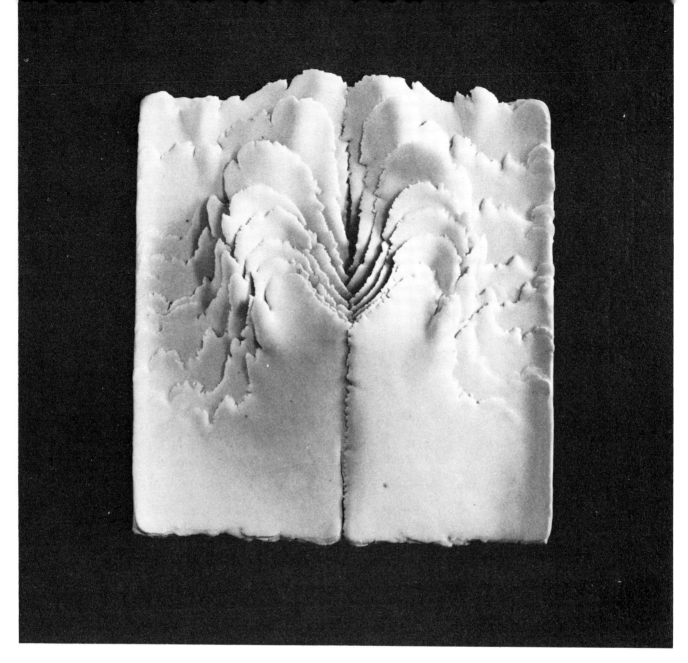

Below: 'Winter Weaving'. Hand-built and thrown porcelain dish, 9 in. (22.9 cm) diameter. Clear glaze, reduction fired to 1300°C. By Ann Mortimer (Canada).

Above: Layered relief, 18½ × 18½ in. (46.4 × 46.4 cm), with bright celadon glaze, mounted in brown-black stoneware. By Christa Gebhardt (West Germany), 1979.

Opposite: 'Figures Trapped in Cushion'. Textile cushion soaked in porcelain slip and modelled, 10 in. (25.4 cm) wide. By Ruth and Alan Barratt-Danes.

Strips of clay can be pressed together to build up slabs either in open-work designs or as sheets leaving distinctive fine lines where overlaps occur and these can be further emphasised by inlaying stains or oxides later when dry. This presents fascinating decorative possibilities because the purity of the porcelain offers no surface distractions to disturb the clarity of line. Strips can even be joined by weaving and pressing as can be seen in the dish on the left made by **Ann Mortimer** (Canada).

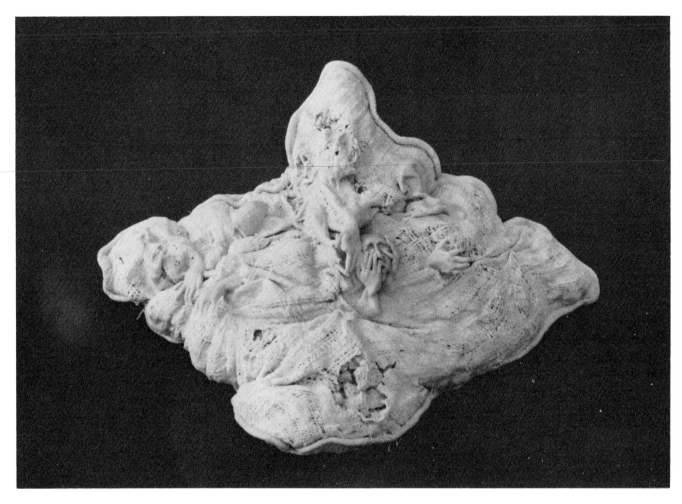

Modelling and sculpting

The work of **Beate Kuhn** has already been mentioned under the section on throwing because, although she is very much a sculptor, all her work is assembled from thrown and cut pieces. She describes some of her porcelain as "little machines to display the translucency of the material".

Ruth and Alan Barratt-Danes have used a variety of techniques to model some disturbing images which are described in their notes to a 1978 exhibition: "The inhabitants of the soft structures, hovering on the fringe of consciousness, find themselves trapped in the enveloping folds of their chairs and realising their predicament, struggle against, or submit to, the over-powering forces that threaten to suppress them. Sometimes their defensive reactions will succeed and they are released, but more often than not the struggle to find a way out is a bewildering and painful

experience, and the conflict is in vain, with the result that they submit to the inevitable situation and become totally enmeshed in an inanimate object that has manifested its aggressive will."

Fabric cushions are made by Ruth to soak in porcelain slip and into which figures are modelled with plastic clay. When fired the textile fibre burns away leaving its "fossilised" ceramic skin from the slip.

They have produced a series of lidded boxes surmounted by frogs which are initially thrown by Alan in one piece and are left uncut until the modelling is complete. When they have been turned and finished in the leather-hard state they are dampened until plastic enough to be manipulated by the apparent force of the frog which has previously been roughly modelled. It is almost as if the animal is attacking the form. The air within the sphere acts as a cushion which helps to retain the fullness of the form rather like a spongy ball. In this way "the frog is dictating where he

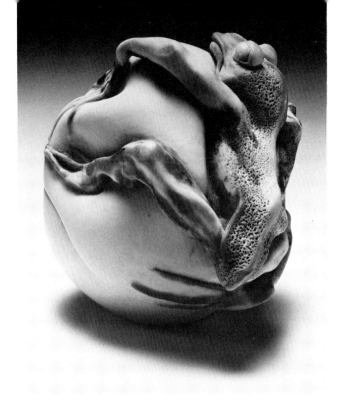

is'' rather than just being stuck on top. The earlier boxes had fairly conventionally fitting lids but later pieces were separated by a much more sympathetic undulating cut line and giving greater interest to the two halves. Most of the modelling is done by Ruth who completes the detailed treatment when the frog is mounted in position.

Body stains are worked into the plastic clay until the colours appear quite dense and Ruth keeps a palette of coloured porcelain available and tones it down by mixing with some of the white body. She finds that modelling with very fine tools directly into the coloured clay which has been applied in particular areas, gives finer detail and greater definition of form than could be achieved by other colouring methods. The ''abundance of frogs'' in their garden are a constant source of stimulus.

When the modelling is finished and the lid has been separated from the base, the frog is cleaned and refined by scraping to bring out the sharpness of detail and colour. Any glaze layer would diffuse the modelling and ''reduce the intensity of the beastie'' so it is normally left in the vitrified bisque state.

The David Leach porcelain body has been put to a more unusual use by Alan and Ruth in some of their narrative pieces. Mixed into a slip with vanadium stain it has been sprayed on to some of the 'mushroom' forms which are the habitat of lustred frogs and snakes. The contrast of the two distinct surfaces adds considerable interest to the final image.

Opposite: 'Cat' assembled from multiple thrown parts, height 7¹/₈ in. (18 cm). Celadon glaze. Fired to 1360°C. By Beate Kuhn (West Germany).

Above left: 'Frog-box'. Thrown and modelled porcelain. The lid was thrown separately. By Ruth and Alan Barratt-Danes.

Above: 'Frog-box'. Thrown in one piece, modelled and cut into two halves. By Ruth and Alan Barratt-Danes.

Below: 'Toadstools with snake'. Porcelain with lustre on snake, height 6 in. (15.2 cm). Texture produced by sprayed, stained slip. By Ruth and Alan Barratt-Danes.

'City'. Porcelain sculpture. Oxidised. By Bob Rogers.

Left: *Thrown and modelled porcelain form, height 6 in. (15.2 cm). By Geoffrey Eastop.*

Bob Rogers has produced a number of small porcelain sculptures on the theme of 'city'. Elongated wads of porcelain are beaten and indented using wooden paddles to create richly-faceted forms, with a vertical/horizontal bias, evoking thoughts of desert towns rising abruptly from the sand.

Bernhard Vogler is a neighbour of the Scheids and Beate Kuhn in Düdelsheim-Büdingen, Germany, but he produces very different work. He is a talented wood-carver as well as a skilful potter who concentrates his energies mainly on enormous pots. However, he uses plaster to model and carve extremely fine details in flat moulds for slip-casting limited editions of porcelain tiles based on biblical themes. He chooses a different story, which he illustrates in time for Christmas each year, signing every tile with the biblical reference and the date. The tiles, which are either round or square, are usually covered with a coloured transparent glaze that runs slightly from the high points revealing the body colour and emphasising the design through the varying glaze thicknesses.

'Daniel in the Lions' den'. Porcelain tile, 6 in. (15.2 cm) square. By Bernhard Vogler (West Germany).

'Cain Killing Abel'. Porcelain tile, 6 in. (15.2 cm) diameter. By Bernhard Vogler (West Germany).

Below: *Porcelain re-arrangeable sculpture with onglaze enamels, 8¼ × 5¾ in. (21 ×15 cm). By Sarka Radova (Czechoslavakia).*

Above: 'The Party'. Porcelain sculpture, 11 in. (27.9 cm) square. By Gillian Still.

Right: 'George'. Porcelain sculpture, height 9 in. (22.9 cm) Oxidised. By Pauline Fowler, 1979. (Student at Cardiff College of Art).

Below: Porcelain sculpture, height 8 in. (20.3 cm), with impressed and applied textures inlaid with stains and oxides. Unglazed. By Peter Simpson, 1979.

Gillian Still, now living and working in Spain, is interested in capturing one particular moment to express through the medium of ceramic sculpture. Her work is figurative and subjects are taken mainly from incidents in daily life but with currents of the surreal and visual humour running through the skein of ideas. She felt that the translation of these ideas directly into clay which could be fired and made permanent was preferable to other kinds of sculpture requiring work in one material for casting later in another. Her early work in porcelain was a disappointment to her because she attempted to handle it as if it were the coarser, gritty clays like T material or crank mixture with which she had previously worked. She soon decided that 'trying to coax life into a flaccid piece of modelling" was almost certain to prove a waste of time and that it was wiser to start afresh. She discovered that she had to change her approach for porcelain and find different methods to overcome the problems, especially porcelain's brittle fragility when bone-dry. Working directly on to kiln shelves avoided breakages which could happen when lifting pieces and placing them into the kiln. Nevertheless, kiln loading is not undertaken unless she is unlikely to be disturbed and when she is in a "tranquil frame of mind"!

She believes it is essential to be absolutely clear in

Opposite: 'Wedding Cake'. Porcelain sculpture, made and fired in three sections before joining. 12 × 22 in. (30.4 × 55.8 cm). Oxidised. By Gillian Still.

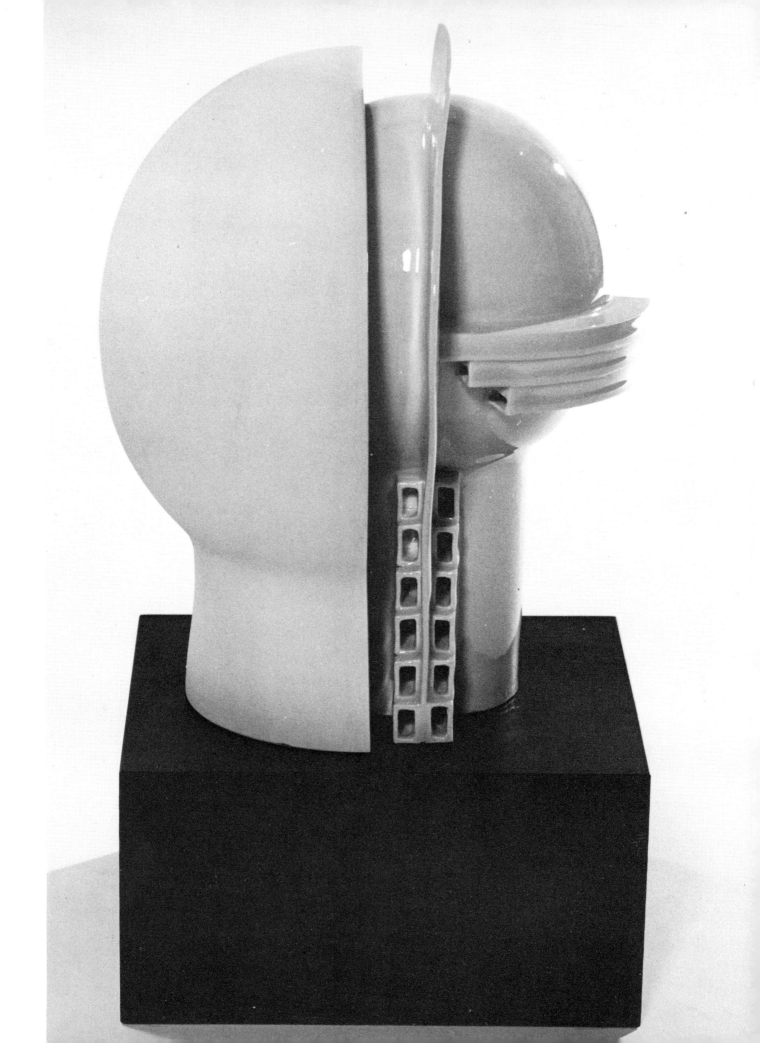

'Oxford Garden Party'. Rolled porcelain figures, height 9½ in. (24 cm). Unglazed. By Audrey Blackman.

'Overlap Interlock'. Three piece slip-cast porcelain sculpture, height 8¼ in. (20.9 cm). By Peter Wright.

'Tree with Birds'. Porcelain, height 3 in. (7.6 cm). By Virginia Doloughan (Ulster).

thinking out, not only the form of the sculpture, but also the method of construction before starting work. Her pieces are hollow-built with inner supports to buttress the natural tendency of porcelain to sag slightly in firing. Figures are worked as quickly as possible in an attempt to keep the forms "fresh and crisp". Over-worked porcelain, she finds, becomes lifeless as a material and this will be reflected in a finished piece.

Her figures are constructed from sheet porcelain rolled into hollow tubes and shaped into limbs. The heads are developed from pinched hollow balls. Parts are joined with slip and the junctions thoroughly smoothed over before any detailed modelling is begun.

Opposite: 'Head'. Porcelain sculpture. By Kurt Spurey (Austria).

125

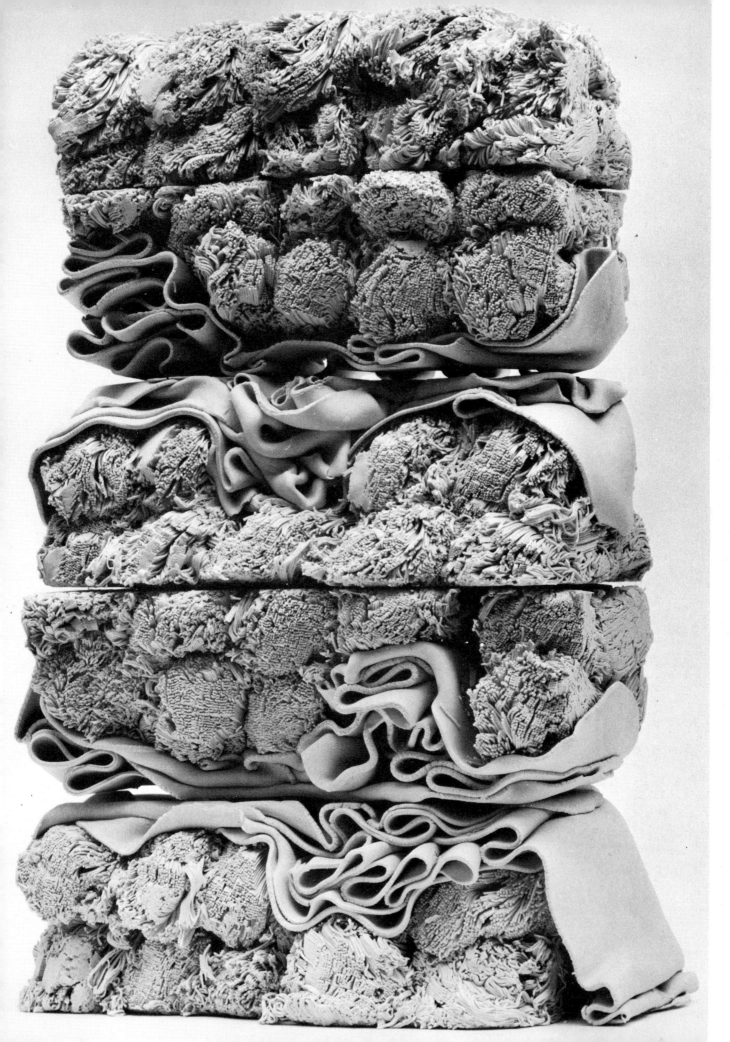

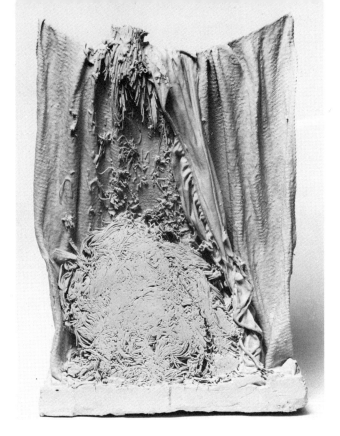

'Suspension'. Porcelain sculpture, 19½ × 13 × 6¾ in. (50 × 34 × 17 cm). Unglazed. Oxidised to 1300°C in an electric kiln. By Nicole Giroud (France), 1979.

The imagery of **Anna Zamorska** (Poland) is inspired by her love of landscape — the earth and the sky. Explaining her approach she says "I try to reproduce in the hardest ceramic material — porcelain — something of the transitory softness of trees, grass and clouds." Much of her work consists of small sculptural units, partially shaped by hand, and these are arranged together in compositions of between 50 and 150 pieces to become 'ceramic landscapes'. She works in a tableware factory in Walbrzych and only uses the materials which are available there. A clear glaze is used, sometimes with over-glaze colours or lustres, but pieces are occasionally left unglazed also.

For **Nicole Giroud** of France, porcelain offers her the opportunity to explore a multiplicity of textures. She uses the white porcelain body from Limoges without added colour or glaze of any kind because she feels that glaze hides the "vitality of the relief work; masking the texture of the body and the structures themselves as if with a garment". Her sculptural work utilises strips, ribbons, shreds and filaments of plastic porcelain extruded through metal grids and composed into a variety of structures. She finds that only porcelain, worked with the help of mechanical means, allows her the freedom to express organic rhythms and movement "nearest to life."

Opposite: 'Threads and Folds'. Porcelain sculpture, 25¼ × 15¾ × 8⅝ in. (64 × 40 × 22 cm). Unglazed. Oxidised to 1300°C in an electric kiln. By Nicole Giroud (France), 1979.

'The Landskyscape'. 72 × 72 × 72 in. (180 × 180 × 180 cm). Part glazed porcelain fired to 1420°C. By Anna Zamorska (Poland).

Two landscaped porcelain boxes. By Anne James.

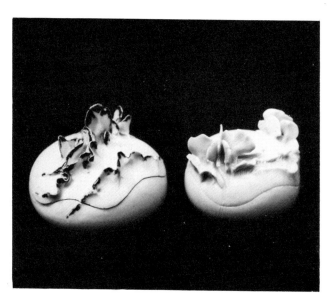

127

Sequence of six photos showing the method used to make a plaster mould in sections. This mould was then used to slip-cast 'Ozymandias'. (See picture opposite). By Glenys Burton, 1979.

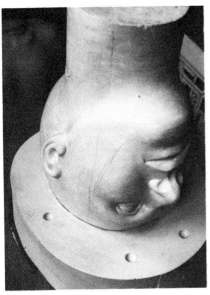

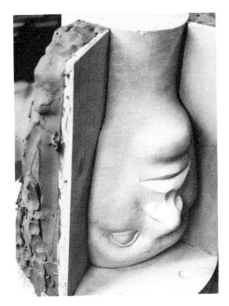

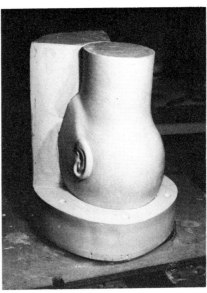

Slip-casting

The advantage of slip-casting is that numbers of basically similar thin-walled pieces can be produced quickly and these require very little finishing. This allows creative energies to be employed in various ways by working upon the pieces or building with them. The final artefact can be as unique and original as any produced by other methods. It first involves the transformation of the porcelain body into a smooth liquid state. This is poured into plaster moulds which are able to absorb the water and retain an even coating of the body adhering to the plaster surface when, after a short while, the excess is drained out. The thickness of the porcelain cast is directly related to the length of time the slip is left in the mould; to the absorbency of the plaster and to the wetness of the slip.

If water alone were to be used to liquify the body material the shrinkage rate and subsequent degree of

Opposite: 'Ozymandias'. Semi-porcelain sculpture height 18 in. (45.1 cm) fired to 1260°C in an electric kiln. The glaze is smoked later in sawdust. By Glenys Barton, 1979.

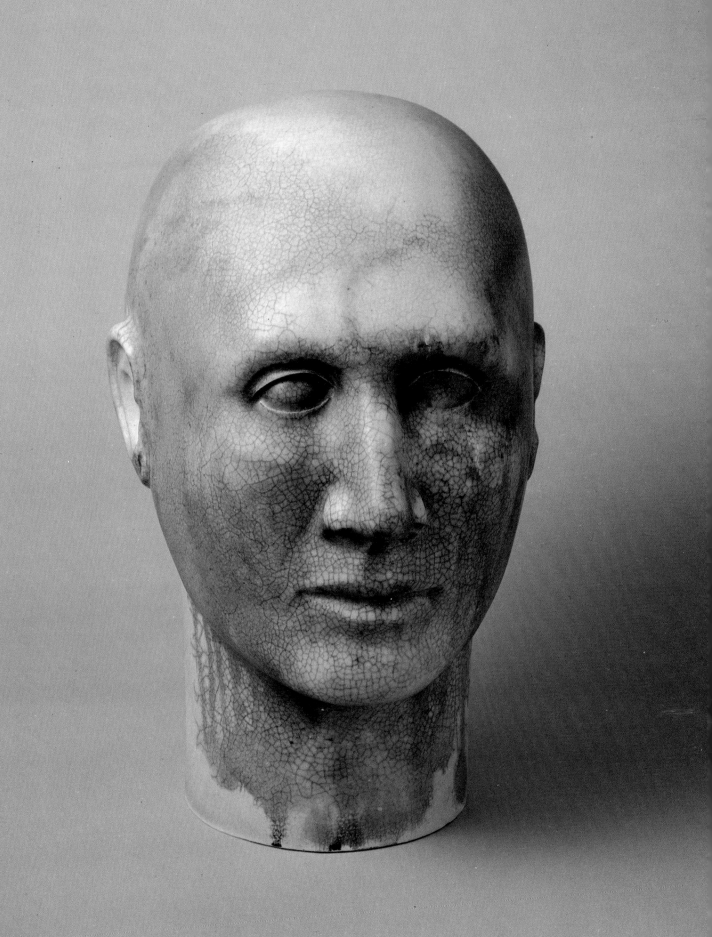

Slip-cast bowls with blue underglaze decoration, 1³/₈–4¹/₈ in. (3.5–10.5 cm). Fired to 1420°C. By Anne Marie Trolle (Denmark).

warping would be unacceptable. At the same time the moulds would quickly become saturated with water and the casts would take far too long to dry and come away from the mould. Sodium silicate and/or soda ash are therefore added, with only small amounts of

Slip-cast and carved porcelain bowl. By Alan Whittaker.

water, to deflocculate the slip, by reducing the electrical attraction of the particles, to the point where it flows easily and dries quickly with a low rate of shrinkage. Deflocculated slip may contain as little as one quarter of its weight in water and has a rather oily texture. Water is drawn off by the capillary action of the plaster leaving the clay deposit to create the form.

This method of forming is particularly useful for bodies possessing little or no plasticity; bone china being a case in point. It is a process often scorned by studio potters and dismissed as inferior to those techniques which require a more intimate involvement and contact between hands and materials and where inevitable variations are more likely to contribute to the individuality of each piece. Slip-casting is an essential part of industrial mass production and therefore represents for many a detached and almost mindless approach to making pots. I have experienced occasions when, having used slip-casting methods in part towards the creation of certain forms, a piece has gained unqualified approval until the techniques involved have been explained. Despite the fact that it has been given further treatment resulting in obviously individual characteristics, the piece seems somehow to have been devalued through revelation of the methods used to produce it! This attitude seems to me to be both narrow and unjustified. If the final visual statement is strong enough to stand alone on merit, and if it satisfies any relevant aesthetic criteria, then it more than vindicates the methods used to reach that particular end.

The two main applications of the slip-casting process, appropriate to contemporary porcelain potters, are towards either sculptural or decorative ends. Sometimes limited editions are made in which only slight or subtle variations occur from one cast to another, when glaze or firing processes provide the differences. **Glenys Barton** is probably the sculptor/artist/ceramist (her work is difficult to categorise) who immediately comes to mind. Others, like **Paul Astbury** and **Richard Shaw** (USA), take plaster casts from existing objects, fragments from everyday life, and use the moulds to slip-cast components for assembly into new and unusual forms. But increasing use is being made of the process to produce simple basic shapes upon which a whole range of decorative treatments may be employed;

Opposite: *'Stack of Cards on Brown Book'. Porcelain sculpture, slip-cast, height 14 in. (35.4 cm). By Richard Shaw (USA), 1977.*

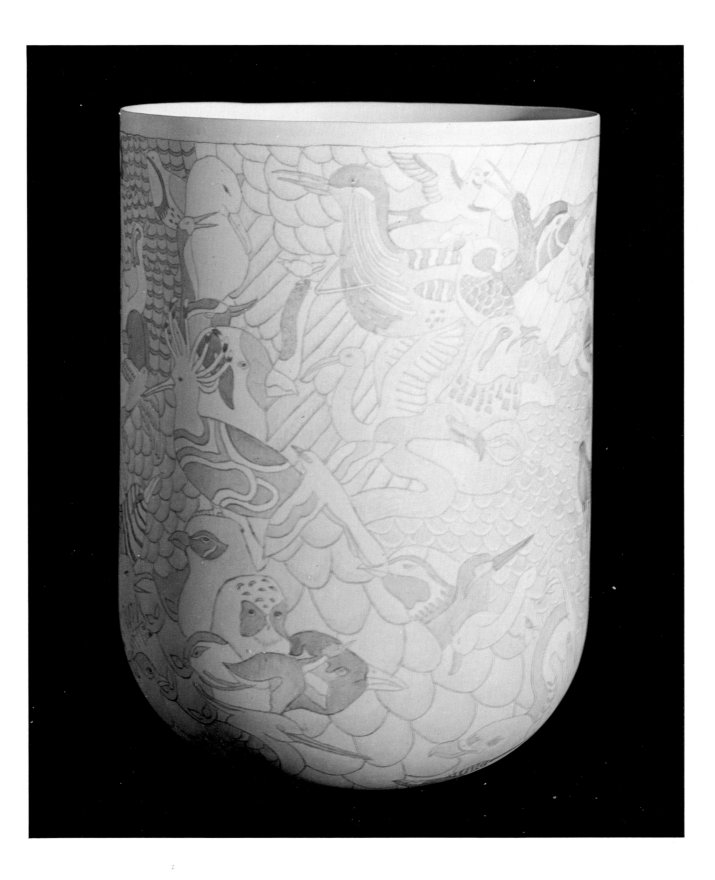

carving, sand-blasting or painting in particular. Quiet, uncomplicated forms may be covered in the most complex designs or painted imagery. The simplicity of such forms allows them to accept an almost riotous arrangement of line and colour without any loss of unity. **Jane Osborne-Smith's** work especially displays a world full of delicate fantasy. The painted decoration is readable, almost as if a mural had been miniaturised to fit perfectly around a piece, without appearing ostentatious or out of place. The painting further defines and complements the form by its continuous, unbroken action.

The moulds used for these simple forms are usually cast in one-piece because no undercutting is involved and the slip-cast form can drop out easily as it dries.

Opposite: 'Large Bird Pot'. Cylindrical porcelain bowl painted in polychrome enamels, height 7⁵/₈ in. (19.3 cm). Oxidised. By Jane Osborne-Smith, 1979.

'Eagles with mushrooms'. White porcelain bowl with bifurcated lid. Modelled white porcelain fishes are attached by means of plaited silk threads and hang inside the bowl. The bowl and lid are painted with polychrome enamels. Diameter 4⁵/₈ in, height 4 in. (11.7 cm, 10.2 cm). Oxidised. By Jane Osborne-Smith, 1979.

Some of **Irene Sims'** pieces are made in two-piece moulds but, in the main, the one-piece variety is all that is needed and provides sufficient scope for imaginative treatment.

Where surface perfection in a slip-cast form is of prime importance, the model, from which the plaster-cast mould is to be taken, is itself usually made from plaster. If the form is to have a circular section it will be smoothly finished by turning on a lathe. When the walls of the model are either parallel or widen without interruption of contour towards the rim, a one-piece mould presents no problems. The plaster

133

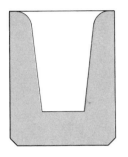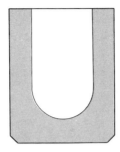

Simple one-piece drop-out moulds for slip-casting.

model is thoroughly soft-soaped by working up a lather over the surface with a soft brush. This is then wiped off with a soapy sponge before wiping again with a clean sponge which has been dipped in water and squeezed dry. This process is repeated two or three times (omitting the water-sponging on the final occasion) to impregnate the plaster surface with soap so that it will resist water and release the subsequent plaster cast.

The model can, in fact, be made of any material and some will release the mould without any need for a soft-soap separation film. Clay models can give fairly smooth surfaces, especially when made from a porcelain body, finely turned on the wheel.

Ideally, the final mould, 100 parts water to 130 parts plaster, should be equal in thickness (about two inches constant) to ensure its even performance in casting slip later. If the mould is thinner in some places it will absorb less water and retain less slip on its surface than thicker sections. A retaining wall, or cottle, of linoleum or tin plate, is positioned around the model and any gaps are sealed with clay.

Plaster is always added to water by sprinkling and, in mixing, care is taken not to whip air into it. One hand kept beneath the surface of the water can usually ensure a smooth mix by continuously agitating with the fingers. When ready, plaster is poured evenly and steadily over the model to avoid trapping air bubbles on its surface and continued until about 2 inches above it. The casting is more satisfactory if sufficient plaster is mixed to complete the operation in one go and it is wiser to make up a little too much to be certain of this.

The plaster heats up and swells slightly as it sets and the model should not be removed until the plaster is cool. Any sharp edges on the outside of the mould are then rounded off to prevent breakages which could contaminate the slip or other clays. It is very important not to allow any stray plaster to come into contact with clay-working surfaces because the smallest fragments trapped within the wall of a pot will absorb

atmospheric moisture and expand to break the surface. This sometimes happens several months after firing. For this reason many potters keep all plaster well away from their main working area.

Some potters prefer to obtain their casting slips ready prepared because the balance of deflocculant and water is a delicate one. (**Kurt Spurey** and **Irene Sims** both use slips prepared for industrial mass production.) But, apart from the non-creative chore of preparation, casting slips are not difficult to make up. Ideally they should be thoroughly mixed in a blunger, but *known* amounts of dry material and water (recorded for future reference) can be mixed by hand in a bucket, if care is taken to ensure an even blending which, following the measured addition of deflocculant, will pass through a 120 mesh sieve. It is first mixed up into a thick creamy consistency and the deflocculant added two or three drops at a time and thoroughly stirred in. The process is repeated until the slip runs smoothly from the fingers and can be put through the sieve. Trial and error methods, cautiously applied, will produce satisfactory results using different ratios of water and deflocculant as seems necessary for individual body composition. If careful records are kept, subsequent mixtures should be straightforward.

Most suppliers of prepared plastic bodies also sell them in dry, powder form and will suggest casting slip recipes to guide those who wish to make up their own. Some suppliers manufacture reliable casting slips for delivery in airtight plastic drums.

Frank Hamer suggests the following deflocculant recipe.[30]

Sodium silicate 140°TW	1 fluid oz.
Sodium carbonate	1 oz.
Hot water	2 fluid oz.

The powdered David Leach body from Podmores[32] makes up into a good casting slip based upon the following proportions:

P1035 powdered porcelain body	110 lbs. (50 kg)
Sodium silicate 140°TW	350 fluid oz. (99 mls)
Water	52 fluid oz. (29.6 ltrs.)

(simply divide these figures by ten to arrive at a manageable bucketful).

It is essential to store all slips in airtight containers because they will quickly be spoilt by exposure to the

Opposite: *Two slip-cast porcelain forms, inlaid with coloured slip, height of tallest 8 in. (20.3 cm). By Irene Sims, 1979.*

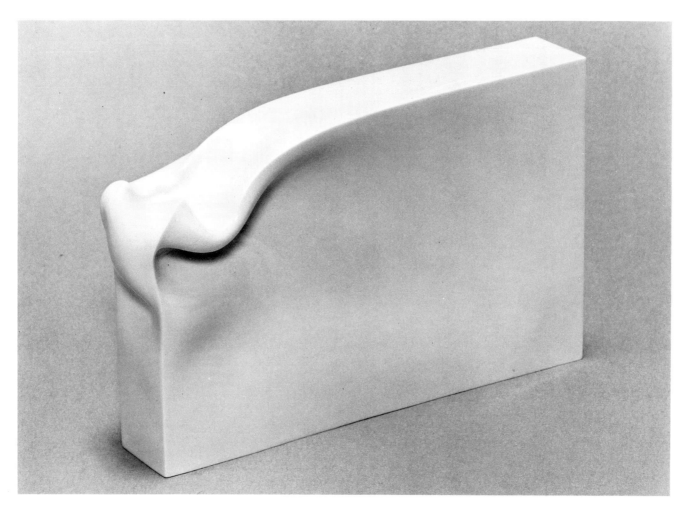

Above: 'Touch'. Slip-cast porcelain, distorted by hand, 13¾ × 2⅜ × 8⅝ in. (34.8 × 6 × 22 cm). By Kurt Spurey (Austria).

Below: *Simple slip-cast forms from a one-piece mould. Pinched tops. Porcelain with various copper glazes, height 4 in. (10.2 cm). Reduction fired. By Peter Lane, 1979.*

air. If a skin should form on the surface it should be removed and not mixed in. Some potters overcome this problem by using a film of oil to protect the surface from contact with the air. Every time a batch of slip is to be used it should be thoroughly stirred and resieved. Excess slip from the mould may be poured back into the container but any which has been in contact with the plaster or has dried should not be returned. It can be re-used if separately made up again with fresh additions of deflocculant, but its performance may be less satisfactory than new slip.

The length of time the slip remains in the mould is best judged by the eye. As the water is absorbed into the mould the level of the slip will drop and it should be topped up with more slip to ensure an even

Slip-cast bowl, height 3¾ in. (9.5 cm). By Jacqueline Poncelet.

thickness for the full height of the walls. Tipping the mould slightly will reveal the wall thickness. Extremely thin walls are possible and, if bentonite is not used, warping should be minimal. Almost paper-thin pieces have been cast in bone china by **Jacqueline Poncelet** and others. For small casts I usually find that up to 30 seconds is quite sufficient with the David Leach body slip, and gives a thickness of around 1/16 in. which is quite sufficient for most small scale work.

Once the wet shine has disappeared the cast is trimmed, usually within 15 minutes or so as cast forms dry quickly. They may be carved and joined to other pieces quite soon after removing from the mould. Sometimes the cast will stick on one side a little and may need some gentle encouragement to release it from the mould. A one-piece cast can be eased clear without too much difficulty by placing the fingers vertically down the side which is already free and smoothly applying very slight pressure, but, beyond this, it should not be forced. If the mould is of even thickness the problem is less likely to arise.

137

FOUR
DECORATIVE PROCESSES

The whiteness and compact nature of the porcelain body invites any of a variety of decorative treatments. Unlike many stoneware bodies which contain impurities that bleed through and enliven the glaze surface in a reduction firing, porcelain does not alter dramatically. Calculated 'chance effects' are more likely to be confined to certain coloured glazes. This freedom from visual interference allows and encourages potters to use precisely-placed decorative elements to complement the forms. Whether the surface is cut, carved, scratched, inlaid or painted, the body will not intrude. In most cases textural interest of any kind is created solely by the potter. Applied design, therefore, can be minutely controlled. The fire gives the work permanence but it cannot conjure up those random qualities which often bring stoneware pieces to life. Such contribution would be alien to the material in every way. The enrichment of porcelain surfaces is within the gift of the potter to a greater degree in this sense and he cannot rely on the kiln to do the work for him. Clearly, this constitutes much of the appeal of porcelain.

Carving and Incising

The surface of porcelain can be cut and scratched at all stages from wet to dry but I prefer to carve into it when leather-hard so that the clay retains a slight resilience

while remaining firm enough to resist distortion under pressure. In this state it is a delightful material to carve and incise. It cuts smoothly and cleanly with sharp tools, leaving a crisp edge. Even loops of thickish wire are unlikely to tear the surface if pulled through at the right stage of drying. This is something that can only be gauged through practice, and it is useful to remember that porcelain, normally a creamy colour in the plastic state, rapidly turns white as it dries.

The major disadvantages of carving porcelain in a bone-dry condition, apart from it being a slow and painstaking process, are its brittleness and the excessive amounts of dust created (one of the greatest hazards in working any dry clay). When dry, the material will often chip along the edges of incised lines in a way that is difficult (but not impossible) to control, and the urge to blow dust away in order to reveal the design must be resisted at all costs. Extra fine particles settle everywhere, to be stirred by the slightest movements so that they hang in the air and are

Opposite: Porcelain dish, 9 in. (22.9 cm) diameter. Thrown and incised (using dental tools). The incised lines are filled with stained porcelain slip. By Caroline Whyman, 1979.

Right: Porcelain bowl, thrown and carved with 'hills and trees', 11 in. (27.9 cm) diameter. Oxidised with shaded glazes. By Peter Lane, 1976.

Carving the rim of a thrown and turned porcelain bowl.

Piercing holes in the wall of the bowl to define the trees.

Incising to connect the hills. Note the supporting left hand.

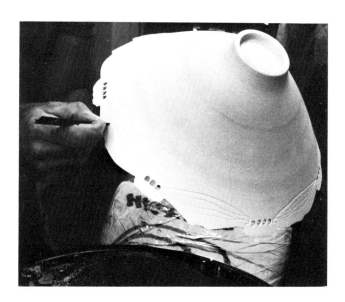

The left hand supports the bowl while final contours are incised and bevelled.

breathed by the unwary. In fact, potters who prefer incising or scraping dry porcelain should *always* wear a face mask covering the nose and mouth. These are cheap enough, not too uncomfortable in use, and they will thwart any attempt at dust-blowing. Despite the most careful precautions, it is inevitable that some dust will be formed and regular washing of workshop surfaces is strongly recommended.

Cutting into the surface of clay was one of the earliest and most natural means of decorating pottery. Some of the finest incised decoration in the history of ceramics was produced by the Chinese potters of the Sung Dynasty. Their beautifully flowing, stylised plant designs were accentuated by bright, fluid glazes pooling in the depressions. Crisp lines and subtle gradations of tone were created by bevelled cuts outlining the areas of the pattern so that the glaze darkened as the depth increased.

Above: *Porcelain bowl, thrown and carved, 11 in. (27.9 cm) diameter. Celadon glaze, fired to 1280°C. By Peter Lane, 1979.*

Below: *Porcelain bowl, thrown and carved, 10 in. (25.4 cm) diameter, with cobalt, manganese and rutile brushed over the dolomite glaze. Oxidised to 1280°C. By Peter Lane, 1977.*

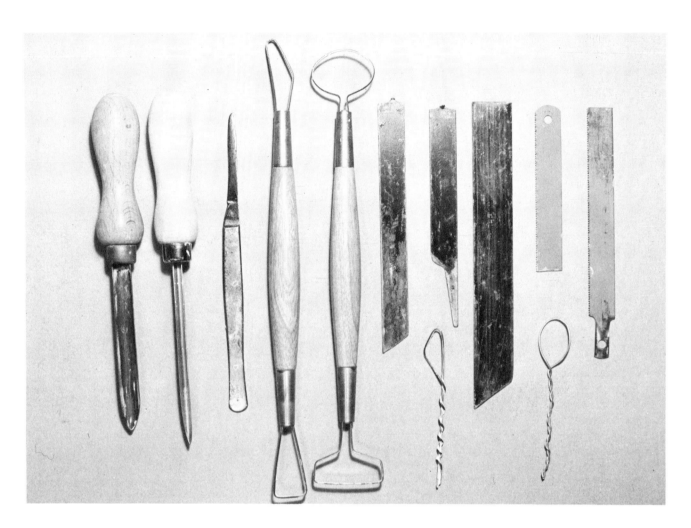

Carving tools used by the author.

Left: *Porcelain bowl with combed rim, 7 in. (17.7 cm) wide. By Colin Pearson, 1979.*

This kind of carving is best undertaken when the clay is quite firm or the tool may judder, resulting in uneven removal of waste material. I often like to draw linear patterns with a purpose-designed tool (made from metal-strip) making a clean, right-angled incision of consistent depth and width. This is followed by another tool which shaves a bevel, or shallow horizontal V-section, along one side of the cut line. Equally, a needle or similar sharp point can be used to outline the design ahead of the bevelling tool. The vertical edge of the incised line is more likely to be torn using the latter method, but, in either case, any obtrusively sharp or jagged parts can easily be softened later.

Porcelain bowl with incised slip decoration, 6 in. (15.2 cm) diameter, and porcelain lidded box incised and inlaid with oxides, height 2½ in. (6.3 cm). By Sheila Casson, 1979.

Right: Fluted vase in three-colour agate ware porcelain, height 9 in. (22.9 cm). By Robin Hopper (Canada).

The free hand should, wherever possible, support the wall immediately behind the points at which pressure is being applied because open forms, such as bowls, are particularly vulnerable unless treated with care and sensitivity. Carving the inside of a bowl places considerable stress upon a very small area around the tool, especially near the rim, but when working on the outer surface some of the pressure is distributed along the curve of the form, lessening the risk of fracture. **Dorothy Feibelman** works on both sides of the dry clay walls when carving her trellis patterns because she finds it impossible to cut through safely any other way. She normally carves porcelain in the dry state, before bisque firing, when it is extremely brittle, using a sharp scalpel, razor blades and steel wool. She has attempted to use a dentist's drill but the vibration proved to be too fierce. She has also

Two delicately carved porcelain bowls with marqueterie inlay, 4 in. (10.2 cm) diameter. Oxidised. By Dorothy Feibelman, 1977.

experimented with various kinds of flour and starch, such as obtained from rice and potato, mixed into the clay which stiffens it for carving and causes only a minimal loss of translucency.

Various tools can be used to pierce right though the walls when still leather-hard, and a gentle pressure with a rotational cutting action is the safest and most satisfactory method. Holes made in this way can be enlarged and shaped with a potter's knife or a tapering blade of metal-strip. Gradual removal of unwanted material is generally wiser than risking the destruction of the piece by trying to take too much too quickly. With patience and care a very fine lattice can be cut in porcelain which would be quite impossible to achieve in a coarser body. But, apart from the aesthetic considerations, any sort of piercing must be sympathetically approached to avoid weakening the form to the point where it may collapse in the firing.

A fine grade of wire wool can be finally used to round off sharp edges and rims provided that all the dust with its fragments of metal is discarded. Some potters prefer the nylon pads, made for cleaning saucepans, to lessen the risk of metal contamination in clay, although meticulous organisation of workshop space with a view to cleanliness reduces such problems. A barely-damp sponge may be used where outer edges are concerned but it can rarely be

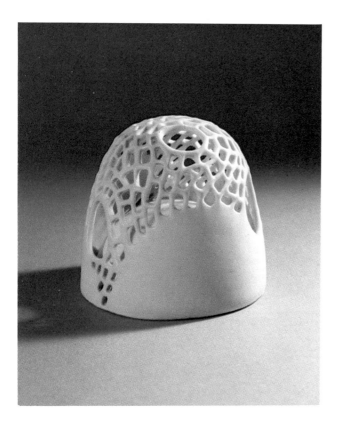

Slip-cast and carved porcelain form, height 3 in. (7.6 cm). Oxidised to 1280°C. By Alison White, 1976. (Student at Keswick Hall College of Education).

Sheila Casson carving bowls with applied rims.

Right: *Three shallow bowls with carving, 6 in, (15.2 cm) diameter. By Deirdre Burnett, 1979.*

compressed enough to deal with more confined areas of the design.

Sheila Casson adds thrown sections to the rims of simple cylindrical or bowl forms with rounded tapering bases and then, piercing right through the wall, carves them into distinctive features. Since the additions are usually confined to one side and much higher at one point, the unbalanced weight makes such pieces prone to warp. This need not necessarily be detrimental to the form.

Two large porcelain flasks made from thrown and assembled sections. An inner wall is placed behind the pierced centre decoration. By David Eeles, 1979.

Right: *Diagrammatic view of the five thrown sections in one of David Eeles' fretwork vases.*

Below: *Translucent porcelain bowl in 'sky' series, height 2¾ in. (7 cm), diameter 5¼ in. (13.3 cm). By Victor Margrie, 1968.*

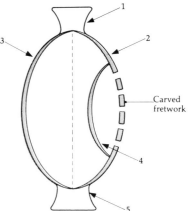

Carved
fretwork

The pierced flasks of **David Eeles** are constructed from several thrown parts including an inner wall behind the carved area (see above). Double skinned walls with pierced-work designs, often of great intricacy, can be traced back through different periods of ceramic history reappearing from time to time in a variety of forms.

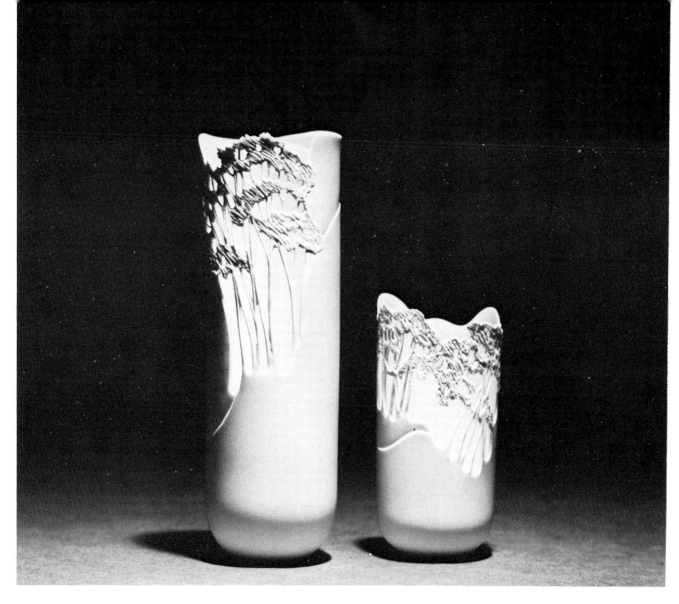

Analogies can be readily drawn between the pierced forms found in nature: seed cases, sponges, bones, coral etc., and some of the pinched and carved porcelain of **Mary Rogers**. The smoothness of the material allows so much to be cut away that the final structure may consist of no more than a network of ceramic threads and still survive the fire.

The ultra-fine carving of **Irene Sims** has already been mentioned. Her favourite tools are surgical scalpels but they quickly become blunt and have to be changed frequently. Her slip-cast pieces in porcelain or bone china are worked on when leather-hard. Any texturing of the surface is carried out before the walls are pierced. Horizontal groundlines running around the pot are indicated in pencil and a guide cut made along them for the wall to be pared down to, leaving a tiny ledge. The bevelling is softened using a damp, soft-haired paintbrush. Surprisingly, few pieces are lost through breakages at this stage but losses due to cracking (mainly in the tree trunks) or warping are sometimes as high as 50% in the glost kiln fired to 1240°C.

Two cylindrical forms, slip-cast and carved, the tallest 7 in. (17.7 cm). By Irene Sims, 1979.

Two seed pod forms, pinch-built and carved, 3 in. (7.6 cm) long. By Mary Rogers, 1979.

147

Group of fluted pieces by David Leach.

Left: *David Leach fluting. Note the supporting left hand.*

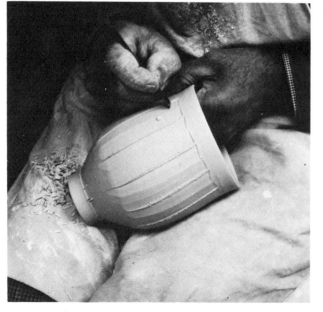

The bold, fluted carving of **David Leach** is well-known and much-admired. He uses two or three variations of his vertical fluting achieved through holding the tool at different angles and altering the spacing of the strokes. To be successful this type of decorative treatment must be tackled in a confident, relaxed manner with controlled rhythmic movements. The basic tool is simply a strip of metal, hacksaw blade or, sometimes, a sharpened bamboo tool. Fluting is done at the leather-hard stage and he rests the pot in his lap, with his left hand holding and supporting the wall at the point of carving.

Some of the most highly-skilled and meticulous carving in porcelain comes from **Karl Scheid** (West Germany). Few can equal his control and versatility of design. Although not consciously adapted from nature he acknowledges that similar patterns of repetitive elements that ornament his work may be found in natural objects. He often draws vertical guide-lines on the pot with a pencil when the clay is in the right condition and begins carving at the bottom. Each horizontal line is also drawn in as the work proceeds. The whole process requires intense concentration and takes a very long time. Some of the most complex carving may take up a whole day and certainly no more than three of the 'simpler' designs can be finished in that time. Razor blades and strip-metal loops made from alarm clock springs, are the tools he uses. The real pleasure for him is in the successfully completed piece where every detail of form, ornament and glaze are perfected in harmony. "A goldsmith's work is very fine, so why should not hand-made porcelain have similar quality?"

In my own work I normally use a loop of wire for carving flutes. Different thicknesses of wire can be bent into a variety of looped shapes for cutting appropriate widths and depths. The loop meets with less resistance from the clay than a solid blade and,

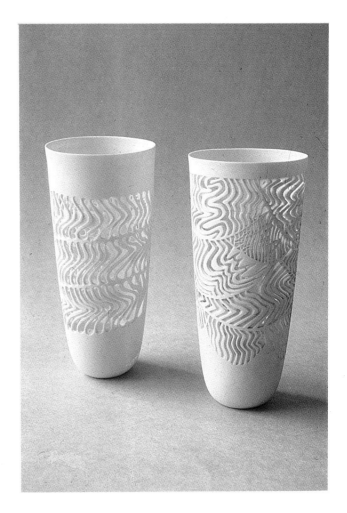

Two porcelain vases, slip-cast, carved and sand-blasted. By Alan Whittaker.

Below: *Carved porcelain, height 4¾ × 5⁷/₈ in. (12 × 15 cm). By Karl Scheid (West Germany), 1975.*

Right: *Carved porcelain bottle, height 4³/₈ in. (11 cm). By Karl Scheid (West Germany), 1975.*

Porcelain bowl with 'clouds'. Carved rim. Oxidised to 1280°C. By Ian Pirie, 1979.

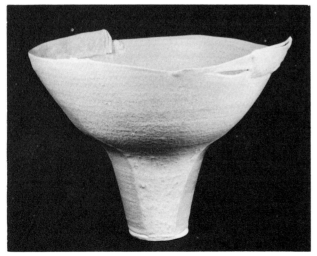

Left: 'Edge-scape Vessel,' height $8\frac{1}{4} \times 10\frac{3}{4}$ in. (20.9 × 27.3 cm). By Sally Bowen Prange (USA), 1979.

particularly when made from wire, smooth directional changes of movement present few problems. One stroke is usually sufficient and will leave a clean-edged flute whereas a blade tool requires several strokes to shave away successive layers to the chosen depth or section. On the other hand a strip blade is used exclusively in carving my 'landscape' bowls because directional variations are gradual and flowing, and are executed with relatively shallow, bevelled cuts. These bowls, initially thrown and turned quite thin, especially towards the rim, are carved when 'firmly

leather-hard'. Not so soft that burrs appear at the
edges of the carving and not so dry that the waste
material falls away like a damp powder. There is just
enough strength and resilience to withstand carving
and piercing at this stage without distortion. The
horizon line of the rim is cut first and the edge scraped
and refined with a flexible kidney steel, always
supporting the wall with the palm of the other hand at
the point of pressure. Then the walls are pierced by
rotating the point of the scalpel or metal strip tool into
the wall surface, with the left hand again supporting
and feeling for the point to emerge. Once the holes are
large enough to accept the full width of the blade they
can be gently shaped and related to each other to
suggest the trunks of trees grouped together. The
profiles of foliage and the outlines of the hills are
drawn in with another strip-metal tool especially cut

Porcelain bowl with painted and incised slip relief decoration under a celadon glaze, 3½ in. (8.8 cm) diameter. By Agnete Hoy.

and shaped with a hooked end. The walls are bevelled
down to this line.

Agnete Hoy carves into leather-hard porcelain with
bamboo tools which she makes herself from pieces
taken from her garden. She likes to keep all her
working methods as simple as possible and treats each
piece individually. Occasionally she builds up the
surface with a thick slip made from the body and
models or carves this in relief. Sometimes the slip is
stained with cobalt or manganese. If some of the
carving is subsequently hidden by the glaze she feels
that it "adds to the mystery".

151

Many potters have re-shaped or carved the rims of their pots at one time or another. The smallest nicks removed from the rim of a dish or bowl alter the character of the piece. Superb examples of 'foliated' porcelain were produced by the Chinese and it is a form of treatment, unspectacular but effective, which appears timeless. **Bill Brown's** foliated bowls are deeply indented, cut and re-shaped, while the broad rims of **Ian Pirie's** bowls are carved to suggest billowing clouds above misty, airbrushed landscapes.

Faceted forms are made by leaving the walls thick enough to allow for cutting with a knife or length of taut wire when almost leather-hard. **Antoine de Vinck** (Belgium) and **Betty Woodman** (USA) have both used this method of carving.

Three lidded porcelain jars with carved sides. By Antoine de Vinck (Belgium), 1979.

Below left: *Deeply foliated porcelain bowl with celadon glaze. Oxidised to 1280°. By Bill Brown, 1979.*

Below: *Porcelain lidded jar with cut diagonal facets. Fired to 1300°C. By Betty Woodman (USA), 1975.*

Slips and Oxides

The whiteness of porcelain provides a perfect ground for the application of colour with oxides and prepared stains. One technique is to stain the porcelain itself by wedging oxides directly into the plastic body by layering. The usual method is to wedge and beat the clay into a manageable block which is then cut horizontally with a wire into even slices. The powdered oxides or stains are sprinkled between the slices and the complete sandwich is thoroughly re-wedged. The clay should contain sufficient moisture, without being sticky, to counteract the drying properties of the added powders. Speckling can occur unless the oxides are finely ground and cobalt oxide is the most likely to offend in this respect. Grinding with a pestle and mortar for a few minutes beforehand will help to reduce the particle size to more acceptable levels. This method of oxide addition can be unreliable because it is difficult to judge the final intensity of colour unless careful records are kept of the body: stains, weight ratio, and the distribution of the pigment is also dependent upon the evenness of the wedging process. However, few potters use large amounts of coloured porcelain prepared in this way at any one time, because it is normally used for inlays in small quantities for decoration. It has the advantage that it can be mixed and used immediately, or stored in polythene until required. It must be remembered that the true colours are not revealed until the final firing.

Porcelain which incorporates body stains is normally left unglazed or it may be covered by a transparent glaze (usually shiny) so that the design can be seen. Matt and opaque glazes tend to hide the colour unless the oxides are present in sufficient strength and quantity to stain the glaze itself. Even so, the crispness of the design and any subtle variations are likely to be lost under such glazes.

Inserting stained pieces into balls of porcelain prior to throwing is one of the simplest applications. **Joanna Constantinidis** and **Marianne de Trey** among others, have used the material in this way. A prepared ball of porcelain body is sliced open to receive the stained

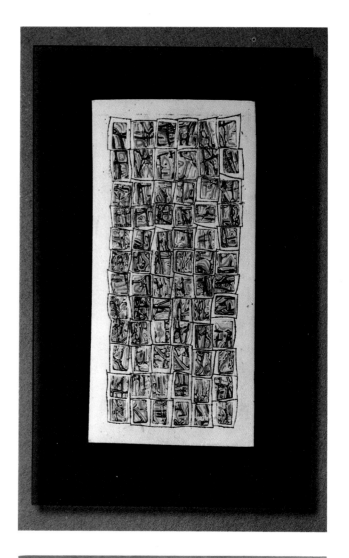

Above right: 'Accumulation'. Inlaid porcelain slab, 7 × 5 in. (17.7 × 12.7 cm). Oxidised to 1260°C. By William Hall, 1979.

Right: Three pieces of thrown porcelain inlaid with copper-stained body inserted prior to throwing. Note the characteristic spirals. Reduction fired to 1280°C. By Marianne de Trey, 1979.

wads and the whole is slapped firmly together again to ensure a smooth bond. Pushing the thumb into the centre between the coloured inserts when throwing will guide them towards the outside of the pot wall where they will appear, spiralling upwards. Several colours can be used but the patterns are not completely predictable. The resultant slurry formed during throwing is best discarded or else kept quite separately to be modified later and brought up to strength with further additions of stain for re-use.

Agate, Neriage and Marqueterie Techniques

Similarly, for agate ware, two or more differently coloured porcelains can be laminated together and lightly wedged prior to throwing. The striations so formed are variable and only revealed when the slurry is cleared from the surface before removal from the wheel. **Robin Hopper** (Canada) makes agate ware in which he creates extra visual interest by cutting or fluting the surface into rhythmic, rippling patterns.

Thin strips, coils, pellets or shaped pieces of the stained plastic material can also be inlaid by placing on to a slab of the white body and rolling in. The inlays will spread according to the degree and direction of rolling but, with practice, it can be reasonably controlled. Adhesion is helped by slightly dampening the underside of the pieces to be applied. If they are made too wet or sticky, subsequent rolling may pick up some of the colour and muddy the surface. It can, of course, always be scraped clean again when drying but it need not be necessary to do this if carefully used in the first place. A sheet of paper laid over the slab before rolling will help to keep the work clean. Any of the constructional methods previously discussed may be used to build with the decorated slabs and any smears which may occur during joining are cleaned up later. Clearly, the colour relationships may be reversed by inlaying white porcelain into the stained body.

Relatively small sheets of porcelain clay may be rolled extremely thin, damped with a sponge, layered and rolled again. Slices taken vertically through the

Above left: *Unglazed porcelain, inlaid, thrown and polished (blue, grey and white). Oxidised to 1280°C. By Peter Lane, 1979.*

Left: *'Folded Form'. Blue and white agate porcelain, height 8½ in. (21.5 cm). By Robin Hopper (Canada), 1977.*

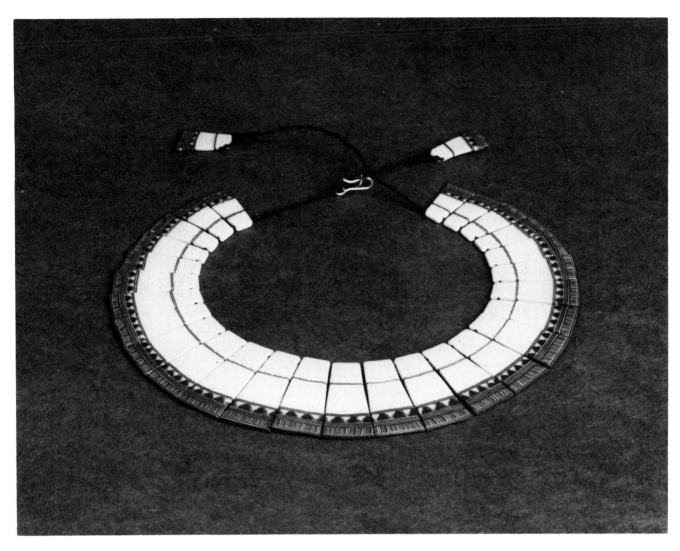

Inlaid porcelain necklace. By Dorothy Feibelman, 1979.

layers give stratified sections which can be used or manipulated further and inlaid as pattern into other slabs. Or a wider slice containing several layers can be rolled up like a carpet from which a spiralled section can be cut. Slices thus taken may be combined with other variations to embellish, or even construct, slab-built forms.

Dorothy Feibelman is one potter who has thoroughly explored this latter technique. Her work is richly ornamented with precisely placed motifs of inlaid agate showing great delicacy. She has been working in porcelain since 1968 and feels that she has now reached the point where she is in control of the material. Translucency is an important element in her work and she scrapes her pots down to an almost eggshell thinness.

She finds that the addition of colouring oxides is likely to alter the fluxing temperature of the body and this may be compensated by adjustments to the basic recipe (if known). When the ingredients in the body remain in the same proportions, irrespective of the amount of colourants added, certain mixtures may blister and bloat at the otherwise normal firing temperatures. If this happens it suggests that that particular mixture has been over-fired to the point where it has begun to 'boil'. Layers so affected within a stratified batch of inlay may separate or at best mar the form and destroy the crispness of the pattern. All stains and mixtures should be thoroughly tested, and modified where necessary, to ensure compatability at the given temperature.

Three porcelain bowls, marqueterie ware, height 2–4 in.
(5–10.2 cm). By Dorothy Feibelman, 1979.

Dorothy Feibelman uses mainly cobalt, copper and iron oxides for most of her colours, and adjusts the body recipe slightly for each. In some of the blues she uses chromium oxide to temper the cobalt.

Apart from its suitability for the kind of work she is doing, she feels that porcelain appeals to her "because it is at the finer end of the scale, rather like silver and gold". It is hardly surprising, therefore, that much of her work is fairly small, possessing some of the qualities of jewellery, and that she also makes necklaces of exquisitely incised porcelain beads or slices.

Dorothy Feibelman's method of inlaying coloured porcelain is an extremely demanding and lengthy process. When making a bowl, for example, she rolls out a thin sheet of porcelain clay and places it into a mould. Then individual segments or slices of agate inlay are carefully moistened and pressed in position to form the pattern on the inside of the bowl. The edges of the segments, where they are to butt up against others, must also be moistened to make strong lateral joints. When the inlaid pattern is complete the bowl is left to dry bone-hard in the mould before the most difficult part of the process begins. The bowl is removed and painstakingly scraped away on the underside to reveal the agate pattern passing right through and forming the body of the piece. Intense concentration and great sensitivity are necessary if the bowl is to survive this treatment and the wastage rate is high. She estimates a loss rate of about seventy-five per cent over the combined stages of drying, scraping and firing. Patience and fortitude is required of all those who would try this technique and although clearly uneconomic, a well-designed and properly executed piece can more than justify the effort involved.

Gary Wornell-Brown prepares his inlays without recourse to rolling at any time yet he produces the most delicately controlled wafers of inlaid porcelain no more than $\frac{1}{64}$ in. thick. These pieces are mounted with a thin layer of strong adhesive on to an opalescent glass sheet, elegantly framed with aluminium moulded-strip and clear glass set on a Perspex stand. The 'pictures' are reminiscent of random slices of a white, veined rock, or of biological sections, but with a range of soft, gentle colours shading from brown-purple, blues and greys. Translucency alters the colour and tonal relationships when the piece is back-lit, and certainly adds to the interest, but although this is an attractive, intentional quality, it is not essential to its enjoyment. All his work is in the David Leach porcelain body.

A small ball of soft plastic porcelain is slapped, stretched and thinned by throwing it down at a sharp angle along the flat surface of a smooth plaster slab. The slab has been carefully cast on glass, to present the most perfect working surface. It is thoroughly dampened to prevent too much loss of plasticity from the porcelain body as it is alternately slapped and peeled off the plaster slab. Despite this precaution the body still has a tendency to dry as it stretches and this is successfully countered by spraying water vapour around the immediate working area to maintain a damp environment.

Stained porcelain agate, stretched paper thin, is laid on to equally thin white body material which is slapped again across the plaster slab. Tiny slices taken from the edge of the porcelain sandwich with a razor-sharp knife are inlaid as linear elements by further slapping and the design is manipulated in a variety of other ways until he is satisfied with the result. Sometimes Gary Wornell-Brown also presses patterned sheets of his ultra-fine inlay into the surface of small solid balls of white porcelain which are then left to dry for two months before once-firing to vitrification and polishing with 'wet and dry' carborundum paper to become tactile 'pebbles'.

Mixing and applying slips and oxides

An even distribution of colouring oxides can be achieved by mixing with the powdered body into a porcelain slip. Dry materials can be accurately weighed giving reliable percentages of stain. Another advantage of mixing dry is that individual adjustments can be made to the body composition (where the recipe is known) if the fluxing power of added oxides causes any problem such as bloating. The slip can be allowed to stiffen and then worked into a plastic condition, or it can be applied to the surface of a leather-hard piece by painting, spraying, sponging, trailing, pouring or dipping. It is also possible to apply

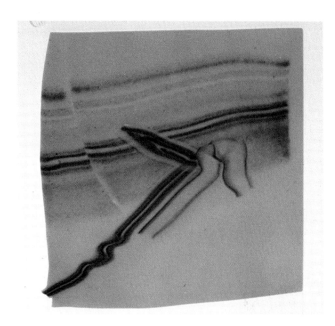

Inlaid porcelain slice, height 4 in. (10.2 cm). Mounted on opalescent glass and framed with clear glass and aluminium. By Gary Wornell-Brown, 1979.

Below: *Foliated porcelain dish with cobalt edging. Crackle glaze inlaid with gold lustre for emphasis. By Gary Wornell-Brown, 1979.*

to a bone-dry pot, but only brief contact with the wet slip should be allowed, because dry porcelain is brittle and so absorbent that excessive wetting at this stage, especially when only parts of the form are treated, can lead to distortion or collapse.

Sheila Casson incising through slip on porcelain boxes prior to bisque firing.

Porcelain bowl, incised and inlaid with manganese dioxide, under a white glaze. By Sheila Fournier, 1979.

Sheila Casson uses a coloured slip on thrown boxes and bowls to provide the ground for her sgraffito designs which are cut through the slip layer to reveal the contrasting whiteness beneath. The slip contains sufficient oxides to show clearly through the covering glaze. The slip layer is fairly thin and the tool does not need to bite deeply so the piece remains fairly smooth to touch and the incisions can hardly be felt when filled with glaze. She often uses a wax-resist for areas of the design prior to dipping into slip and this broader treatment complements the fine linear elements of the sgraffito work.

Robin Hopper uses slip expansively, enriching broad areas with flowing layers and shapes to re-create, in a pictorial way, forms and patterns of nature inspired by the Canadian landscape around him. His feathery, tree-like patterns of mocha diffusions are made by mixing oxides with weak acids and applying this to the edge of a freshly slipped area. The acid produces the characteristic patterns by clearing branching channels through the slip and allowing the body to be stained by the oxides. Manganese dioxide or cobalt oxide are most commonly used for this purpose.

Much of **Sheila Fournier's** porcelain is incised with fine lines into which she brushes manganese dioxide. Any oxide spreading beyond the line is scraped away when the piece is dry. She mainly uses a semi-matt white glaze over these pieces and the design remains very clear.

Nick Homoky's incised linear designs are carved with a pocket knife and inlaid with heavily-stained porcelain slip, blobbed on with a brush until the depression is proud of the surface. This is left to dry for scraping away later. Ten to fifteen per cent of the body stain is used for the inlay together with a ''pinch of bentonite'' (about one per cent) plus 25 per cent of soda feldspar to flux. He finds that bentonite aids painting and carving. Oxides are either used neat (manganese dioxide, copper carbonate, cobalt carbonate) or they may be mixed with commercially prepared stains. Neat oxide additions to the slip are usually kept within five per cent otherwise he finds that their fluxing power partly vitrifies the bisque so that it resists the glaze. After bisque firing to 950°C the inlay is rubbed down further. When firing glaze over inlays he 'soaks' the kiln at 1260°C to avoid pinholing. Many pieces are left unglazed but are thoroughly

Two thrown unglazed porcelain pieces incised and inlaid with stained slip. Both pieces are vitrified and smoothly polished. By Nick Homoky, 1979.

Nick Homoky inlaying slip.

159

Slab-built bottle, height 16 in. (40.6 cm). Black porcelain, two slips applied with oxide mocha diffusions and orange overglaze enamel. By Robin Hopper (Canada).

Above right: *Slab-built porcelain with impressed textures inlaid with oxides, 5 × 4 in. (12.7 × 10.2 cm). By Maggie Andrews, 1979.*

Below: *Porcelain bowl with dribbled oxide decoration, height 4 in. (10.2 cm). By Emmanuel Cooper.*

Below right: *'Two carrier bags'. Slip-cast and decorated with underglaze crayons, height 4¼ in. (10.7 cm). By Joan Hepworth, 1979.*

rubbed down until absolutely smooth, with a fine carborundum paper and plenty of water, because he feels that the vitrified and polished surface is serviceable and too good to hide.

Gordon Cooke brushes oxides and stains into some of his slab-built pieces, which have been impressed with textured plaster stamps and bisque fired. The raised elements of the design are sponged clean leaving the colour in the depressions.

Maggie Andrews treats a variety of impressed textures in a similar way.

A number of potters are now using underglaze crayons, composed of ceramic stains, to draw directly

Set of porcelain bowls with blue and rust pigment brush decoration. Lime/feldspathic glaze. By Derek Emms, 1979.

Below right: *Porcelain dish with design in copper oxide, reduction fired under a celadon glaze. By Peter Beard, 1978.*

on to the bisqued surface. The white ground is well-suited to receive the colour and the crayons can be controlled rather more easily than a brush. **Keith Campbell** (Canada) has decorated press-moulded dishes and **Joan Hepworth** enlivens her slip-cast porcelain, both using underglaze crayons with a transparent glaze over the design.

Oxides mixed with water and applied by brush can be painted on to porcelain in the 'green' (unfired) state; when bisqued as underglaze pigment; or on top of the unfired glaze. Oxides quickly settle in the container unless a suspending agent (such as a small amount of bentonite is also added) and the water should be stirred with each brush stroke. Possibilities seem infinite and may be illustrated further by considering the painting of a simple band of colour. In the green state the band may be scratched through in parts with a variety of tools of different widths to reveal the white body underneath, or it may be brushed over a 'resist' of paper, wax, latex or masking tape. (These treatments are also used with coloured slips). The character of the glaze subsequently used will determine the final colour and effect. The same

decorative treatments may be employed on bisqued ware except for sgraffito (although even this *is* possible on soft porcelain bisque). On the friable surface of unfired glaze much more care is necessary because it is difficult to rectify mistakes. The intensity of the fired colour is dependent upon the thickness of the glaze in relation to the amount of brushed oxide.

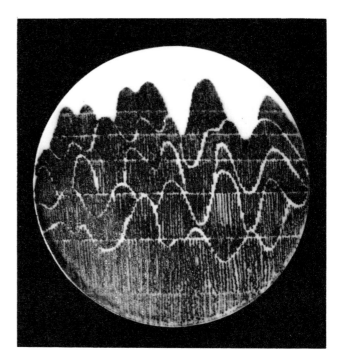

161

Porcelain bowl with banded oxides, 10 in. (25.4 cm) diameter. Oxidised. By Lucie Rie, 1979.

Press-moulded porcelain plate, 13 in. (33 cm) diameter, decorated with underglaze crayons and orange lustre. Oxidised. By Keith Campbell (Canada).

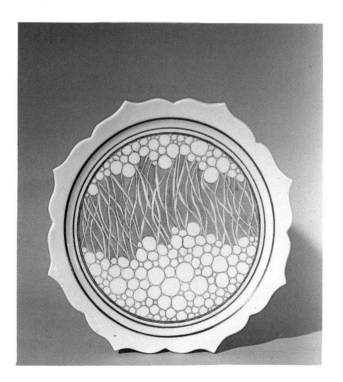

This can only be judged through practice. The edges of brushed bands can be softened or made paler by diluting the mix with water and fading out the colour as the pot revolves on the wheel. Unfired glaze can be highly absorbent and is liable to lift away from the body if overbrushed or if wetted too much. The oxided band can still be lightly scratched but the more usual method of retaining the natural glaze colour is to paint on some kind of resist beforehand. Wax emulsion works quite well if the brush is well-charged with liquid colour (a dry brush tends to leave too much oxide on the wax) but wax is almost impossible to remove when a mistake is made, in which case the only solution is to remove all the glaze and start again from the beginning. Latex resists can be thinned with water and are remarkably effective although rather unkind to brushes, and errors can be corrected easily because the thin rubber skin pulls cleanly away, barely disturbing the surface.

Freely applied oxides brushed over glaze is a more popular treatment with potters who wish to introduce touches of colour ro relieve a surface, define a form or generally add visual interest.

Using a fairly dry brush, oxides can be painted over a white glaze covering incised or carved areas so that the *depressions* remain clear of colour. This is a method I have often found useful where one basic glaze provides the ground for a range of subtle colour variations (see page 141).

Oxides are brushed on to emphasise rims and edges by **Mary Rogers, Deirdre Burnett** and many others. Heavy saturation by oxides produces a dark, metallic appearance and this has been exploited in different ways by **Lucie Rie** and **Val Barry**. Manganese dioxide in particular fluxes and runs with reflective, brassy highlights.

The 'landscape' dishes of **Ian Pirie** are air-brushed and painted with two mixtures of oxides in the form of slips:

Iron:
2 parts red iron oxide
1 part black iron oxide
1 part ball clay

Cobalt:
2 parts red iron oxide
1 part black iron oxide
1 part cobalt oxide
2 parts China clay

For air-brushing, it is preferable to sieve both through a 200 mesh sieve to prevent clogging. **Ian Pirie** finds that black iron helps to create a granular effect rather

Two porcelain bowls, heavily brushed with manganese dioxide. Oxidised. By Val Barry, 1979.

Porcelain dish with airbrushed slips. By Ian Pirie, 1979.

Valentine box, porcelain with gold lustre. By Glyn Hugo, 1979.

like a black and white photograph. Very even glazing is required on his flatware such as plates and the lids of boxes, so all pieces are dipped, mainly using tongs or dipping wires. The two oxided slips give a wide variety of tones and colours through the use of different glazes over them.

Impressing

The ability of plastic clays to retain impressions is still one of the most enjoyable decorative properties—and probably the oldest. The range of patterns and textures is only limited by the individual potter's imagination and invention. All manner of things may be used to impart texture. Even soft textile materials may be laid on and rolled over to make an impression. The possibilities are infinite.

Particularly effective results can be achieved by inlaying pellets, coils or strips of white, plastic porcelain into slabs of the same material. Pieces may be added on and rolled level with the existing surface or they may be projecting for greater prominence. Clustered filaments of clay can be pushed through the mesh of a sieve and added in numerous ways for extra visual interest. Light rolling bonds the inlay but leaves an indented line around the edge of each fragment. The line will remain visible without any further treatment but it can be given emphasis by brushing in oxides and cleaning the top surface in the green state with fine wire wool or, when painted on to bisqued ware, with a damp sponge. Alternatively, a coloured, transparent glaze such as celadon will fill the line with darker colour.

'Trees'. Thrown porcelain bowl with painted lustres, 10 in. (25.4 cm) diameter. By Peter Lane, 1979

Gordon Cooke trails extremely fine threads of white porcelain slip with very rapid movements across a plaster slab and uses these in tiny cut lengths for pressing into rolled-out porcelain sheets to create textural variations. The slip used for this purpose is deflocculated but is slightly thicker than normal casting slip.

Lustres

The movement towards more colourful studio ceramics is illustrated further by the increasing use of on glaze enamels and lustres. Commercially prepared lustres are available in a wide range of iridescent colours, as well as in silver, platinum, gold and copper which give brilliant, reflective surfaces on smooth, shiny glazes. Matt glazes will also accept lustres but the effect is likely to be less dramatic. **Glyn Hugo** occasionally uses gold lustre directly on to the body, without any glaze, quite successfully.

Before firing, lustres are mostly brown and can be thinned with oil of lavender essence if they seem rather glutinous. They consist of metallic salts mixed with resin and oil of turpentine (or lavender) and are fired in oxidation to 750°C, where the combustible material burns away causing a local reduction to take place. This reaction deposits a bright film of metal on the surface of the glaze.

Soft-haired brushes are normally used to apply the lustres; they are best reserved solely for this purpose and must always be thoroughly cleaned after use. If brushed on too thickly, lustres are liable to flake off

Geoffrey Swindell spraying paraffin on the unfired lustre to break the surface tension.

Above right: *Geoffrey Swindell blending further lustre colours.*

Below: *Porcelain bowl, 11 in. (27.9 cm) diameter, lettered with gold lustre. By Mary White, 1979.*

when fired, and a moderately thin, even layer is preferable. Brush marks tend to level out in the firing but may remain slightly visible with some colours.

Fascinating visual textures are produced when the surface tension of the lustre medium is broken before it has dried on the pot. This can be accomplished with paraffin or detergent liquids. A tiny drop is all that is required to make the painted lustre retreat in a widening circle immediately on contact. With care this phenomenon can be controlled and exploited to good effect. **Geoffrey Swindell** has developed this technique to a very fine art. After brushing on a lustre he sprays it briefly with paraffin through an airbrush or, sometimes, squirts washing-up liquid on to the surface. As the medium moves and contracts fresh lustres are laid on producing richly-beautiful colour combinations. He also uses a gold lustre to rub into the crackled dolomite glaze on some pieces and wipes away the excess with thinning essence on a cloth. The residue remaining in the crackles gives a fine network of pink lines.

Mary White's early training in calligraphy is well-demonstrated in the lustred lettering applied to her porcelain bowls, boxes and teapots. Often the form of the pot dictates that the lettering be written upside-down yet this never seems evident in the finished piece. Bowls in particular, tend to be lettered to commemorate special occasions and are usually commissioned. But she also uses gold lustre to add

Large porcelain vase assembled from thrown sections. Height 13 in. (33 cm), with lidded porcelain box. By David Eeles, 1979.

Right: David Eeles painting with glaze on raw glaze. Note that there is little indication of the final colour at this stage.

sparkling threads of textural interest to a dark or coloured glaze.

When **Oldrich Asenbryl** decided to introduce clearly defined blocks of colour into his pieces in 1975 he turned to lustres and enamel colours sprayed, or printed by silk screen processes, on to the glaze. The "clean, dense, uncontaminated surface was a much more suitable material than stoneware to offset the colours". He found that a shiny, translucent glaze provided the right base for this treatment. It gave them "a definite feeling of wetness and fluidity after the

'Extended Movement'. Porcelain sculpture with enamels, 36 × 36 in. (90.2 × 90.2 cm). By Oldrich Asenbryl, 1979.

glost firing". Recently he has been using matt (mostly barium) glazes to achieve a more neutral background. As his sculptural pieces are mostly slab-built and extruded, translucency has been unimportant to him.

The lustres of **Alan Barratt-Danes** are fired for 20–22 minutes in heavy reduction at 800°C in a small gas kiln. The glaze is taken to 960°C and the kiln turned off and allowed to drop in temperature to 800°C when it is relit and the reduction is started.

His basic glaze consists of:

    85% Alkaline frit
    10% China clay
     5% Whiting

To this glaze, metal salts are added in various proportions to give different lustre effects:

Copper oxide	2%
Silver sulphide	2%
Cupric sulphate	2%
Silver carbonate	2%

Opposite above: 'Perforated space'. Slip-cast sand-blasted porcelain sphere, 8 in. (20.3 cm) diameter. Oxidation fired. By Ann Mortimer (Canada), 1976.

Opposite below: Porcelain bowl, slip-cast, carved and sand-blasted. By Alan Whittaker.

He also recommends the following combinations of metallic salts:

Copper oxide	2%	Silver sulphide	2%
Silver sulphide	2%	Cupric sulphate	2%
Copper oxide	2%	Silver sulphide	2%
Silver sulphide	5%	Cupric sulphate	5%
Copper oxide	5%	Silver carbonate	2%
Silver sulphide	2%	Cupric sulphate	2%
Copper oxide	2%	Silver carbonate	2%
Silver carbonate	5%	Cupric sulphate	5%
Copper oxide	5%	Silver carbonate	5%
Silver carbonate	2%	Cupric sulphate	2%

The lustre salts are carefully sieved into the glaze through a 200 mesh lawn.[33]

168

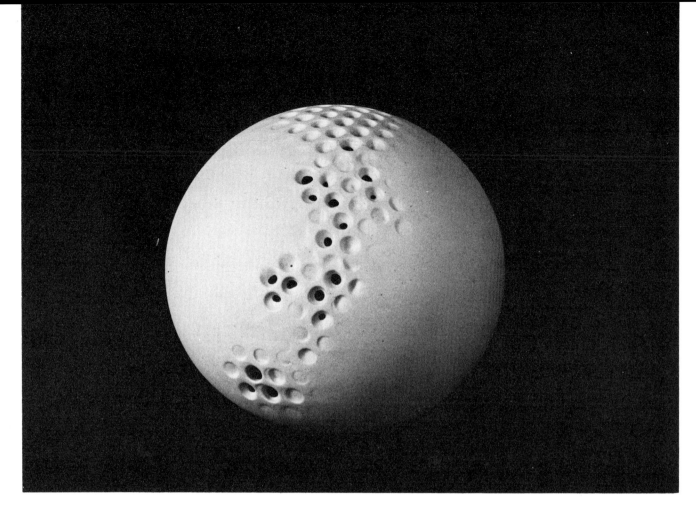

Sand Blasting

This is a technique used by **Paul Astbury, Ann Mortimer, Geoffrey Swindell** and **Alan Whittaker** among others, to texture and even cut right through the glaze and body of porcelain after the final firing. Sand blasting is carried out in a box with two armholes and a glass window so that the operator, wearing rubber gloves, can be protected from flying grit while observing his work. The gun normally operates at a pressure of between 160–180 pounds per square inch, with silicon carbide grit 300–400 mesh size. The grit is constantly re-cycled as it drops through a trap in the floor and is directed back through the gun. **Alan Whittaker's** pierced pieces are slip cast in plaster moulds which he brushes with lithium carbonate or talc (as releasing agents). Sufficient of this material often adheres to the cast to give a thin glazed appearance to the surface between 1230°–1250°C. He carves part of the way through the wall in the leather-hard state and sand blasts the design further when the body has been fired to vitrification (currently he is using one body formulated to mature at 1230°C). After it has been thoroughly rubbed-down and polished with 'wet and dry' carborundum paper, an adhesive plastic tape is used to cover the parts of the piece which are to remain untouched by the grit. Final sand blasting to create his filigreed patterns often takes as long as two hours with the piece held in one hand and the gun in the other. Alan has recently designed some vases, bowls and jewellery boxes incorporating similar delicate tracery for the Rosenthal Studio, Germany.

FIVE

GLAZES FOR PORCELAIN

I doubt if any potter can deny the thrill of unpacking a glost kiln full or porcelain, especially when experimenting with glazes or where the results are not totally predictable, as in a reduction firing. The transformation is so complete. The marriage of body and glaze seems so perfect and natural that a successful firing of porcelain is one of the most exciting and satisfying experiences.

The subject of glazes is fascinating, vast, exciting, daunting, straightforward, fraught with difficulties, or surrounded by mystique and secrecy, according to your knowledge, interest, involvement or point of view. Some potters enjoy the mathematical aspects of glaze chemistry while anything beyond the basics remains a mystery for others. A lifetime could, quite happily, be spent juggling with materials, formulae, atmospheres and temperatures in pursuit of an infinite range of colours, surfaces, textures and effects without making anything worthwhile on which to display them. Similarly the other extreme holds true. Even the most excellent forms may be disguised under a lifeless or unsympathetic glaze, appearing diminished in character and impact. Most good potters manage to strike a balance, neither over-indulging in glaze technology, nor dismissing the opportunity to experiment and broaden understanding.

It may reassure anyone who views with abhorrence and incomprehension, the prospect of glaze calculation by molecular theories to learn that many potters who are currently working in porcelain, share

this dislike of figures and analyses. The overwhelming preference is for the empirical approach, allied to a little basic knowledge and common sense:

Keith Campbell: "I am more interested in the other parts of making and only use glaze chemistry when I have to."

Derek Davis: "I tend to have a pragmatic approach to glazes — I play it by ear using three or four basic glazes which can be superimposed over each other."

Marianne de Trey: "I'm not much of a chemist but do, when necessary, use a tri-axial blend to change either texture, or fit, and find it worth the effort."

Ruth Duckworth: "Technology does not basically interest me. It's simply a means to an end."

Geoffrey Eastop: 'I am not particularly interested in the chemistry of glazes. My main concern is the problem of assessing the character of a glaze in relation to the form of the object."

Tina Forrester: "I dislike glazing and am not particularly interested in the chemistry or experimenting, although I do, of course, make tests from time to time. Most of my glazes are standard recipes slightly altered. The exact origins are forgotten."

Sheila Fournier: "The chemistry does not interest me."

Anne James: "The chemistry interests me very much but I find it so demanding that if I get involved I would have to work so hard at it that I'd never make any pots. So I use recipes which are available and adapt them empirically, sometimes by line blends."

Kurt Spurey: "I am not especially fascinated by chemistry. Glazes always seem to be at their best when one becomes familiar with them through repeated use."

Irene Sims: "The chemistry of glazes does not interest me particularly. I am using one commercially-prepared transparent glaze at present."

Geoffrey Swindell: "I am not interested in glaze chemistry and have very little knowledge of it."

Opposite above: *Porcelain bowl, height 3 in. (7.6 cm). Mineral glaze containing lithium. Reduction fired to 1360°C. By Margarete Scholl (West Germany).*

Opposite left: *Porcelain bowl, height 5½ in. (14 cm), width 7¼ in. (18.5 cm). The first glaze layer is a celadon with latex resist painted on top and the pot re-dipped in a tenmoku (iron-bearing) glaze. Reduction fired to 1360°C. By Ursula Scheid, (West Germany), 1977.*

Glaze Compostition

Many standard stoneware glazes work equally well on porcelain although there may be differences in colour and surface and some are more prone to flux. The rougher surface of stoneware 'keys' and retards the flow of glaze. Porcelain on the other hand allows the glaze to flow more easily over its smoother body. This can effect the optimum firing temperature of a glaze according to the nature of the body used. The essential glass-former is silica to which is added one or more fluxes to bring the melting point within the range of available kilns. To make a satisfactory glaze capable of remaining on vertical surfaces, the viscosity of the mixture is improved by the addition of alumina. Fortunately, there are naturally-occurring rocks which already contain these elements chemically-combined in a variety of forms. The high temperatures involved simplify the task of successful glaze composition because the readily available glaze-forming agent, feldspar, will itself melt and become a stiff glass between 1250°C and 1300°C. Normally, around 50 per cent of feldspar in a porcelain glaze makes a good starting point. As much as 100 per cent is possible but unlikely to be satisfactory in practice.

Feldspars contain all the ingredients of a 'natural' glaze. They consist of silica and alumina combined with certain alkalis, notably potassium (potash) and sodium (soda). These two types known as orthoclase (the most common) and albite, respectively, are more likely to be used, although there are ten other forms which are also termed true feldspars, together with many other feldspathic materials known as feldspathoids (i.e. Cornish stone and nepheline syenite). Lime feldspars (anorthite) and barium feldspars are less commonly used, as lime is usually introduced more profitably into glazes in the form of whiting, and barium is added in its carbonate form. Lithium feldspathoids (lepidolite, petalite and spodumene) have found increasing favour with potters wishing to expand their glaze palettes. They are used as auxiliary fluxes and can produce a brilliant colour response in conjunction with various oxides. **Margarete Schott** (West Germany), who constantly experiments with glazes, has developed some exciting and unusual colour variations using lithium minerals.

Although feldspar may be used alone to make a glaze, other materials are normally added to make a more satisfactory melt, to improve the fit, to achieve particular surface characteristics or to encourage different colour responses. When a recipe merely indicates a given proportion of feldspar it may be assumed that it is in the form of potash, but, generally speaking, it is possible to substitute other forms for all or part of that amount.

Cornish stone, also known as Cornwall stone, China stone, Carolina stone, is often used as a major constituent of glaze in place of true feldspar, for it contributes extra properties through the additional alkalis (potash, soda, calcia and magnesia) in its composition. One of the best and most reliable glazes used by many potters consists of as much as 85 per cent Cornish stone with the remaining 15 per cent taken up by whiting. This makes a reliable basic glaze. Excellent on its own, over porcelain it usually gives a milky white in oxidation and a greyish white in reduction. It is prone to craze heavily on low silica bodies, such as the standard David Leach porcelain, producing an attractive crackle which can easily be stained for greater emphasis. It is also very useful as a glaze to apply under or over matt coloured glazes to lend variety to both colour and surface. The absence of clay in the recipe, other than the small percentage of kaolinite present in the stone, means that it does lack adhesion prior to firing and its dry powdery surface can be rubbed off by careless handling.

Opposite: *Three porcelain bottles with crystalline glazes. By Diane Creber (Canada).*

Below: *Porcelain bottle vase, height 5⅞ in. (15 cm), with celadon glaze. Fired in reduction to 1300°C in a wood-burning kiln. By René Ben-Lisa (France), 1979.*

Below right: *Thrown porcelain box with tenmoku glaze. Reduction fired to 1260°C. Height 5⅝ in. (14.2 cm). By Hein Severijns (Holland), 1979.*

The lower melting point of nepheline syenite together with the possibility of unusual and interesting colours makes it another useful substitute for potash feldspar. It is especially valued to introduce soda into a glaze. **Peter Simpson** developed a number of nepheline syenite glazes for use on his fungoid pieces and some of his recipes are listed on page 191.

The best porcelain glazes are usually composed of a very simple combination of minerals and the function of each is not difficult to learn. The number of separate ingredients rarely exceeds four or five and to these are added any necessary colouring oxides. Once the rôle of the various glaze-forming minerals is understood, the choice of ingredients can be made to suit individual purposes, and be designed to fit particular bodies and mature at given temperatures.

"The final glaze partially combines the physical properties of the constituent oxides and partially displays new properties. New properties are those belonging to its amorphous state and include its physical hardness, resistance to chemical attack and to abrasion, its colour, transparency, opacity, and its surface texture. The combined properties from the oxides which are displayed by the new state are those of hardness and the overall rate of expansion".[34]

In addition to the feldspathic base extra silica is usually included in the form of flint or quartz to improve the fit, hardness and durability and to give greater stability to the glaze. China clay provides further silica but is mainly used for its high alumina content and up to 25 per cent is often present in a porcelain glaze, particularly when purity is required. Ball clays are also used and have rather better adhesive properties than China clays in the unfired state. Their smaller particle size helps to keep the glaze slop in suspension but at the same time increases shrinkage. Sometimes a glaze recipe may include amounts of both China clay and ball clay, but if a high proportion of the glaze is to be made up of clay, it is usual to substitute a portion of calcined clay to prevent excessive shrinkage.

Silica, therefore, forms the largest part of the glaze, while other materials are added to modify the performance and appearance of the glaze. Alumina contributes viscosity to the molten glaze and helps to prevent re-crystallisation on cooling. Crystalline

Thrown and pinched porcelain bowl, height 3 in. (7.6 cm), with copper red glaze. The darker red spots come from copper carbonate painted on to the glaze before firing. By Peter Lane, 1979.

glazes are the only ones which contain little or no alumina so they are often notoriously fluid in the kiln.

The higher the maturing temperature of a glaze the greater will be its percentage of silica plus alumina and the corresponding need for added fluxes will be less. **Nigel Wood** explains this very well in his book *Oriental Glazes*. He points out that the "sum totals of the silica and alumina percentages" govern the maturing temperature more than any other ingredients, and he suggests that the following guidelines will give good glazes, provided that the silica content is between 60–74%, within the temperature range 1220°–1310°C. The higher the temperature the more silica is required if the glaze is "not to become glassy and prone to run".

> "Cones six to eight — silica + alumina 73–80% of total glaze.
> Cones seven to nine — silica + alumina 78–82% of total glaze.
> Cones eight to ten — silica + alumina 80–85% of total glaze."[35]

He goes on to say that "A high alumina figure does not necessarily mean a high maturing temperature" because "a high-alumina glaze with a low silica percentage can still run badly if the SiO_2 + Al_2O_3 total is low, because the silica also plays a part in hardening the glaze. Seventeen per cent alumina represents the normal limit in Chinese glazes, and the commonest amounts of alumina in these glazes are found to be between 10 and 15 per cent".

In addition to the figures given above, of course, the remaining percentages of 15 to 27 per cent are made up with fluxes according to requirements.

Potters talk of 'dolomite glazes', 'barium matts', 'lime matts', 'magnesium glazes' and so on because it is the flux which dictates much of the character of a glaze and exercises considerable influence over its reaction with colouring oxides. The high temperatures offer a much wider choice of fluxes than are available in earthenware. Those most commonly used by porcelain potters are derived from various forms of calcium, barium, magnesium, zinc, lithium and, of course, potassium and sodium which are normally introduced as constituents of feldspar.

Whiting (calcium carbonate) is the most important source of calcium and is therefore widely used as the principal flux in porcelain glazes. By itself whiting is a refractory material but it becomes an active flux and combines readily with feldspar. It is used in amounts up to twenty-five per cent of a glaze. Beyond this it becomes something of an anti-flux, due to its

Three deeply fluted porcelain pots, largest height 6 in. (15.2 cm) with dolomite glaze, showing the characteristic pink where the glaze runs more thickly. Reduction fired to 1280°C. By Peter Lane, 1979.

refractory nature, and only imparts a dry dullness to the surface. Celadon glazes especially work well in the presence of calcium.

Some potters are using wollastonite, a natural calcium silicate fairly new to ceramics, to replace part of the whiting and flint for its uniform composition, greater fired strength and improved resistance to thermal shock. **Sheila Casson** includes about 14 per cent in her celadon glaze (recipe given on page 188).

Barium is not such a strong flux as calcium but it is often used in its carbonate form to produce matt or semi-matt glazes or to encourage the development of unusual colours. It is poisonous in its raw state, and like all ceramic materials, should be handled with care.

One of my favourite glazes contains 20 per cent barium carbonate and behaves extremely well in both oxidation and reduction atmospheres. Colours are generally clean and clear but if applied too thickly the glaze can become unpleasantly dry. The full recipe and suggested colouring are given on page 190.

Magnesia glazes enjoy considerable popularity for their smooth, buttery appearance. Although slightly soluble, magnesium carbonate may be used, but more often talc or dolomite are preferred because they also

bring other oxides to the glaze. Dolomite, a double carbonate of calcium and magnesium which exists as a natural rock, is often introduced into high temperature glazes, to help create a matt surface through the development of tiny crystals of calcium and magnesium silicates on cooling. So many potters employ their own slight variations of Daniel Rhodes 'high alumina matt' glaze (No. 32) containing 22.4 per cent of dolomite, that it has become the all-purpose, standard formula for good or ill. Most of the familiar cream, slightly speckled, reduction-fired domestic stonewares which seem to predominate up and down the country owe their being to this well-known, over-exposed recipe. My own version merely simplifies the proportions given by Rhodes and may be welcomed by other non-mathematical minds.

(Cone 9)		**Val Barry's** version (Cone 9)	
Potash feldspar	49	Potash feldspar	50
China clay	25	China clay	25
Dolomite	22.5	Dolomite	20
Whiting	3.5	Whiting	5

It is generally reliable and well-behaved on both stoneware and porcelain. Its characteristic cream colour appears when used over iron-bearing bodies in a reduction firing but in oxidation it gives a rather dead

175

Three porcelain bottles, tallest 5⁷/₈ in. (15 cm). Fired in reduction to 1280°C. By Robert Deblander (France), 1979.

white. However, it seems even more ideally suited to use on porcelain. In reduction the magnesium gives an attractive pink (in heavy reduction it tends towards a rather dense, mottled purple) and its slightly increased fluidity on porcelain allows the body to show whitely through on thin edges, emphasising any fluting or carving. In oxidation the crystalline structure sparkles in the warm-white surface and the much better fusion of the porcelain body with the glaze makes it more attractive than when used with oxidised stoneware. This particular glaze in oxidation responds well to brushed or sprayed oxides. According to thickness of application, cobalt carbonate produces a variety of shades from pale pink/purple through violet to a deep electric blue; copper carbonate gives colours ranging from light to dark salmon-orange to a matt, crystalline black; red iron oxide appears as a hot gingery-brown. Many variations are possible by combining these and other colouring oxides in different proportions. Rutile is also useful to include in small amounts where broken

textures of colour are required. Mixed with cobalt, rutile is likely to develop green colours.

Despite the apparent opacity of this dolomite-matt glaze, porcelain will often retain considerable translucency when thinly potted and where the glaze remains white; the David Leach body particularly so.

Linear incisions filled with manganese dioxide show up quite well under this glaze without too much bleeding or loss of clarity. **Sheila Fournier** uses this technique.

Talc is a magnesium silicate, obtained from steatite or soapstone, normally used as a source of magnesia with similar effects, and it also contributes silica to a glaze. Its low expansion rate helps to improve the body and glaze fit and reduces the risk of crazing.

Bone ash is occasionally used in small amounts to contribute a degree of opalescence to a glaze and may produce effects similar to a Chün glaze.

Zinc oxide, another flux, is rarely used in amounts of more than five per cent. Larger proportions often make a glaze prone to pinholing with a very dry, uneven surface. It is sometimes used in conjunction with titanium dioxide for crystalline glazes. Colours tend to be dull and uninteresting although copper can give strong turquoise greens in the presence of zinc. In the presence of large amounts of zinc oxide some glazes may be susceptible to attack by acids commonly found in coffee, vinegar, citrus fruits and so on.

Choice of Glaze

To further understand the nature of these glaze ingredients and their reaction upon one another at high temperatures a number of simple tests may be conducted with small amounts of raw materials fired on test tiles. The table below shows part of a test tile of materials for 1250–1280°C, suggested by **Paul Barron** (see *Ceramic Review* Number 20). A small amount of the powdered material is thoroughly mixed with water into a thin paste and dropped in place on the marked out bisque tile 'like a tiny meringue' about ½ in. diameter and ⅛ in. thick. Further tests can be made after assessing the fired results. 50/50 blends of complementary pairs of these and other materials can be mixed and applied in a similar way to other test tiles. This simple investigation will help, in a visual and tactile way, towards understanding the rôles played by the various glaze constituents.

Broadly speaking, to increase the melting of a glaze the percentage of flux is raised; to decrease melting the percentage of flint, quartz, china clay, ball clay or hard ash is increased; 'fattening' the glaze requires the percentage of clay or feldspar etc. to be raised.

Individual porcelain bowl with copper glaze in white and red, height 4¾ in. (12 cm). Reduction fired to 1300°C. By Stig Lindberg (Sweden), 1979.

Three thrown and beaten porcelain bottle forms, height 3 in. (7.6 cm). 'Sunflower seed' pattern cut through glaze. By Anne James, 1979.

Test tile: glaze constituents. 1250°C–1280°C.

Igneous rocks	Cornish stone	Feldspar	Nepheline syenite
Clays	China clay	Ball clay	Red clay
Fluxes	Whiting or Limestone	Mixed wood ash	Leadless (medium) Frit
Refractories	Flint or Quartz	Grass ash (hard)	Tin Oxide

Armed with this basic information concerning the nature of available glaze materials tests can be conducted to compose glazes for particular purposes. Thousands of tried and 'proven' recipes have been

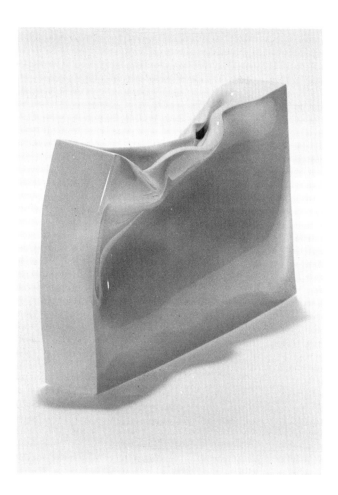

Porcelain form. The 'wetness' of the glaze emphasises the fluid movement of the form. By Kurt Spurey (Austria), 1978.

Transparent glazes

Transparent glazes are essential to allow certain kinds of decorative treatment to remain clearly visible: e.g. over neriage designs, agate and marbled patterns, underglaze crayons. In these instances the glaze contributes very little to the piece other than protection for the surface and 'varnishes' the colours for sharper contrast.

Transparent glazes are perhaps at their best when used over incised, impressed or carved decoration especially when tinted by the presence of iron to become celadons. These glazes on porcelain are still as appropriate, beautiful and popular as when they first appeared in China and Korea. Small percentages of iron oxide in a clear lime glaze produce subtle greys and greens and pale blues. Even the slightest scratch on the body of the pot collects enough glaze to become clearly visible due to the darker colour arising from increased depth of glaze. Among the finest celadon wares currently being produced are the strongly-fluted teapots and bowls of **David Leach**. Glaze, decoration and form seem so admirably suited; fruits of a long tradition, timeless in their appeal but still unmistakably individual in concept. The carved ornament of **Karl Scheid** is often enhanced by one of his own celadon glazes. He has conducted thousands of glaze tests for his own studio purposes and also for industrial applications. (The Scheids' workshop has enormous numbers of glaze test rings — ribbons of clay formed into rings — threaded on strings.)

While transparent glazes reveal designs in or on the body of a piece they do have the disadvantage of a reflective surface which can interrupt the form. Very few potters attempt to use such glazes without some kind of decorative treatment. One of the exceptions to this rule is **Kurt Spurey** who has been working with thin slip-cast slabs to build rectilinear forms which he then deforms, trying to create "tension out of the difference between the hard technical shape of the block and the softness of the deformation". The high gloss and reflective property of the transparent glaze emphasises the fluid plasticity of the form so that it almost appears to move.

There can be no such thing as a definitive glaze for porcelain, or any other ceramic medium. The choice of surface, translucency, colour and visual texture, together with tactile qualities, remains a personal one; what appeals to one potter may be anathema to another. There are, however, areas of general agreement and it is felt that matt or semi-matt glazes

published and much time and effort can be saved by deciding to take one or two of these as starting points for experimenting with surface and colour, although there is never any guarantee that your results will match those described in another potter's recipe, because there are so many variables. The composition of minerals from one source will probably differ from those obtained elsewhere and in combination there may be considerable variation. However, the proportions of the ingredients to hand can be adjusted to control the performance of any glaze to suit the body, selected firing temperature and kiln atmosphere. Possible combinations are infinite and most potters settle for three or four basic glazes which will offer them a wide enough choice of visual and tactile interest. Colouring oxides under, over, or within the glazes extend the possibilities further and even wider permutations appear when doubled glaze alternatives are considered.

Red porcelain bottle, 9 × 4 in. (22.9 × 10.2 cm). By Elsa Rady (USA), 1978.

Porcelain bottle with 'sang de boeuf' copper glaze, 9 × 7 in. (22.9 × 17.7 cm). Fired to 1300°C. By Derek Davis, 1979.

offer greater scope for most sculptural surfaces. Since mattness is due to crystallisation, undissolved material or colour additions, it is inevitable that this will partially impede translucency. At the same time matt glazes usually have far more character and sublety than their glossy counterparts.

Often the most exciting results come from the application of one glaze on top of another, particularly when one is glossy and the other matt, and when one or the other, or both, contain percentages of colouring oxides. Glazes used in this way behave differently and give results which could not be achieved by mixing them together prior to application. Quite different effects may happen when the position of the two glazes is reversed – both colour and surface qualities are likely to alter. The most logical combinations apart from glossy and matt, are light and dark, or coloured and plain.

Some of the most exciting colours I have produced on porcelain have resulted from a matt barium glaze containing two and a half per cent tin oxide and one per cent copper oxide under the Cornish stone glaze referred to on page 173. Rich variations of red, mauve and purple, arising from copper in reduction, develop according to the positioning of pieces in the kiln. Copper reds require porcelain bodies if they are to be seen at their best and, although the colours in themselves may not be attractive to everyone, their successful creation can be intensely rewarding to a potter. The brightest colours often come from small amounts of copper oxide that would hardly be sufficient to stain the glaze if fired in oxidation. The effects of oxidation and reduction may be evident in the same piece, so delicate is the balance between the two where copper is concerned. This variation adds to the interest when the boundary line between the two is not too abrupt.

Crackle glazes

These glazes are specially prepared to have a high rate of thermal expansion. They contract on cooling to a greater degree than the body which supports them. They are not easy to control in the sense that crazing can be precisely dictated, and sometimes the pattern of lines becomes over-complex. It is thought that some of the early Chinese pieces we admire to-day for their decorative crackled glazes may not originally have been crazed. When a glaze is not kept under compression this crazing may continue over periods of many years and the lines become stained through normal use. However, it is a form of decorative treatment which on the 'right' piece is distinctive and appealing, and seems admirably suited to porcelain. The classical associations of crackle glazes may be responsible for their relative neglect by contemporary potters. **Christine-Ann Richards** is one of the few who has made them a feature of her work. Any potter who 'discovers' crackle glazes will find that sharpening the resolution of the lines is extremely satisfying. Chinese ink is brushed over the crazed glaze and allowed to dry before being wiped clean with damp newspaper and the piece finally washed, revealing the permanently-stained crackle lines. (**Agnete Hoy** relates how she was told to only remove crackle glazed pots from the kiln with a silk handkerchief so that no grease would affect the passage of ink.) This method of staining seems infinitely preferable to the Chinese technique remarked upon by Père d'Entrecolles during the early part of the eighteenth century. In one of his letters he reported that "after it has been fired it is boiled for some time in a very fat broth, and after that placed in the foulest sewer, where they leave if for a month or more".[36]

Salt-glazing

Salt-glazing can produce interesting effects on porcelain and it is a method used by **Jane Hamlyn, Mary Rich** and a few others. Copper, iron, manganese and cobalt in particular can provide interesting colour variations when applied to the pieces in a ball clay slip. **Anndelphine Wornell-Brown** uses an ordinary

Above left: *Three porcelain pots with pink crackle glaze. By David Leach.*

Left: *Winged porcelain bottle, with blue-green crackle glaze, height 7 in. (17.7 cm). By Colin Pearson. (In the collection of W. Lenzen).*

Carved salt-glazed porcelain milk jug and sugar bowl, height 3½ in. (8.8 cm) and 2¾ in. (7 cm). By Beate Nieuwenburg (Holland), 1977. (In Museum Boymans-van Beuningen, Rotterdam.)

commercial washing soda in place of the salt to produce brilliant, heavily textured green colours on her porcelain slab-built sculptures. The effects are similar to salt-glaze but without its accompanying chlorine fumes.

Beate Nieuwenburg (Holland) fires all her porcelain to 1300–1320°C in an oil-fired kiln with salt-glaze. She finds that the combination of incised decoration and salt-glaze is "just perfect". She uses the Limoges porcelain body for its excellent throwing properties and translucency.

Testing Glazes

Despite the fact that most potters tend to work with just a few glazes which they know well, there is often room in the kiln for the odd test tile. **Margarete Schott** is constantly formulating and testing glazes for colour and texture. Her basic mixtures consist of feldspar and quartz (in the ratio of 1 : 1 or 2 : 1) plus alkaline earths and some clay substance. Her most recent

experiments involve the use of a lithium feldspar, fluxed with barium or calcium, with perhaps three per cent bentonite and very little clay. She works empirically and returns to the formula when the results are too unusual. Although she has made hundreds of tests she still tends to use a limited range but concentrates upon the colour variations.

Robin Hopper described his method of testing glaze recipes in *Ceramic Review*[37]. He took approximately 50 known glazes designed for Cone 9 and worked out an average for the basic ingredients, not including the major colour-affecting fluxes. In this way he arrived at two recipes, one a matt and the other a shiny variation. His first experiments were based upon his 'average' glaze consisting of:

Feldspar	35
China clay	12
Ball clay	17
Whiting	12
Flint	7

which produced a total of 83 parts. To bring this sum up to 100 parts for straightforward calculation of colour percentages, one or more of the colour-affecting fluxes could be added to make up the requisite 17 parts. This system gave him a successful matt glaze, and the subsequent development of a shiny version merely meant removing the China clay (12 parts) and replacing it with flint (making the total of flint 19 parts).

181

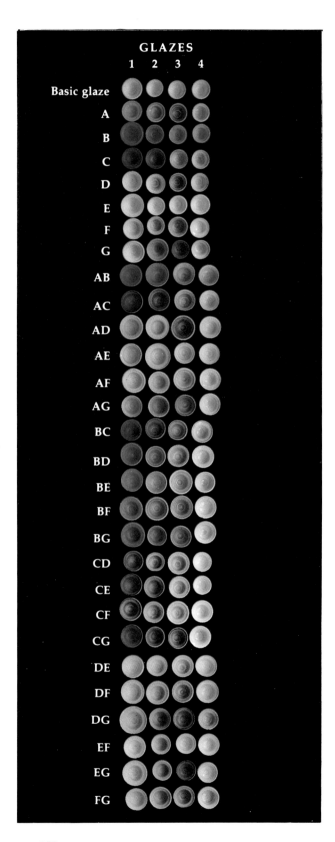

	GLAZES			
	1	**2**	**3**	**4**
Basic glaze				
A				
B				
C				
D				
E				
F				
G				
AB				
AC				
AD				
AE				
AF				
AG				
BC				
BD				
BE				
BF				
BG				
CD				
CE				
CF				
CG				
DE				
DF				
DG				
EF				
EG				
FG				

Line-blending

This is one of the simplest ways of testing colour additions to a glaze and this is the method which I normally use. In order to illustrate this I made up seven two-hundred gramme batches of dry materials, for each of four separate glazes, using the following recipes for oxidised firing:

Glaze 1 (Emmanuel Cooper)[38]
1260°C

Nepheline syenite	50
Barium carbonate	50
Bentonite	3

This glaze has a very dry surface.

Glaze 2 (Peter Simpson)[39]
1250°C

Nepheline syenite	80
Whiting	10
China clay	10
Bone ash	2
Barium carbonate	6

A smooth matt glaze.

Glaze 3 (Eileen Lewenstein)[38]
1250°C

Feldspar	4
Whiting	31
China clay	40
Flint	18
Dolomite	7

A satin matt glaze with a slightly crystalline surface which encourages the formation of mottled and variegated colours. Best applied thickly for textural interest.

Glaze 4 (Emmanuel Cooper)[38]
1250–1260°C

Borax frit	45
Whiting	10
Zinc oxide	27
Flint	30
Rutile*	4

A shiny, crystalline glaze with a good colour response but inclined to run if thickly applied and over-fired.

* In glaze 4 (which already contained 5% rutile) 4% tin oxide was substituted for test E.

Left: *Vertical layout showing colour variations between the four different base glazes, all fired in an electric kiln.*

Percentages of colouring oxides were added to each batch of glaze and mixed with equal amounts of water. These mixtures were then sieved through a 120 mesh to disperse the colourants and are poured into labelled jam jars. The pattern of blending is best demonstrated by the following example:

A = 1.5% Copper carbonate; B = 0.5% Cobalt carbonate; C = 4% Manganese dioxide; D = 2% Red iron oxide; E = 5% Rutile*; F = 5% Uranium pentoxide; G = 5% Tin oxide + 1% Chrome oxide.

A	B	C	D	E	F	G
	A+B	A+C	A+D	A+E	A+F	A+G
		B+C	B+D	B+E	B+F	B+G
			C+D	C+E	C+F	C+G
				D+E	D+F	D+G
					E+F	E+G
						F+G

Above left: *Porcelain bottle. Mineral glaze containing lithium brushed over with copper oxide. Fired in reduction to 1360°C. By Margarete Schott (West Germany).*

Above: *Porcelain bottle, height 4½ in. (11.5 cm). Fired in reduction to 1360°C. By Margarete Schott (West Germany), 1976.*

Each glaze is thoroughly stirred every time it is to be used. Purists will argue that it is impossible to be absolutely accurate but I have found in practice that the method described above is a sufficiently reliable guide to the colour and textural possibilities of glazes.

Equal amounts of each mixture are ladled into another small container and stirred before applying, by pouring and dipping, on a tiny, bisqued bowl, the base of which is painted or incised with identifying letters. Including the seven initial mixes a total of twenty-eight glazes is very quickly made up. Within certain recognised limits the chosen colourants and their amounts are quite arbitrary. Several more such as

Carved and incised porcelain teapots. By Petra Van Heesbeen (Holland).

Below: *Slab-built porcelain piece. By Michel Morichon (France).*

Opposite: *Margarete Schott trailing glaze on glaze.*

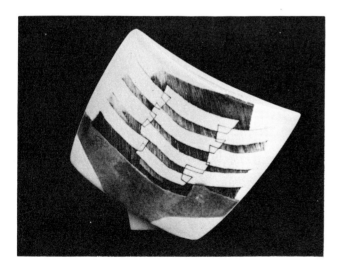

vanadium, antimony, nickel, iron chromate, and ilmenite, as well as prepared stains may also be used. If two test bowls are glazed with each mixture one set can be fired in oxidation and the other in reduction with the prospect of quite different results.

It must be remembered, when mixing up a larger batch of a particular choice later, that the oxide percentages must be *halved* where two of the initial glazes have been mixed or the results will not be the same. For example, glaze test A + B is equivalent to 100 parts glaze plus 0.75% copper carbonate and 0.25% cobalt carbonate.

The same percentage of colouring oxide in one base glaze may give very different effects in another. With so many variables involved the potter's palette of glazes and colours is truly infinite and the spirit of adventure and the excitement of discovery will, surely, never disappear.

A great deal has been written on the subject of high-fired glazes over the last few years far beyond the scope of this book and a number of excellent works are available dealing more specifically with all aspects of glaze technology (see bibliography on p. 222).

Glaze Application

The method of applying glazes affects the thickness and possibly the performance. Thin porcelain can be difficult to glaze because it quickly becomes saturated with water and takes a long time to dry. I cope with this problem by spraying several light layers of glaze, allowing each to dry before the next is sprayed on. This builds up an even thickness without runs. Warming up the pot a little beforehand does help if dipping, as does a thicker glaze mix, but a degree of

unevenness is almost inevitable with the latter method. **Margarete Schott** uses uneven thicknesses and dribbles of glaze to give variety of colour and texture under brushed oxides. She also trails glaze on glaze with a slip trailer. In the main, I prefer to keep my glazes as smooth as possible on porcelain and for this reason I spray almost every piece.

Spraying is the only way to achieve subtle gradations of tone or colour by overlapping and

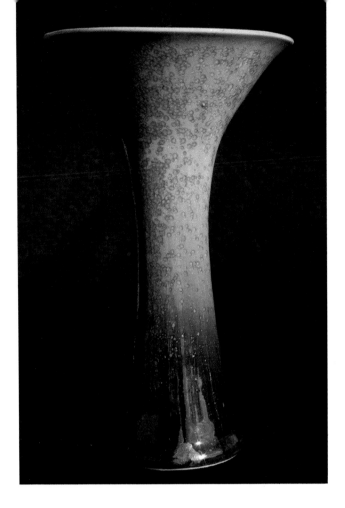

merging one glaze into another. The nozzle of the spray-gun can be positioned to give a fan of spray and this permits a remarkably fine degree of control in shading glazes, or for use over a template or mask. Glazes sprayed over latex resists also offer many possibilities for pattern and colour interchange. It is best to allow time for the glaze to build up gradually or the water content will cause dribbles away from the non-absorbent latex. Quite complex designs can be painted with this resist and if the lines or areas of latex are linked together the whole network can be easily removed to reveal the clear-cut pattern when the glaze is dry. If only one or two glazes are to be dipped the latex works equally well. Wax resists tend to be less successful under sprayed glaze than when they are dipped, and I feel that they are less versatile than the latex version.

All the other methods used for stoneware can be applied to glazing porcelain. Raw glazing is used especially by those potters engaged in vapour-glazing with salt in a 'once-fired' process. Painting with coloured glazes on to the unfired glaze is one of the techniques employed by **David Eeles**.

Crawling

The surface of bisqued porcelain even when fired to 1000°C is still slightly soft and dusty. It should be carefully wiped over with a damp sponge before glazing or it may cause the glaze to crawl. Crawling usually results from applying the glaze to dusty or greasy surfaces, or with too great a thickness of glaze (especially when double-dipped), and if the glaze layer cracks on drying. It can also be attributed to too much refractory material in the composition. Excess amounts of plastic clays in the composition, such as bentonite, may be another cause of crawling. Matt glazes can also crawl away from edges and rims if the method of raw-glazing is used.

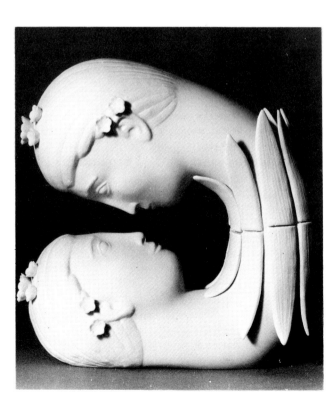

Opposite: *Incised porcelain bowl with cut rim, height 7¼ in. (18.4 cm). By Elsa Rady (USA), 1978.*

Porcelain vase, height 10¼ in. (26 cm); with ash glaze. By Jean Girel (France), 1977.

'Narcissus'. Slip-cast sculpture in unglazed porcelain. By Stig Lindberg (Sweden).

187

GLAZE RECIPES

The following recipes, contributed by the potters under whose names they appear, are given as parts by weight but in most cases the amounts total 100 and percentage additions of colouring oxides may easily be calculated.

Base glazes (minus colouring oxides) may be used in either oxidation or reduction to the maturing temperatures given, although potters have indicated their own preferences in most of them. Colouring oxides can then be added according to taste and to suit the chosen method of firing.

Oldrich Asenbryl
1280°C (Reduction)

Potash feldspar	60
Whiting	27
China clay	28
Flint	65
Talc	20.5

Potash feldspar	33
Whiting	20
China clay	15
Quartz	32

Nepheline syenite	70
China clay	10
Flint	10
Dolomite	5
Barium carbonate	20

Val Barry[39]
1240°C (Oxidation)
White with small crystals

Potash feldspar	18
Whiting	12
China clay	31
Quartz	15
Zinc oxide	23

Peter Beard
1300°C (Reduction)
Clear glaze

Potash feldspar	20
Whiting	23
China clay	25
Quartz or flint	32

Blue celadon glaze

Potash feldspar	60
Quartz	20
Whiting	15
China clay	5
Red iron oxide	1

"This glaze settles easily: use Epsom Salts as a suspender."

René Ben-Lisa (France)
1300°C (reduction)

Feldspar	60
Whiting	15
Quartz	25
China clay	5
Barium Carbonate	5

A celadon is obtained by adding 5 parts yellow ochre to this glaze, and a tenmoku by adding 10 parts red iron oxide.

Audrey Blackman
1280°C (Oxidation)

Shiny glaze:

Cornish stone	20
China clay	30
Whiting	23
Flint	27

Matt glaze:

Feldspar	56
China clay	24
Dolomite	24
Whiting	2

"To avoid cracking I warm my electric kiln overnight at 20% input of electricity, after that I raise the temperature at 100°C per hour. At 1280°C I soak for one hour and then lower the temperature slowly to 1104°C before switching off."[40]

Michael Casson
1280°C
White glaze

Cornish stone	33
Whiting	7
Ball clay SMD	4
China clay	6
Magnesium carbonate	2

"This is a good glaze used alone; over slips; or with painted decoration. Best in reduction."

Sheila Casson
1280°C
Celadon glaze: grey-green
(Reduction)

Cornish stone	40
Potash feldspar	6.6
Wollastonite	13.4
Flint	13.5
Porcelain body	20
Red iron oxide	1

"A blue-grey celadon is made by adding 0.1 manganese dioxide and .05 cobalt cabonate to this glaze."

Russell Collins[39]
1280°–1300°C
(Oxidation or reduction)

Potash feldspar	30
Whiting	18
Quartz	39
China clay	11

Delan Cookson
1280°C
(Reduction)

Feldspar	49
China clay	20
Dolomite	22
Whiting	4
Flint	5

"This glaze is semi-translucent, silky-matt."

Feldspar	83.5
Whiting	24
Ball clay	7
Flint	23
Zinc oxide	7.5

"This glaze is blue-white, translucent with a satin shine. It has nice pooling characteristics in incisions and hollows."

Iet Cool-Schoorl (Holland)
1250°C
(Reduction)
Titanium blue glaze

Feldspar	45
Whiting	11
Talc	1
China clay	1
Red clay	4
Titanium dioxide	4.5

1250°C
Copper red glaze
(Reduction)

Petalite	35
Dolomite	5
Flint	10
Barium carbonate	10
Copper carbonate	1
Tin oxide	1

Emmanuel Cooper[41]
1250°–1260°C
(Oxidation)

Potash feldspar	55
Whiting	10
Barium carbonate	20
Zinc oxide	10
Ball clay	5
Nickel oxide	2

"Gives a rich glaze effect over porcelain – pale green with dark specks, but be warned, the glaze has a tendency to run and form a dark mauve pool of glaze (unless used with) a precise firing temperature and glaze thickness."

Emmanuel Cooper (from Bill Gordon)[41]
1250–1280°C (Oxidation)

Potash feldspar	35
Barium carbonate	40
Zinc oxide	15
China clay	5
Flint	5
Nickel oxide	1–3*

* for matt pink/blue glaze

Emmanuel Cooper[39]
1260°C (Oxidation)
Pink/beige glaze

Potash feldspar	40
Whiting	20
China clay	10
Flint	20
Zinc oxide	3
Rutile	7

Emmanuel Cooper[36]
1260°C (Oxidation)
Black/green speckle

Potash feldspar	50
Whiting	10
China clay	10
Flint	6
Barium carbonate	20
Copper carbonate	2

Harris Deller (USA)
1305°C (Reduction)
Chun glaze

Potash feldspar	42.1
China clay	1.8
Flint	27.2
Whiting	2.6
Colemanite	8.8
Dolomite	8.8
Zinc oxide	1.7
Barium carbonate	4.4
Tin oxide	2.6

"My base glaze. I use it for a clear copper red and a celadon. For red add ½% Copper carbonate; for celadon add 1–3% red iron oxide; for tenmoku add 10% red iron oxide."

Marianne de Trey
1280°C (Reduction)

Feldspar	33
Wood ash	33
Flint	33
Bentonite	2

Ruth Duckworth (USA)
1280°C (Oxidation or reduction)

Feldspar	40
China clay	20
Whiting	30

Johannes Gebhardt (West Germany)
1280–1300°C (Reduction)

Potash feldspar	53
Whiting	22.3
Kaolin (from Hirschau)	24.7

"This glaze gives a good waxy surface at cone 9/10 when applied medium thick". Presumably other China clays could be substituted for the Hirschau kaolin and it can be further modified by adding small amounts (up to 5%) of titanium dioxide or extra kaolin.

Jean Girel (France)
1300°C (Reduction)

Clear celadon glaze

Powdered granite	60
Flint	25
Whiting	15

A bluish celadon (Chün) glaze

Pumice stone	75
Tobacco ash	25

Jane Hamlyn
1280°C (Reduction)
For raw glazing

Nepheline syenite	10
Ball clay	4

"Very simple, giving different results with different ball clays. Raw glazes with more than one third ball clays need to be used when pots are leather-hard to avoid crawling."

Glyn Hugo
1300°C (Reduction)
Copper red glaze

Potash feldspar	35
Whiting	20
China clay	15
Quartz	20
Barium carbonate	10
Black copper oxide	0.75

"This base glaze can be used as a starting point for various copper reds."

Sylvia Hyman (USA)[36]
1260°C (Reduction)
Deep green celadon

Potash feldspar	50
Whiting	10
Ball clay	12
Flint	20
Dolomite	6
Zinc oxide	2
Red iron oxide	1.5

Stephanie Kalan (USA)[39]
1300°C (Oxidation or reduction)

Feldspar	31
Whiting	11
China clay	13
Flint	28
Barium carbonate	22

Feldspar	20
Whiting	13
China clay	20
Flint	33
Barium carbonate	14

Beate Kuhn (West Germany)
1350°C (Reduction)
Matt white

Potash feldspar	22
Whiting	12
China clay	10
Flint	40
Magnesium carbonate	16

Peter Lane
1280°C (Oxidation or reduction)

Potash feldspar	65
China clay	5
Barium carbonate	20
Dolomite	10

With oxides added, this glaze gives rich colours in both reduction and oxidation (best when soaked for an hour in the latter to ensure a smooth melt). Excellent under Cornish stone 85: whiting 15 in reduction (with various colouring oxides staining the barium glaze). The proportions given in the line blend example (on page 183) give good results as a starting point.

David Leach[42]
1270°C (Reduction)
Jade green celadon

Cornish stone	25
China clay	25
Whiting	25
Quartz	25
Red iron oxide	2

"With only ½% red iron oxide this recipe gives a bluey-green Ying Ch'ing celadon"

David Leach[42]
1300°C (Reduction)
Tenmoku

Cornish stone	66
Whiting	11.5
China clay	7.5
Quartz	15
Red iron oxide	7.5

David Leach[39]
1280°C (Reduction)
Yellow celadon

Potash feldspar	31
Whiting	14
China clay	7
Quartz	33
Talc	12
Red iron oxide	3

"This tends to give a mustardy-yellow glaze which is dependent upon the thickness of application and temperature, it can crystallise."

David Leach[39]
1260–1280°C (Reduction)
Grey Korean celadon

HP stone or feldspar	60
Whiting	7
China clay	5
Quartz	24
Barium carbonate	2
Bentonite	1
Black iron oxide	1.5

"This glaze should be lawned as fine as possible, say 200 mesh to disperse the bentonite. If applied thickly it gives a very pleasant characteristic crackle."

David Leach
1260–1280°C (Reduction)
Orange to red glaze

Nepheline syenite	50
Calcined red clay	50

(Not *all* red clays will work). "The red clay should be calcined at 600°C to remove plasticity or over-contraction. The glaze is applied thickly over another glaze and will fire red at 1260°C and orange at 1300°C.

Michel Morichon (France)
1400°C (Reduction)
Blue/red glaze

Silica glass	44
Whiting	20
Barium carbonate	10
Dolomite	10
Zinc oxide	5
Alumina hydrate	7
Copper carbonate	4

"Alternate oxidation and reduction, finishing with a period of oxidation. In the last minutes saturate the kiln with a heavy period of reduction. Very vigorous glaze, red in depth, turquoise on the surface but transparent, with local saturation of copper and metallic carbon residue."

Ian Pirie
1280°C (Reduction)
Blue-green celadon

Potash feldspar	13
Cornish stone	10
Whiting	25
China clay	27
Quartz	25
Talc	7
Red iron oxide	1

"Without the red iron this becomes a semi-transparent white glaze."

Mary Rich[39]
1280°C (Reduction)
Raw glazes used in combination with salt-glaze

Soda feldspar	4
Grolleg kaolin	1
Black ball clay	.5
Whiting	1.5'

"This gives a soft, sugary pink with copper carbonate under light reduction."

Soda feldspar	1.5
Cornish stone	0.5
Dolomite	1.5
Whiting	0.5
Kaolin	2
Black ball clay	1

"A mottled, pale pink glaze."

Karl Scheid (West Germany)
1360°C (Reduction)

Potash feldspar	38.3
Whiting	21.3
China clay	20.2
Quartz	10.2
Titanium oxide	4.0

Hein Severijns (Holland)
1260°C (Reduction)
Tenmoku

Sodium feldspar Maffei	29.7
China clay ECLP No. 6	7.4
Whiting	14.8
Quartz, milling 10	36.1
Red iron oxide/ red ochre	6.9/5.0

Peter Simpson[39]
1240–1260°C (Oxidation or reduction)

Nepheline syenite	74
Whiting	13
China clay	7
Flint	8
Bone ash	2
Barium carbonate	8

1250°–1280°C (Oxidation or reduction)

Nepheline syenite	80
Whiting	10
China clay	10
Bone ash	2

Peter Simpson[39]
1260–1280°C (Oxidation)

Nepheline syenite	50
Whiting	3.5
Dolomite	23
China clay	25

1240–1260°C (Oxidation)

Nepheline syenite	40
Whiting	7
China clay	20
Flint	20
Dolomite	20
Bone ash	2
Barium carbonate	6
Zinc oxide	6

Carl-Harry Stålhane (Sweden)
1400°C (Reduction)

Feldspar	27
China clay	33
Nepheline syenite	8
Flint	30
Bentonite	2

Gillian Still
1260–1280°C (Oxidation)

Nepheline syenite	33.6
Dolomite	13.4
Whiting	7.3
Zinc	5.9
China clay	22.5
Flint	17.4

"I use this glaze for everything."

Geoffrey Swindell
1280°C (Oxidation or reduction)

Potash feldspar	48
China clay	24
Dolomite	24
Whiting	4

Mary White[39]
1260°C (Oxidation)

Potash feldspar	50
Whiting	8.5
China clay	7.5
Flint	20
Zinc oxide	4
Magnesium oxide	10

Glazes in general use by several potters:

Cornish stone	80
China clay	20
Whiting	20

1280–1300°C Oxidation or reduction but best in reduction. A good general purpose glaze with an attractive satin surface.

Cornish stone	60
China clay	20
Dolomite	20

1280°C Oxidation or reduction

SIX
FIRING PORCELAIN

Committing the fruits of many hours of labour to the heat and flame of the kiln is the supreme act of faith undertaken by potters. Few other craftsmen are required to risk everything through such a severe test of their skill and expertise. The excitement and satisfaction of a successful firing bring unparalleled rewards but which can, probably, only be fully appreciated by potters themselves.

Kilns are sometimes blamed for failures and disappointments but most potters adopt a philosophical approach towards this final act of the creative process. They accept that any shortcomings are due to some misjudgement in the making or firing of the work. They recognise that the basic principles of kilns and firing are simple enough and most problems are not difficult to analyse and solve. Much of that which applies to the firing of stoneware is also appropriate for porcelain, although porcelain is less tolerant of mistakes.

The performance of each kiln depends upon its construction, proportions, insulation, the fuel used and its efficiency; the directional flow of heat; the way in which it is packed, and the degree to which the atmosphere and the rise in temperature is controllable. Factors such as siting and weather conditions can also affect performance. With so many variables each kiln fires best to its own independent pattern. Where live flame is involved, even kilns built to identical plans can differ. In addition no two firings ever seem to be exactly alike. But understanding comes through practice, and potters soon acquire an affinity with their kilns which enables them to sense when adjustments are necessary. No amount of words can replace first-hand experience.

Opposite: *Carved porcelain teapot, height 11 in. (27.9 cm), width 6½ in. (16.5 cm). Reduction fired to cone 12 with celadon glaze. By David Keator (USA).*

It would be wrong to be dogmatic about firing methods and it is more profitable therefore, to consider the essentials relating to high temperature wares in general, and porcelain in particular.

Packing the Kiln

Nothing is more aggravating than finding that an otherwise perfect piece has been spoilt by bits of kiln debris sticking to the glaze. Kiln shelves must always be thoroughly checked before each firing and impacted bat wash and drops of glaze carefully removed to preserve a clean level surface. Deposits of volatilised glaze can accumulate and cause pots to stick to them unless protected by some refractory material. The usual bat wash consists of approximately equal amounts of flint and kaolin. **Margarete Schott** uses three parts quartz to two parts kaolin mixed with water and applied with a paint-roller. **Peter Beard** prefers to use calcined alumina. **David Leach** suggests a mixture of nine parts aluminium hydroxide to one part kaolin.

Sometimes glaze spots must be chipped away, leaving the shelf pitted, and particular care must be taken when placing pots on or near damaged parts. Bat wash only superficially fills the depression and, in any case, should not be applied too liberally if the surface is to remain smooth. It has been found useful to place porcelain glost ware on to bisqued 'setters' made from the same body. These are flat discs or rings of material, dusted with bat wash or alumina, which will shrink at the same rate as the pots they support. Placing the setters on a thin layer of silica sand, or aluminium hydroxide ensures an even smoother movement on contraction. A setter will protect the

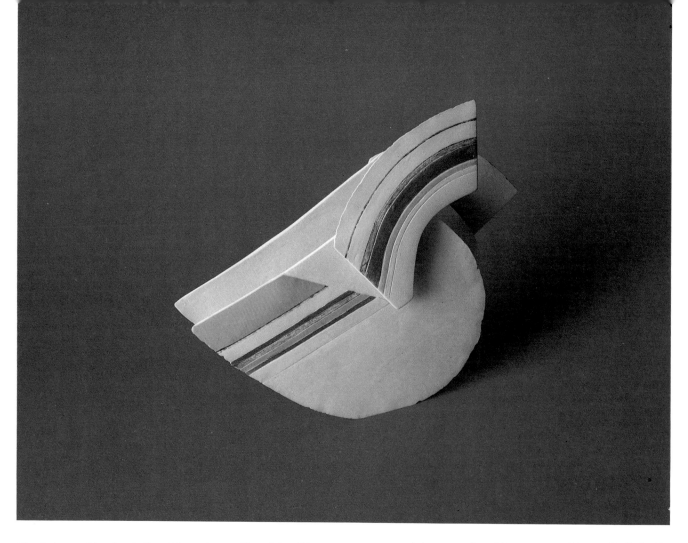

'Bowl shape with wings'. Porcelain sculpture, 7½ × 9 in. (19 × 22.9 cm). Inlaid slip and painted enamels. By Eileen Nisbet, 1979.

foot from the effects of dragging across the shelf when the pots shrink. It helps to avoid the risk of 'plucking' and reduces warping problems. Plucking occurs when the foot sticks to the shelf at one or more points during contraction and fragments are plucked out of the base of the ware. These razor-sharp slivers of vitrified porcelain remain to catch unwary fingers and must be completely removed from the shelf before re-use.

Michael and Sheila Casson use ceramic-fibre paper rings as setters, while some potters make fresh porcelain discs for every piece. I very rarely use setters of any kind and have been fortunate enough not to have suffered this particular problem. **Alan Whittaker** sometimes uses a ceramic-fibre wool to support, as well as to protect, bowls in the kiln when no glaze is involved. This fibre can be obtained in various grades and forms. Although first developed in 1942 it did not become commercially available until 1952. It is an extremely versatile material which is also used for kiln insulation and hot-face linings. It consists mainly of combinations of alumina and silica (zircon is included in more expensive versions) melted in an electric arc furnace. The molten material is blasted with a jet of

steam as it is poured and is converted into a fluffy bulk fibre which can be used to produce different thicknesses of blanket, wool, board or paper, and it can also be cast in numerous other forms.

Porcelain, especially when thinly potted, is prone to warp during firing unless very carefully sited in the kiln. **Dorothy Feibelman** fires her tiny marqueterie ware bowls in bisqued moulds, made from stoneware clay, in an attempt to overcome this problem. Some distortion, however slight, seems unavoidable due to the 'pulling' power of the inlays she uses, but firing the pieces in this way, and protected by saggars, allows the bowls to "relax" while supported in the mould.

Nick Homoky fires his handled bowls, with the handle pointing up at an angle of 45°, resting in a bed of sand to avoid distortion.

Eileen Nisbet takes particular care to fire the thin rolled shapes, which are the component parts of her slab sculptures, very slowly in order to keep them flat. She keeps her kiln shelves meticulously clean by rubbing them down with carborundum between firings and uses no placing powder or bat wash. Firing to 1240° vitrifies the David Leach body she uses and gives ample translucency to outline the thinly-scraped edges.

The relatively low temperature used by **Eileen Nisbet** gives some indication of the wide firing range of the material. Other potters using the same body take it to temperatures from 1250°C to over 1300°C. **Gary Wornell-Brown** fires all his work to 1335°C in reduction without any problem. The flat sheets of **Eileen Nisbet** would not survive such temperatures without distortion and she has found that 1240°C is her optimum working figure. Even so, she places great emphasis upon the need to take these once-fired pieces through a very gently firing pattern which involves switching the kiln on to a low setting overnight. Full power is only used towards the end of the firing cycle, and the kiln is switched off as soon as the temperature of 1240°C is reached.

Kiln Shelves and Props

When placing bats (shelves) in the kiln, the undersides and edges must be inspected for loose material which might drop on to pots beneath. Bats are best supported at three points for stability and to minimise any tendency to warp. Various types of props are used to support and separate the shelves. They are usually of tubular construction and are obtainable in different lengths, sometimes with interlocking, castellated ends for further extension.

I once suffered considerable losses when one of these props collapsed under the bottom shelf during the reduction firing of a tightly-packed glost kiln.

Three support points for each kiln shelf will help to avoid warping while providing a more stable structure than any other arrangement.

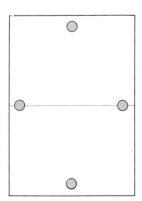
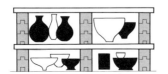

Marqueterie bowl in blue and white porcelain, height 3 in. (7.6 cm). Oxidised to 1280°C. By Dorothy Feibelman.

Since then I have preferred to trust in blocks cut from insulating firebrick. These have never let me down and, supporting very heavy loads, have remained serviceable through scores of firing. It is necessary to dust the tops and bottoms of the blocks with calcined alumina where they come into contact with the shelves or they may stick and break away on removal. Each successive prop must be placed directly above the ones beneath so that the whole weight is taken by the kiln floor.

The greatest stability of shelf structure is achieved when the smallest pots are placed at the bottom of the kiln and the sizes are gradually increased towards the top. High props, (unless they are very sturdy ones) placed at the bottom levels, present the risk of a teetering, unsafe structure. The enormous pressure from above can exaggerate the effects of heat and cause the props to collapse. Therefore, it is helpful to arrange pots beforehand, according to height, to work out the most economical kiln placing. Every piece must be completely dry and the bottoms cleaned of all traces of glaze.

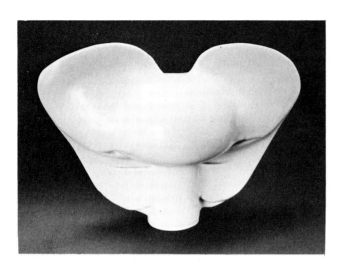

Slab-built porcelain form, 8 × 5 in. (20.3 × 12.7 cm). Oxidised to 1280°C. By Marianna Franken (Holland).

Heat Circulation

In 'live' kilns, where raw fuels are used, it is wise to bear in mind the direction and passage of the flames and to allow for the circulation of heat to all parts of the kiln. If the shelves are placed too closely together in an unstaggered arrangement some sections are likely to be isolated and the firing will be uneven. This problem does not apply so much to electric kilns where constant, radiated heat is involved.

Another concern in live kilns, packed with porcelain, is the need to prevent the flames from impinging directly upon the ware. This can be dealt with in a variety of ways. One of these is to pack the ware in saggars for protection but not many studio potters today use this method; most rely on bag walls to deflect the flames. There are no rules governing this procedure and each potter has his own ideas and methods which work for him.

I first fired my oil kiln with bag walls built up with four courses of bricks, bringing the top a good two feet above the floor of the fire-boxes. The height of these walls was gradually reduced in practice until only one course of bricks remained. The kiln has performed well with this arrangement for many firings. Some kiln designs demand very high bag walls or baffles and, even with similar kilns to mine, other potters may prefer to operate with different bag wall arrangements.

Particular pieces may also be protected by the judicious siting of stoneware pots (or insulating bricks) where the flame is likely to be too fierce. Direct flame upon porcelain can result in warping and distortion of a piece through uneven shrinkage. Flashing may interrupt the uniformity of the glaze with loss of colour, especially where copper reds are concerned. For this reason it is usual to place unprotected porcelain towards the centre of the chamber. Even in small, electric kilns potters try to keep porcelain as far away from the elements as possible. They also try to prevent hot spots developing. These can be caused when shelves are placed too close to the elements and contribute to unevenness in firing temperature. It also reduces the life of the elements. Closed-in forms like bottles present fewer problems because their compact shape resists warping.

A closely-packed kiln is likely to fire more evenly than one in which there are dense areas and empty spaces. Radiated heat from the pots themselves in a well-packed kiln also aids efficiency and less fuel is wasted in heating non-productive space.

Heat Measurement and Control

A pyrometer attached to a thermocouple is useful to indicate atmospheric temperature inside the kiln chamber but, ideally, pyroscopes (cones, bars or rings composed of ceramic materials designed to flux at given temperatures) should always be used to give an accurate indication of the actual *heat work* done. This is dependent upon the ratio of temperature to time. The usual practice is to have three cones. They should be placed where they may easily be observed but where they will not fall against any pots as they melt. The first to fall acts as a warning that the required temperature is approaching. The second cone indicates that the

Pyrometric cones before and after firing to cone 9 (1280°C).

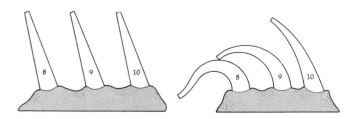

heat has completed its work to mature body and glaze, while the third serves as a guide to prevent over-firing. Combinations of cones vary according to individual needs but I normally rely upon Staffordshire cones (numbers 8, 9 and 10) representing temperatures of 1250°C, 1280°C and 1300°C respectively. These are set in heavily-grogged clay or crank mixture in a horizontal line reading from left to right. The clay is dried out completely before placing in the kiln so it survives quite rapid temperature rises.

My kiln chamber is a three foot cube (excluding the fireboxes), and two sets of cones, one towards the top and one towards the bottom, provide sufficient information to judge the progress of a firing in combination with readings taken from the pyrometer. Larger kilns are sometimes more difficult to heat evenly and cones placed at strategic points around the chamber will soon search out hot and cold spots. If these variations persist over a number of firings, the kiln design may have to be altered or some adjustment

27 cu ft down-draught oil fired kiln used by the author based on a design by S Kent (CoSIRA). This kiln has two Dine burners supplied by pumped oil (BP Distoleum or similar) and compressed air. The effective placing space is a 36 in. (90.2 cm) cube.

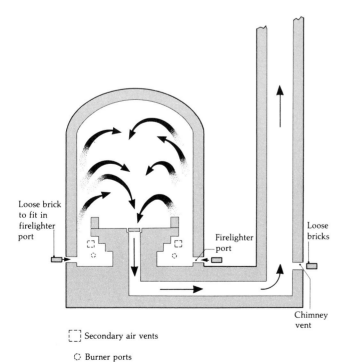

Loose brick
to fit in
firelighter
port

Firelighter
port

Loose
bricks

Chimney
vent

⌐¬ Secondary air vents
L⌐ Burner ports

Porcelain bottle, thrown with indented body. By Geoffrey Eastop.

to flame circulation can be made. Occasionally, a different arrangement of shelves can solve the problem. Some potters, however, utilise these variations in heat to fire pots with glazes fluxing at different temperatures in the same kiln.

Despite the many variables surrounding kiln firing, it is generally accepted that an average temperature rise of about 100°C is normal for glost firing. Potters using identical kilns often adopt quite independent firing patterns to achieve similar temperatures and effects. Some will stress the need to 'soak' the kiln (i.e. to maintain a constant temperature for a given period)

at one or more points in the firing. This is usually towards the end of a glost firing to ensure the proper maturation of glazes. Others will rapidly cool down the kiln immediately the cones have melted, until the temperature has dropped to about 1000°C. Some may inject more heat or adjust the atmosphere during the cooling process. Once a potter has found a successful firing pattern, he may be reluctant to risk a change.

A small capacity kiln can be fired quickly in a uniform way but larger kilns often require a longer firing cycle in order to equalise the temperature.

Kiln Atmospheres

Firing is most easily conducted in an electric kiln but this leaves little room for the calculated risk which makes flame firing so exciting. Electric kilns provide a rather clinical oxidising atmosphere by easily-controlled radiated heat. There are numerous types which need not concern us here.

Elements are usually spirals of Kanthal A1 wire set

Above left: *Individual thrown porcelain with light cream-coloured glaze. Oxidised to 1250°C. By Stig Lindberg (Sweden).*

Above: *Thrown and carved porcelain, height 5 in. (12.7 cm), with oxides brushed over a white dolomite glaze. Oxidised to 1280°C. By Peter Lane. (In the collection of W. Lenzen.)*

in grooves within the soft insulating brick lining the floor, walls and door. The energy input and temperature rise is controlled by either a simple three-position switch (low, medium, high), a graduated energy regulator or simmerstat (calibrated 0–100), or by some sort of automatic device.

It is common practice with many potters to fire their bisque or 'green' ware by electricity while the glost ware is reserved for fuel-burning kilns. Electric kilns for studio use are somewhat limited in size for maximum efficiency because the heating elements are comfined to the periphery of the chamber. Therefore the most economical interior dimensions are based on a cube.

Potters have to work much harder to compound glazes which have sufficient liveliness in texture and

Three lustre-painted porcelain pots. These pieces are bisqued and then glost fired to vitrification at 1280°C. Following lustre application they are given a further firing to 730°C. By Geoffrey Swindell, 1979.

colour to compensate for the absence of those extra qualities obtained under reducing conditions. Craftsmen who are restricted to firing in electric kilns often spend considerable time on decorative treatments which require the work to be left unglazed, or they may use glaze merely as a varnish possessing little character in their own right. Sometimes an otherwise unremarkable glaze forms the base upon which on glaze enamels or lustres are painted and re-fired at lower temperatures.

Porcelain fired in an electric kiln does seem to lack that indefinable extra depth which is more readily apparent in ware matured under reducing conditions.

Nevertheless, excellent pieces are regularly produced from electric kilns as may be witnessed in the work of potters such as **Eileen Nisbet**, **Mary Rogers**, **Irene Sims**, **Lucie Rie**, **Mary White**, **Nick Homoky**, **Gordon Cooke**, **Ray Silverman**, **Geoffrey Swindell** and many others.

While it is possible to create reducing conditions in electric kilns by introducing resinous wood or mothballs, it is at considerable cost to the elements and is not advised. A safer method, sometimes used to obtain reduction effects, is to include small amounts of finely-ground silicon carbide (400 mesh) in the glaze composition. This encourages local reduction. Copper reds can be obtained by adding between one and four per cent of silicon carbide to an alkaline base glaze containing about one per cent copper oxide, but the effects are somewhat erratic.

199

Carved porcelain covered jar, 14 × 9 in. (35.4 × 22.9 cm). Celadon glaze. Fired to 1300° in reduction. By David Keator (USA).

'Veined convolvùlus'. Pinch-built porcelain bowl with painted oxides, height 3½ in. (8.8 cm). Oxidised. By Mary Rogers.

Reduction firing

Reduction firing enjoys its popularity for those particular qualities, already referred to, which it brings to porcelain. Renewed interest in oriental porcelains has certainly contributed to its attractions and it is now the method of firing most commonly preferred by studio potters.

The individual differences which occur under reducing conditions are unacceptable for most types of industrial production. But the fire, properly controlled, works for, rather than against, the studio potter who values the uniqueness of each piece. Variations of colour and surface are prized for their extra interest. Occasionally, the firing may impart special qualities to a particular piece due to its position in the kiln and the prevailing atmosphere at that point. In the oxidising atmosphere of the electric kiln results are almost totally predictable, with fewer surprises or excitements.

The most economical use of heat in reduction firing is secured in down-draught kilns. These were first introduced by the Chinese, who used many-chambered kilns, built on sloping sites, known as climbing kilns. Waste heat from the first chamber is directed through the second, then the third and so on, before finally reaching the chimney. When the first chamber has reached temperature, the fireboxes of the pre-heated second chamber are stoked up. The process continues until all chambers are fired.

David Eeles has built a large, three-chamber, wood-fired kiln based on this principle at his pottery in Dorset. He experienced some problems with hot and cold spots during firing in parts of the kiln and decided that the bag walls were deflecting too much heat from certain areas near the floor. To overcome this he removed the bag walls completely, and now places saggars packed with pots near the entry flues to act as a baffle against the fiercest flames. Gaps between the saggars allow the heat to circulate more freely to all parts of the kiln. The saggars, which occupy about half the placing space in this way, were made from a mixture of fine-grain, China clay Molochite (70%), China clay (15%) and ball clay (15%), using coiling and throwing techniques.

It is interesting to note that the first time David Eeles fired this kiln it was difficult to prevent it firing much too quickly, which in turn led to some unevenness. The remedy has been to reduce the size of the flues connecting the chambers, and to allow outside air to enter at the base of the chimney to slow the draught.

The type of kiln more commonly used by studio

Porcelain bowl. Reduction fired to 1300°C. By Johan van Loon (Holland).

Right: 'Trees'. Thrown and carved porcelain bowl, 12 in. (30.4 cm) diameter. With sprayed and shaded glazes. Oxidised to 1280°C. By Peter Lane, 1977.

potters consists of a single chamber. Although the principles remain the same (i.e. retention of heat within the chamber, easy control of temperature and atmosphere, coupled with economy), designs vary according to the construction materials; choice of fuel; site position and individual requirements. Oil, gas, coal, coke or wood may be used. At one time, oil was the cheapest alternative to wood and many kilns were built to burn it, especially in rural areas where piped gas was unobtainable. It now seems possible that the constantly rising cost of oil could soon prohibit its use by the studio potter.

Porcelain lidded jar with reduced copper and iron speckles, height 8 in. (20.3 cm). By Tina Forrester, 1979.

Vast quantities of wood (particularly soft woods like pine or spruce) which have an open grain structure are required for each firing of a wood burning kiln and constant attendance is necessary throughout the whole period. Gas is more straightforward but does not provide the same sense of excitement and personal involvement.

Reducing atmospheres are essential for the development of certain colours such as the celadons and copper reds. When reduction is induced during the firing, carbon is deprived of oxygen, and combustion is incomplete. This releases free carbon (visible as smoke), hungry for oxygen, and the chemical reaction is continued with oxygen extracted from the colouring oxides present in the glaze. These elements are thus *reduced* to their metallic state. The intensity of the colours produced vary according to the percentages of oxides present, the character of the base glaze and the amount of reduction obtained.

The most versatile are the oxides of iron and copper. Iron, normally tan, brown or black in oxidising atmospheres, can give the most delicate range of greys, greens and blues through deep olive to rust red and black depending upon the proportions used. The oxides of copper, normally green in oxidation (turquoise or blue in alkali-base glazes), yield an amazing variety of pinks, reds and purples under reduction.

Peter Beard sometimes "fumes" the kiln with copper vapours "to give pale pink lines over pieces.

Porcelain bowl with iron oxide brushwork, height 5 in. (12.7 cm). Reduction fired to 1280°C. By Thomas Plowman.

Right: Three small porcelain forms thrown and modelled, height 3 in. (7.6 cm). By Anne James.

This is done by placing small pots full of copper oxide in the kiln''. The results are impossible to control so careful placing is necessary.

The majority of porcelain glazes only require light to medium reducing conditions to produce the best results. Too heavy reduction, especially in the early stages of firing, may lead to bloating of the body. Porcelain bodies fired in reduction usually have a colder, slightly bluish tint due to faint traces of ferrous iron in their composition.

The atmosphere within the kiln and the speed of temperature rise is mainly governed by two related

Cast porcelain bottles with matt grey and brown glazes. Reduction fired. By Stig Lindberg (Sweden), 1979.

factors, Firstly the input of fuel and secondly the rate of combustion. The latter depends upon the ratio of carbon to oxygen, once kindling temperature is reached. These amounts must be regulated by the potter, who can either increase or decrease the input of fuel, or air, or both. Where gas or oil is used, the adjustment may be made to the burner settings or to the primary air available at the burner port. The difference between oxidation and reduction is delicately balanced but quite logical to follow in practice. When the burners are operating at their optimum settings it may prove more convenient to leave them as they are and to control the atmosphere by dampers or secondary air vents.

The process of combustion is best explained by comparing it with a bonfire. On a windy day the match may be blown out unless shielded from the draught. In other words, the rush of air must be restricted to the amount needed to sustain combustion. Once the fire is kindled, a strong breeze hurries the flames along so that all material is quickly consumed. A sudden addition of fresh material will momentarily slow the flame and produce smoke (i.e. the balance is disturbed until more oxygen is available). If too much fuel is

Stemmed porcelain bowl with copper red glaze, height 7⁷/₈ in. (20 cm). Reduction fired. By Iet Cool-Schoorl (Holland), 1979.

Above right: *Blue and white salt-glazed porcelain teapot with paper-resist pattern of trees, height 6½ in. (16.5 cm). By Jane Hamlyn. (In the collection of Mr and Mrs R. Hubbard.)*

piled on too quickly the fire may even be extinguished. But, on a still day, it might be necessary to fan the flames to ensure that sufficient air reaches the area of combustion. To put the bonfire out, it is smothered with non-combustible material such as earth or turf, preventing the access of air.

In a kiln, the atmosphere within the chamber is more precisely controlled, especially when the firebox is hot. All that may be needed to ensure that sufficient reduction takes place in the middle stages of a glost firing (around 1000°C) is to slow the rate at which the fire passes through the chamber and up the chimney. To achieve this the flue may be restricted by the use of dampers, or air can be allowed to enter through ports cut in the base of the chimney causing a back-pressure inside the kiln. The latter method works best in the oil kiln I use. As the firing continues and the temperature rises, combustion accelerates to the point where restriction of the air supply must be more severe in order to maintain the same degree of reduction.

Some potters like to fire with a light reducing atmosphere from around 1000°C right through to the end, with or without a period of oxidation at the finish. Others prefer to take it in alternating steps, with

perhaps half an hour reduction followed by a similar period of oxidation until the final stages.

Potters learn to judge the degree of reduction taking place in the kiln by the amount of smoke visible at the chimney, the colour of the flame in the firebox; and by the appearance of the chamber viewed through the spyholes. When the kiln is oxidising the flames will look clean and the pots will be sharply visible with no evidence of smoke at the spyhole or at the chimney.

Salt-glaze firing

Several potters are currently applying salt-glazing techniques to porcelain. In Britain many of these have graduated from the Harrow School of Art Studio Pottery Course. Salt is extremely corrosive and severely reduces the life of a kiln. Some measure of protection can be gained by frequently washing all surfaces with aluminium oxide. The kiln furniture also must be treated, and some potters use an aluminium paint for this purpose.

Salt-glazing is a once-fired process in which salt is thrown directly into the firebox when the maturing temperature of the porcelain body is reached. The salt vapourises, releasing sodium which combines with the silica of the body to form a thin glaze. Successive salting at intervals during the firing builds up thicker layers of glaze.

Joanna Constantinidis uses a technique of firing salt-

Three 'poppy' pots with indented rims brushed with oxides. By Ray Silverman, 1979.

glaze within individual saggars to which dry salt has been added before the kiln is fired. She tries to obtain a lustrous effect by spraying a mixture of copper and iron oxides on to porcelain and this, together with the salt, produces a glazed surface with colours ranging from pale flesh-pink to rich rust-red. (The interior of

the saggars themselves are often very beautiful!)

The saggars are sealed with a mixture of clay slurry and sawdust so that the lids can easily be removed after the firing. When under pressure to complete work for an exhibition she has fired a salted saggar in an electric kiln but would not recommend this as a general practice. Salting is, in any case, rather unpredictable, and colours and surfaces vary considerably. At one time she used sawdust, but it burnt away too quickly with limited effect. Then quite by chance, one of her students offered her a quantity of mustard seed, which she substituted for sawdust as a reducing agent, and found that its denser structure burnt more slowly and effectively for her purpose. She now uses mustard seed to encourage local reduction within a saggar.

Bloating

One of the major problems in firing porcelain, especially in an electric kiln, is body bloating. Quite large blisters sometimes appear within the body wall and are the source of much comment and suggestion concerning causes and remedies. It is a problem which may ruin the pots in one firing while a subsequent firing, under apparently identical conditions, leaves the pieces unblemished. Certainly, if the firing is too rapid, carbonaceous matter may be trapped within the body. This will turn to gas as the firing proceeds which may be unable to escape when the pores are sealed by glaze.

The David Leach body recipe favoured by many potters in Britain has gained an unenviable reputation for its tendency to bloat if unsympathetically fired in oxidation. Over a number of years bloating is the only serious problem which several potters have experienced with this body in electric kilns. However, I have found it to be remarkably well-behaved and completely reliable when fired in reduction atmospheres. I take about ten hours to reach 1000°C and a total of seventeen to eighteen hours to 1280°C and this longer firing cycle (normally twelve hours in the electric kiln) probably ensures the complete dispersal of carbon gas.

David Leach himself fires his oil kiln oxidising to 1000°C in approximately six to seven hours. He then 'soaks' it for one hour, maintaining 1000°C for the duration of this period, in order to burn off any residual carbon before the body vitrifies and prevents the escape of gas. **David Eeles** takes the precaution of soaking his *bisque* firing at 1000°C for up to three hours to serve the same purpose. **Eileen Lewenstein** also soaks her bisque ware, but only for half an hour at 1000°C.

This annoying problem of bloating can be avoided if either the bisque firing is taken a little higher to burn away the volatiles, or if the time allowed for gases to escape is increased by soaking at the top bisque temperature. Alternatively, a slower rise in

Two thrown porcelain bowls, height 3 in. (7.6 cm). Pieces of stained porcelain have been thrown with the white body creating inlaid spirals. The pot on the left has been fired in a closed saggar containing salt. By Joanna Constantinidis, 1979.

temperature between 1000°C and 1100°C during the glost firing should provide a similar opportunity.

Bloating may also be caused by over-firing the porcelain body, when the fluxes present in the body begin virtually to boil and bubble. If the surface of the body is sealed off during firing before the gases caused by decomposition in over-heating have escaped, bloating will be the inevitable result.

An example of bloating by overfiring porcelain.

SEVEN

COLLECTING STUDIO PORCELAIN

Anyone familiar with crafts in Britain will be aware of the tremendous revival of interest which has taken place since the late 1950s. The injection of public money following the setting-up of the Crafts Advisory Committee in 1971 confirmed the new-found status of the crafts movement. Inevitably the Crafts Council, as it was renamed in 1979, has drawn as many critics as it has admirers, not least because of the dangers in fashioning a 'public taste' through sponsorship.

The Crafts Council has been instrumental in focusing the attention of craftsmen and public to a remarkable degree in a very short space of time. Through its exhibitions, its *Crafts* magazine and other publications, it has publicised and promoted craftsmen, their products and their rôle in society, thereby giving extra impetus to the rapidly expanding movement.

As far as ceramics are concerned, the enormously successful and much respected Craftsmen Potters' Association (established in 1955) has also had a considerable influence in Great Britain. Its popular bi-monthly magazine *Ceramic Review* is a useful reference source for all who have any interest in pottery.

There can be no doubt that public appreciation of fine craftsmanship has developed enormously over the past decade, stimulated by the above and other organisations in different countries, and by the ever-increasing number of good galleries.

However, few of the private galleries in Britain at present show the work of potters from other countries, probably because the choice among native craftsmen is so wide and few gallery owners claim any deep knowledge of contemporary porcelain from elsewhere. During the 1970s a number of good quality

crafts shops and galleries have been opened in which fine ceramics may be closely examined and handled. The best of these impose stringent standards in the selection of work for sale and in many cases pieces are attractively exhibited on well-lit display units.

In addition, the lead given by the Crafts Council and the Victoria and Albert Museum in jointly establishing a highly selective crafts shop within the museum was quickly followed by the Castle Museum, Norwich and several other provincial museums with similarly energetic management. At the same time more museums are collecting contemporary ceramics and making them available for study. Opportunities therefore exist in abundance for any who would acquaint themselves with current developments. Regular looking will undoubtedly sharpen the eye of the collector and ease the problem of trusting to one's judgement in the hope that time will not devalue (in the aesthetic sense) the attraction of any chosen piece. Although work displayed in public collections acquires a status which may or may not be justified, it does provide a point of reference.

Taste and fashion can be dictated to some extent by the frequent exposure, through the media, of the work of particular craftsmen, so that demand for their artefacts far exceeds the supply. Prices are often pushed beyond the means of many people. Yet the choice open to collectors, be they casual or dedicated, is very wide and compared with the fine arts ceramics remain reasonably priced.

Newcomers may well be confused by the never-ending conflict of 'craft versus art' in ceramics today. "When is a craftsman an artist and when is an artist a craftsman? Is the hand versus head concept valid? History can give one whatever answer one wishes. All attitudes have been accepted, refused, exploited and developed. The fact is human values are constantly changing and the human condition can be varied depending upon the initiative, daring

Opposite: *Interior of the Craftsmen Potters' Shop, Marshall Street, London (headquarters of the Craftsmen Potters' Association — 'CPA').*

dedication and talents of the individual."[43]

Edward Lucie-Smith, the art historian, writing in *Ceramic Review* in 1977[44] claimed that "nobody knows any longer what a good pot is and nobody can draw the line between what is primarily ceramics and what is primarily sculpture. This wouldn't matter so much if it hadn't led to a decline in standards of judgement. Because people no longer know how to categorise what they see they've also lost the power to say whether or not it strikes them as being any good. Rather than condemn something which they feel might in fact lie outside their own area of expertise, they mutter 'Oh well, I suppose it's all right if you like that sort of thing'. Aesthetic unease, like other forms of unease, tends to breed whimsicality, because the making of jokes is a way of trying to link incompatible impulses and aims. Fun ceramics make me reach for my hammer."

While I can sympathise with this view, I do not believe that it should be necessary to find convenient labels either to justify or refute the validity of work. At the same time one must acknowledge that some ceramics may be the product of a kind of self-conscious exhibitionism, designed to attract attention but having no real depth or substance. The dilemma of judgement is best resolved through constant looking, learning and assessing over a period of time. Countless millions of pottery vessels have been made by hand but, like performances of a familiar concerto played by different musicians, each pot is an individual expression.

Potters "are second class artists to no-one. The pot-maker may pursue a more humble aim than the sculptor but the processes he goes through involve him in a very similar area of concern, that of abstract concepts. The problems start in the area of 'non-pot' where there is a less recognisable frame within which to work."[45]

Bernard Leach blames "the acquisitive impulse of the collector" for the creation of "many false values".[46]

Jon Catleugh, himself a collector, wrote in *Ceramic Review*[47] that "the young potters are no different from the young of any generation inasmuch as they question the validity of the work and tenets of the previous generation; they are very alive to their future and cannot see that the dogma they have inherited is valid for themselves. The older generation had a very clear idea how to define a potter and his place in society. But what of Mr X, who has just spent three stimulating years at the Royal College with all the technical facilities that were there available to him? . . . He would have seen that there are many

semi-industrial techniques available for all the dull, repetitive work, leaving his imagination free to invent . . . He has discovered that there is more to pottery than just clay. If he is a sculptor who prefers to work in porcelain rather than in stone, where does he fit in?"

But collectors (or indeed anyone interested in purchasing modern ceramics), are faced with a bewildering choice. How does one begin? What is 'good'? What criteria should be used in making judgements? Where is the line drawn between gimmickry and genuine creativity? How much weight should be attached to the opinions of others?

Lionel Phillips, who has been collecting ceramics since 1970, believes that before starting a collection it is wise to "look at the work in the best galleries and keep on looking until you are able to distinguish the good from the bad."

Most of the collectors I know have an instinctive 'feel' for the pieces they buy. W.A. Ismay, who has a fairly comprehensive collection of British ceramics, says that when he looks at pots his "hand and eye pick out preferences (based perhaps on the maker's lively and sensitive use of the materials) quite quickly. I can usually rationalise the choice later but the choice itself I can only call instinctive." He rates contemporary studio porcelain very highly in the sense that it interests him "more than any other porcelain since Sung China and other oriental names of associated character. Later oriental porcelain is too ornate for my taste and modern studio porcelain is the first European porcelain to come from one pair of hands. The piece can be chunky and solid but take glaze as no other body does (or be thinner, and reveal incising or facet-cutting under a pale, transparent glaze as no other surface can); it can be delicate and dry-surfaced; it can be smooth, fragile and markedly translucent; it can be an abstract exploration of the quality of the clay and of light itself."

Jon Catleugh believes there can be no other criterion than personal taste. He suggests that one should choose that which one considers good. "You have got to live with it. If you take other people's advice the chances are that they have commercial interests or they may have an interest in being fashionable. There is virtually no investment incentive for buying — yet." For him "craftsmanship is of prime importance, provided it is combined with a true, first-hand vision. We do not greatly care for, say, West Coast 'funk', where originality appears to be all important and how it is made of no importance at all. Bad workmanship palls incredibly quickly. Modish novelty looks very sad after a year when the next novelty has been

declared OK by some colour supplement journalist.''

He looks also for a true understanding of the ''hitherto impossible potential of the clay: **Jacqueline Poncelet's** paper-thin, slip-cast bone china; **Angela Verdon's** 'lace'; **Dorothy Feibelman's** inlay. Since we make a point of getting to know our favourite potters it is enjoyable to see them in their work and watch their development.''

Bernard Leach once wrote that ''to make a thing oneself is the nearest way to understanding.''[46]

Reginald Hyne is an architect and a collector of ceramics who has built a well-equipped studio in which he enjoys making his own pots. Like the Catleughs, the Hynes like getting to know the potters whose work they collect. All their pots have clear identities which seem to bring the potters closer to them. A porcelain tea service, hand-made by **David Leach**, is in constant use and gives them immense pleasure.

British studio porcelain in particular is rated very highly by many collectors and gallery owners. Celia

Interior of Casson Gallery, Marylebone High Street, London, during an exhibition of porcelain in May 1979.

Colman (Innate Harmony Gallery, London) told me that in her view individual studio porcelain in Britain is of a ''very high quality'' and she believes that it has an ''undisputed mastery''. She also feels that there is ''a certain aura of respect attached to porcelain. Potters working in the medium tend to be more selective in what they show, due to the inherent nature of the material, which demands more care in conception and design. However, although the aesthetic value of modern studio porcelain is there for all to see, only time will prove its endurance and positive acceptance.''

Pan Henry (Casson Gallery, London) feels that ''the porcelain currently being made by the best potters in Great Britain is among the best in the world; it being noted especially for its small scale and delicacy.'' She finds that it is in ''great demand. The public are very enthusiastic about it.''

Interior of Barclaycraft Gallery, Brighton, during an exhition of stoneware and porcelain by Glyn Hugo in 1979.

Joan Crossley-Holland (Oxford Gallery, Oxford) places British porcelain "second to none" but also refers to the "lively interest aroused by avant-garde work in Germany." She feels that "as antique porcelain has been collected for generations, the very name immediately commands respectful attention, even for new studio porcelain." Because the prices for individual pieces are generally lower than for the fine arts she also believes that many collectors are encouraged to persevere. "Nonetheless unique porcelain by leading potters *should* command prices which compare with those for fine arts pieces and set a realistic standard."

Dr. Paul Köster, who runs a much-respected gallery in Mönchengladbach, selects pieces on the basis of artistic quality. The material used is, therefore of secondary importance. However it is clear to him that "since the mid-sixties porcelain has become an increasingly important means of artistic expression, so that in terms of quantity, pieces of porcelain from all the most important European countries occupy considerable space in my stocks." He also feels that England and Germany are "leading countries in ceramic art" at the moment, but considers Ruth Duckworth as belonging more to English art than to American.

The Somers Gallery in Heidelberg held its first exhibition of English porcelain in 1978. Apart from the high level of craftsmanship, the gallery owners appreciate especially the "delicate, refined and light-hearted work" of contemporary English potters.

Hugo Barclay (Barclaycraft Gallery, Brighton) feels that there is a pronounced movement away from domestic ware "particularly chunky, country-style pots, towards the finer, one-off pieces, most especially in porcelain. The influence of the Germanic taste for

212

fine exact porcelain work is very noticeable. This is the main trend today and certainly owes much to the increased public awareness of standards and the appreciation of more skilful work."

All discerning gallery owners in Britain look for high quality craftsmanship and design. Peter Dingley (Peter Dingley Gallery, Stratford-upon-Avon) is less concerned with "originality *per se* than with long-lasting ability to give delight." Although he rates some work very highly he is also suspicious of work which has "more gimmicky shadow than satisfying substance."

Stephen Brayne (Craftsmen Potters' Shop, London) refers to the "immense variety of current work, and the special quality which is recognised by many members of the buying public who prize porcelain above the 'common' stoneware. The translucency and silky texture of many porcelain glazes are the qualities that mainly appeal."

Stephen Scott (Art and Ceramic Gallery, Richmond, Surrey) believes that the public is looking for something "personal and imaginative. Something which is looked into rather than looked at: the artist's personal world." In this respect he selects pieces which exhibit "craftsmanship allied to originality."

Gill Wyatt-Smith (Yew Tree Gallery, Derbyshire) feels that "sculptural porcelain has come into its own very forcibly these last few years and is being appreciated too by gallery visitors, obviously by collectors and also by the general public who enjoy the fineness of porcelain in contrast to the plethora of stoneware, which was so popular for so long. There are many highly-skilled craftsmen working in porcelain at the moment and this really is essential, for porcelain can so easily look clumsy if not expertly handled. The more natural and simple the design of a piece, the more acceptable it seems to be. The contorted and intricately-worked images have their appeal but I feel that this is more a fascination for 'how does he do it?' rather than a fundamental instinctive response to a form which appears completely right for the medium. I would cite **Mary Rogers'** and **Val Barry's** work here as examples of calm, relaxed forms which are nonetheless intricate through their handling of the clay." She regrets that the prices of individual sculptural porcelain are rising so rapidly and believes that this is probably due to participation in exhibitions abroad where such pieces do command much higher prices than in Britain. "This takes them out of the category of general public purchases and into the collectors' class."

In 1975, Garth Clark[48] was calling for "a revolution to break down barriers between the traditions of the makers of pots and the makers of objects."[48] In chapter 1 I referred to the suspicions and jealousies evident in the attitudes of some of those who hold opposing views and entrenched positions. "The snobbery of the fine artist provides the barrier on one side and the mystique and defensiveness of the potter on the other."[45] If we look at the broad spectrum of ceramic tradition there would seem to be no room for dogma concerning *any* aspect. Those collectors who spoke to me of the 'presence' they search for when choosing pieces, recognise this indefinable quality regardless of any kind of categorisation. A potter may take the *idea* of a bowl form (probably the earliest type of pottery utensil) to explore in visual, sculptural, decorative or abstract terms, but if final justification for its existence rests with its suitability for domestic or culinary use this would be a blinkered and unacceptably restrictive view. On the other hand, a simple bowl may possess a quiet, unassuming 'presence' no less impressive than the most complex sculpture whether designed for use or otherwise. Experience tells one the level to which an individual craftsman has been honest to himself and to his materials in expressing ideas. This honesty and sincerity in work, allied to fine craftsmanship in the handling of materials becomes more recognisable as one grows familiar with ceramics through constant study and appraisal. We should remain *open-minded* whatever our personal tastes — and even these may well change with time.

One collector, Mrs. L.L. Epstein, told me "I do not buy functional or purely ornamental pieces. I am aware that 'decorative' is a relative term but any art judgement is also arbitrary and I will buy only ceramics which are a conscious aesthetic expression."

W.A. Ismay feels that one has to "observe some personal principle of conformity if the collection is truly to be one." He also feels that anyone who buys as an investment is an investor, not a collector. "A collection proper, in a sense, dies if it becomes static. But there is something wrong unless, when anything new arrives, everything moves round a little, perhaps, but does so to make room for the newcomer."

He thinks that "it is simpler if one specialises, more fundamental if one collects generally and to some extent gets pieces for actual use. In this way they become part of one's life in general, carrying associated non-usable pieces with them."

The Catleughs' approach to collecting crystallised after their first year. They realised that they did not have to be in "competition with the Victoria and Albert Museum" and they did not need a representative collection of late twentieth-century English ceramics. So they drew up a list of their "twelve preferred

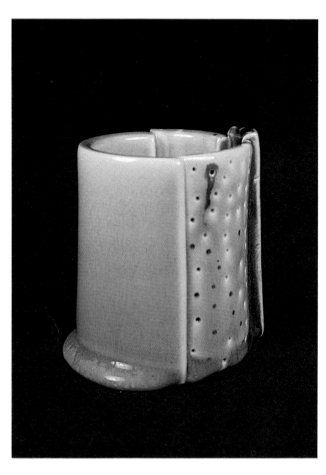

Porcelain cylinder, thrown and cut. Height 4 in. (10.2 cm), with feldspathic glaze. Fired in reduction to 1300°C. By Joe Molinaro (USA), 1979.

potters" and decided to concentrate on the work of these craftsmen. It happened that these were all potters of the younger generation who were "pushing out the frontiers of what could be done with clay." They also decided that they would not buy any more works which showed the influence of the Far East. They are both members of the English Ceramic Circle and at meetings felt that "the world is divided into two classes; pottery people and porcelain people. They looked different, dressed differently and even behaved differently. That was in the days when porcelain meant Chelsea figure groups and Meissen; a certain rococo artificiality." In those days porcelain summed up those things in the eighteenth century for which they had no sympathy. "Then suddenly potters started to realise that this wonderful material had qualities that they wanted to explore. It demanded discipline, attention to detail. It enabled them to work immaculately. How different from the slap-dash

workmanship that the reduced stoneware boys fobbed off on the world as the authentic hand-made look."

As an architect, Jon Catleugh finds himself very much in sympathy with "the elegant precision of potters like **Nick Homoky**." His purchases today are as likely to be from the potters' studios direct, as from exhibitions or shops.

Mrs L.L. Epstein expressed the "light-hearted and joyful aspect" of looking at ceramics. She will "go miles to see an exhibition" and is "full of anticipation all the way to it." Although she admits that one aspect of collecting is the satisfaction of personal taste, it is "essentially acquisitions of objects which speak one's own dialect and which extend the bounds of one's own aesthetic horizon. Any other form of collecting is meaningless to me."

Many avenues are open for specialising with a collection. For example, one may decide to collect porcelain (in the broadest sense) in order to demonstrate the diversity of approaches or the imaginative and sympathetic use of materials and techniques. Another possibility would be to take a theme such as miniature pieces, bowls, bottles, boxes, sculptural forms, lidded pieces, paperweights, particular colours, types of glaze or surface treatment. Or, perhaps to concentrate upon the work of one, two, three or more craftsmen; or, as in the case of some collectors, limit the selection to pieces from one country. A number of private collections, however, are truly international in concept and scale.

The tremendous enthusiasm of many collectors is impressive, not only in the activity of collecting itself but in their knowledge and appreciation of the work involved. This enthusiastic excitement is infectious and, in most cases, is clearly self-perpetuating.

The pressures upon leading craftsmen working in porcelain at the moment can be quite considerable when related to the expectation of serious collectors. In Germany those potters who have achieved wide acclaim, such as **Karl and Ursula Scheid**, find that collectors are constantly expecting something 'new' from them. The potter's concern for sustained excellence means that exhibition work is necessarily limited because, for various reasons, many pieces will be rejected beforehand as of insufficient quality. Prices for the best pieces are, therefore, inevitably high.

Exhibition prices in general must be inflated to cover the considerable costs and overheads involved. An exhibition, in any case, suggests that the pieces are in some way 'special'. Yet, often work available outside specific exhibitions can be of equal interest to collectors because good craftsmen, who believe in

maintaining standards, will ensure that anything
bearing their mark or name will not devalue their
ideals or undermine their reputation. The Scheids
grind away their personal seals from the bottoms of
any pieces which they feel are too good to destroy but
unsuitable to be sold as top quality work.

Collectors soon learn to identify the work of each
individual potter of any worth. Most have an
unmistakable style even though they may make a
whole range of different pieces. Some have a
particular theme or form which they explore to great
depth. This kind of enquiry may continue for several
years. The danger, from the potter's point of view, can

Above left: *Porcelain lidded jar, 8 in. (20.3 cm) diameter. By
Randy Anderson (Canada), 1977.*

Above: *Porcelain lidded jar with carved top and platinum lustre,
5½ × 5½ in. (13.9 × 13.9 cm). By Keith Campbell (Canada), 1978.*

Below left: *Porcelain box with carved lid, raw-glazed, 4 in.
(10.2 cm) diameter. By Andrew and Joanna Young, 1979.*

Below: *Porcelain box with landscape, incised and applied, 3 in.
(7.6 cm) diameter. By David Winkley. (In the collection of Lesley
Coulson.)*

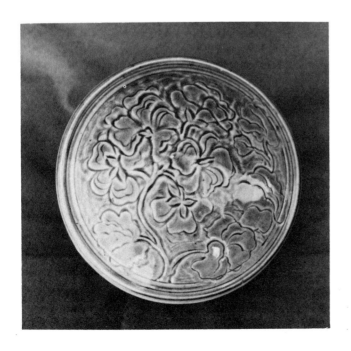

Interior of Innate Harmony Gallery, St. John's Wood, London.

Left: *A section of the interior of Dr Paul Köster's Gallery, Mönchengladbach, West Germany, during a Lucie Rie exhibition 1978.*

be that success achieved through producing one kind of form, or in the projection of an idea in visual terms, may lead to 'type-casting'. The demand for such work may place him on a treadmill that can exhaust freshness and vitality.

But, if the potter's feeling and sensitivity for the material is mature enough, thematic exploration assists both understanding and the realisation of a personal style: **Karl Scheid's** carved bottles; **Colin Pearson's** winged vessels; **Geoffrey Swindell's** narrow-footed pieces; **Gordon Cooke's** slab-work; the fluted wares of **David Leach**; the sculptural expressions of **Mary Keepax** and **Peter Simpson**; and the work of many others comes to mind.

Unfortunately, in a hard commercial world, some

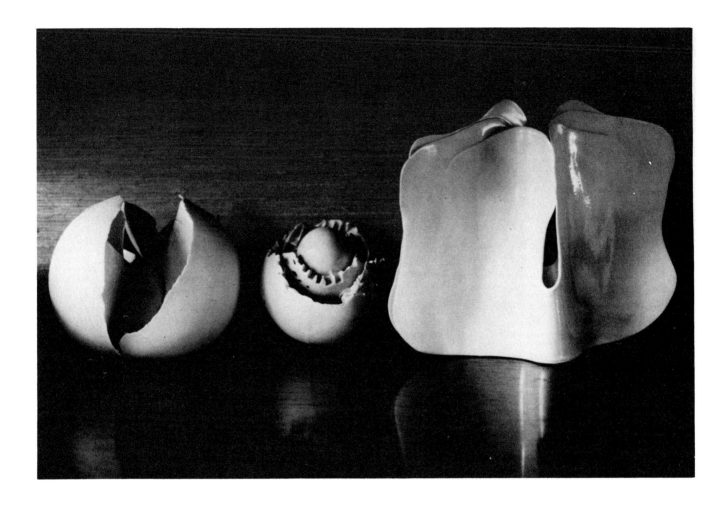

potters do seem to make things in an attempt to be different, in order to draw attention to themselves in an exhibitionist way, without always having any real feeling or belief in what they are trying to say. The indefinable 'presence' is something communicated by the potter through his work and felt by the spectator.

"What it is that moves us within art remains essentially the same, be it in a painting, a piece of music, a poem, a piece of sculpture or a Grecian urn. It is the truth within the spirit of its making (and thus the truth of its maker) that endows an object or work with the power to move us. Man seeks to make and be moved. Both the artist and the craftsman seek to make and to affirm."[49]

The best solutions to aesthetic problems are often remarkable for their simplicity. Under-statement is much more difficult to achieve successfully than over-statement and the best work, whatever the form it takes, expresses the very essence of refined ideas.

Three porcelain pieces by Kurt Spurey in the collection of Dr Karl-Joseph Simons, Aachen, West Germany.

"When thinking of adding a pot to your collection there are two tests worth applying. First, the size must be quite unimportant. You must not feel that it might have been better a little larger or a little smaller. If you do feel the size is wrong, look at something else. Second, the pot must be still. This quality of stillness, which has often been remarked of ancient Chinese pots, is much more than not moving; most solid objects can be still in that sense and the stillness to look for must be central to its nature like the centre of a wheel, the movement all round trapped and brought to a point in the pot. These criteria are immensely demanding. You cannot expect them to be met every time, and you would be right to collect many pieces of pottery that fall short. But now and again you will find something which in shape, decoration and texture meets every test."[50]

217

WHERE TO SEE PORCELAIN

A selection of museums where porcelain of historical interest may be seen:

UK

Bath: Holborne of Menstrie Museum
Bedford: Cecil Higgins Gallery
Birmingham: City Museum and Art Gallery
Bristol: City Art Gallery
Cambridge: Fitzwilliam Museum
Cardiff: National Museum of Wales
Derby: Crown Derby Works Museum
  Derby Museum and Art Gallery
Devon: William Cookworthy Museum, Kingsbridge
Edinburgh: Royal Scottish Museum
Ipswich: Christchurch Museum
Leicester: Museum and Art Gallery
Lincoln: The Usher Gallery
Liverpool: City Museum
London: Bethnal Green Museum
  British Museum
  Percival David Foundation of Chinese Art
  Victoria & Albert Museum
  Wallace Collection
Norwich: Castle Museum
Oxford: Ashmolean Museum
Plymouth: City Museum and Art Gallery
Preston: The Harris Museum and Art Gallery
Shrewsbury: Museum and Art Gallery
Southampton: Art Gallery
Stoke-on-Trent: Art Gallery and Museum
Truro: County Museum and Art Gallery
Worcester: The Dyson Perrins Museum

Austria

Vienna: Österreiches Museum für Angewandte Kunst

Canada

Toronto: Royal Ontario Museum
  (Chinese, Korean and Japanese work)

Denmark

Copenhagen: Bing & Grøndahl Factory Museum
  The Royal Copenhagen Porcelain Manufactory
  Kunstindustrimuseum

France

Limoges: Musée National Adrien-Dubouché
Paris: Louvre
  Musée des Arts Décoratifs
  Musée National de Versailles
Sèvres: Musée National de Céramique

Germany

Berlin: Kunstgewerbemuseum
Darmstadt: Hessisches Landesmuseum
Düsseldorf: Hetjens – Museum
  (Good general collections and contemporary German work)
Frechen: Keramion, Galerie für zeitgenössische Kunst
  (An exciting architectural concept not to be missed)
Hamburg: Museum für Kunst und Gewerbe
Hanover: Kestnermuseum
Köln: Kunstgewerbemuseum der Stadt Köln
Mannheim: Reissmuseum

Holland

Amsterdam: Rijksmuseum
Rotterdam: Museums Boymans-van Beuningen

Italy

Faenza: Museo Internazionale della Ceramica
Naples: Museo e Gallerie Nazionali di Capodimonte
Turin: Museo Civico

Norway

Trondheim: Nordenfjeldske Kunstindustrimuseum

Sweden

Lidköping: Rörstrand Museum
Stockholm: Asiatic Museum

USA

Boston: Museum of Fine Arts
  (Oriental collections)
Chicago: The Chicago Art Institute
  (Chinese and Japanese work)
Cleveland: Cleveland Museum of Art
  (Oriental collection)
Denver: Denver Art Museum
  (Oriental work)
Los Angeles: Los Angeles County Art Museum
New Jersey: The Newark Museum
New York: Brooklyn Museum
  The Metropolitan Museum of Art
  Museum of Contemporary Crafts
  (Changing exhibitions of contemporary work)
Missouri: St Louis Museum
  (Exceptional Chinese ceramics)
San Francisco: De Young Museum
  (Home of the Avery Brundage collection of Oriental Art)
  San Francisco Art Museum
  (Modern American work from the 19th century to the present day)
Seattle: Seattle Art Museum
  (Oriental collections)
Washington DC: Freer Gallery of Art
  (Oriental work)

Some of the many galleries which have fine studio porcelain for sale:

UK

Cambridge: Primavera, 10 King's Parade, Cambridge
Brighton: Barclaycraft Gallery, 7 East Street, Brighton
Derbyshire: Yew Tree Gallery, Ellastone, Nr Ashbourne
London: Atmosphere, 148 Regents Park Road, NW1
   Casson Gallery, 73 Marylebone High Street, W1
   Craftsmen Potters' Shop, Marshall Street, W1
   Craftwork Gallery, 17 Newburgh Street, W1
   Craftwork Gallery, The Market, Covent Garden, WC2
   Innate Harmony, 67 St John's Wood High Street, NW8
   British Crafts Centre, 43 Earlham Street, WC2
Edinburgh: Scottish Crafts Centre, Acheson House, Canongate
Liverpool: Bluecoat Display Centre, School Lane, Liverpool 1
Norwich: Black Horse Craft Centre, 10b Wensum Street
Nottingham: Focus Gallery, 108 Derby Road
Oxfordshire: Exhibit A Gallery, 29 High Street, Wallingford
   Oxford Gallery, 23 High Street, Oxford
Suffolk: Aldringham Crafts, Nr Leiston, Suffolk
Surrey: Art and Ceramic Gallery, 68 Hill Rise, Richmond Hill,
   Richmond
Warwickshire: Peter Dingley, 16 Meer Street, Stratford-upon-Avon

Germany

Darmstadt: Galerie Charlotte Hennig, Rheinstrasse 18, 61
   Darmstadt
Heidelberg: Somers Galerie, Ladenburger Strasse 21, 6900
   Heidelberg 1
Mönchengladbach: Dr Paul Köster Kunstkammer, Albertusstrasse
   4, 4050 Mönchengladbach 1

USA

Illinois: Exhibit A, 233 E. Ontario Street, Chicago, Illinois
New York: The Porcelain Crafts Studio, 74 Fifth Avenue, New York
San Francisco: The Quay Gallery, 254 Sutter Street, San Francisco
   94 108

Canada

The Quest Gallery, 502 8th Avenue SW, Calgary, Alberta

Australia

Blackfriars Gallery, 172 St. Johns Road, Glebe, Sydney, NSW 2037

SUPPLIERS OF CERAMIC MATERIALS

Many suppliers produce comprehensive, well-illustrated catalogues full of detailed, practical information on the use of ceramic materials.

UK Suppliers

British Nuclear Fuels, Risley, Warrington, Lancs. Tel: 0925 35933 *(For depleted uranium U_3O_8)*

Deancraft Ceramic Supplies, 15/21 Westmill Street, Hanley, Stoke-on-Trent, ST1 3EN. Tel: 0782 267226

EEC International Ltd., John Keay House, St Austell, Cornwall, PL25 4DJ. Tel: 0726 4882

Ferro (GB) Ltd., Womborne, Wolverhampton, Staffs. Tel: 09077 4144

The Fulham Pottery Ltd., 210 New King's Road, London, SW6 4NY. Tel: 01 736 1188

Harrison-Mayer Ltd., Meir, Stoke-on-Trent, Staffs, ST3 7PX. Tel: 0782 31633

Podmore Ceramics Ltd., 105 Minet Road, London, SW9 7UH. Tel: 01 737 3636

Podmore & Son Ltd., Shelton, Stoke-on-Trent, Staffs, ST1 4PO. Tel: 0782 24571

Potclays Ltd., Brickkiln Lane, Etruria, Stoke-on-Trent, Staffs, ST4 7BP. Tel: 0782 29816

Watts Blake Bearne and Co Ltd., Park House, Newton Abbot, Devon, TQ12 4PS. Tel: 0626 2345

Wengers Ltd., Etruria, Stoke-on-Trent, Staffs, ST4 7BQ. Tel: 0782 25126

European Suppliers

Aquitex, Rua Sa Da Bandeira 806–2°, Porto, Portugal

British & Continental China Clay Co SA, Rue Blanche 15 (bte 12), B–1050 Brussels, Belgium

Carl Jäger KG, 541 Höhr-Grenzhausen, West Germany

Chematex AB, Koksgaten 18, Box 27049, 200 13 Malmo, Sweden

Comercial Quimica Masso SA, Villadomat 321, 5°, Barcelona, Spain

English Clays (Italy) SpA, Via GB Sammartini 5, 20125 Milano, Italy

Chr. Fahrner A/S, 6 Frederiksberg Alle, DKO 1820, Copenhagen V, Denmark

W B B de France SA, La Gare, Tournon St Pierre, 37290 Preuilly-sur-Claise, France

Fuchs'sche Tongruben KG, Postfach 30, 5412 Ransbach-Baumbach 1, West Germany

H D Pochin et Cie, 22 bis Rue de Paradis, 75010 Paris, France

Podmore Generale SpA, Via Giardini 452, Direzionale 70, Modena, Italy

Podmore, Nederland, Honore Lambostraat 4, Bussum, Holland

N.V Podmore SA, Rue Vanderkinderestraat 540, 1180 Brussels, Belgium

Quiminsa, Villadomat 319,5°,4ᵃ, Barcelona, Spain

K P C L Sapec, Limoges, France

R S Stokvis & Zonen N V, Postbus 426, Rotterdam, Holland

Tropag, Oscar H Ritter (Nachflg) KG, 2 Hamburg 1, Ballindamm 6, West Germany

US Suppliers

American Art Clay Co (AMACO), 4717 W. 16th Street, Indianapolis, IND 46222

Barrett Co Ltd., 1155 Dorchester Blvd., W Montreal 2, Quebec, Canada

Capital Ceramics Inc., 2174 S. Main Street, Salt Lake City, UT 84115

Carborundum Co (Fiberfrax), Box 337, Niagara Falls, NY 14302

Cedar Heights Clay Co, 50 Portsmouth Road, Oak Hill, OH 45656

Clay Crafts Supply, 1004 Taylor Street, Saskatoon, Sas., Canada

Edgar Plastic Kaolin Co., Edgar, Putnam Co., FLA 32049

Ferro Corporation, Frit Division, 4150 East 56th Street, Cleveland, Ohio 44150

Georgia Kaolin Co., 433 N. Broad Street, Elizabeth, NJ 07207

Harrison Bell (associate company of Harrison-Mayer Ltd), 3605A Kennedy Road, South Plainfield, New Jersey

HIRO Distributors, 518 Beatty Street, Vancouver, B.C., Canada

O Hommel Co., P O Box 475, Pittsburgh, PA 15230

House of Ceramics, 1011 North Hollywood, Memphis, TN 38108

Leslie Ceramics Supply Co., 1212 San Pablo Ave., Berkley, CA 94706

Ohio Ceramic Supply Inc., Box 630, Kent, OH 44249

Pemco Division, Glidden Company, 5601 Eastern Avenue, Baltimore, MD 21224

Pottery Supply House, P O Box 192, Oakville, Ontario, Canada

Rovin Ceramics, 6912 Shaefer, Dearborn, MICH 48126

Standard Ceramic Supply Co. Box 4435, Pittsburgh, PA 15205

Van Howe Ceramic Supply Co., 11975 E. 40 Ave., Denver, Co 80239 or 4860 Pan American Freeway N.E., Albuquerque, NM 87107

Western Ceramic Supply, 1601 Howard Street, San Francisco, CA 94103

NOTES

1 Bernard Leach in *A Potter's Book* (Faber and Faber, 1945)
2 William Morris in *Arts and Crafts Essays* (Longman Green, 1899). Taken from *The Arts and Crafts Movement* by Gillian Naylor (Studio Vista, 1971)
3 Bernard Leach in *The Potter's Challenge* (Souvenir Press, 1976)
4 Margaret Medley in *The Chinese Potter* (Phaidon, 1976)
5 Nigel Wood from an article in *Pottery Quarterly*, Vol 12, No. 47
6 Père d'Entrecolles as quoted by Walter Staehelin in *The Book of Porcelain* (Lund Humphries, 1966)
7 George Savage in *Porcelain through the Ages* (Penguin Books, 1954)
8 G. St. G. M. Gompertz in *Celadon Wares* (Faber and Faber, 1968)
9 W.B. Honey in *The Art of the Potter* (Faber and Faber, 1946)
10 Arthur Lane in *Style in Pottery* (Faber and Faber, 1948)
11 Bernard Leach in *A Potter's Book* (Faber and Faber, 1945)
12 Malcolm Haslam in *English Art Pottery in England 1865–1915* (Antique Collectors Club, 1975)
13 From an exhibition catalogue *Art Among the Insulators. The Bullers Studio 1935–52* (Gladstone Pottery Museum, 1977)
14 John Mallet in the catalogue to the exhibition *Glenys Barton at Wedgwood* (Crafts Council, 1977)
15 *Ceramic Review* No 32, March 1975
16 Bernard Leach in *A Potter's Book* (Faber and Faber, 1945)
17 Mary Rogers in *Ceramic Review* No. 9, May 1971
18 Elaine Levin in *Ceramic Review* No 49, January 1978
19 Ray Silverman from his workshop information leaflet
20 Peter Simpson from his notes to an exhibition at Cardiff in 1978 entitled 'Options'
21 Paul Astbury from his notes to an exhibition at Cardiff in 1978 entitled 'Options'
22 Glenys Barton in *Ceramic Review* No 34, July 1975
23 Jeannie Lowe in *Ceramic Review* No. 33, May 1975
24 Translated from the German text of Dr Paul Köster for the catalogue to an exhibition of the Gebhardts' work in his gallery in May 1979
25 Daniel Rhodes in *Stoneware and Porcelain* (Chilton, Philadelphia, 1959; Pitman, London 1960)
26 Richard Parkinson in *Ceramic Review* No 3, June 1970
27 Body recipes from *CPA Newsletter* No 9
28 Body recipe from *Ceramics Monthly* Vol 20, No 6, June 1972
29 Body recipes from *Ceramic Review* No 5, October 1970
30 Frank Hamer in *The Pottter's Dictionary of Materials and Techniques* (Pitman, London, 1975; Watson-Guptill, New York, 1975)
31 Audrey Blackman in *Rolled Pottery Figures* (Pitman, London, 1978; Watson-Guptill, New York, 1978)
32 *Podmores' Catalogue* 1979
33 Alan Barratt-Danes in *Ceramic Review* No 36, November 1975
34 Frank Hamer in *The Potter's Dictionary of Materials and Techniques* (Pitman, London, 1975; Watson-Guptill, New York, 1975)
35 Nigel Wood in *Oriental Glazes* (Pitman, London, 1978; Watson-Guptill, New York, 1978)
36 Père d'Entrecolles as quoted by Joseph Grebanier in *Chinese Stoneware Glazes* (Watson-Guptill, New York, 1975; Pitman, London, 1975)
37 Robin Hopper in *Ceramic Review* Nos 37 and 38, 1976
38 Emmanuel Cooper in *Glazes for the Studio Potter* (Batsford, London, 1979)
39 Glaze recipes from *The Ceramic Review Book of Glaze Recipes*
40 Glaze recipes from *Pottery Quarterly*, No 47
41 Glaze recipes from *Ceramic Review*, No 55, 1979
42 Glaze recipes from the monograph *David Leach* edited by Robert Fournier (Fournier Pottery, Lacock, 1977)
43 Paul Bennett in *Ceramic Review* No 48, 1977
44 Edward Lucie-Smith in *Ceramic Review* No 44, March 1977
45 Glenys Barton in *Crafts* magazine, No 33, August 1978
46 Bernard Leach in *A Potter's Book* (Faber and Faber, 1945)
47 Jon Catleugh in *Ceramic Review* No 31, 1975
48 Garth Clark in *Ceramic Review* No 32, 1975
49 Helen Wilks in *Crafts* magazine, No 33, August 1978
50 Lord Eccles in *Crafts* magazine, No 3, August 1973

BIBLIOGRAPHY

Billington, Dora, *The Technique of Pottery* (Batsford, London, 1966)

Birks, Tony, *The Art of the Modern Potter* (Country Life, London, 1970)

Blackman, Audrey, *Rolled Pottery Figures* (Pitman, London, 1978; Watson-Guptill, New York, 1978)

Boulay, Anthony du, *Chinese Porcelain* (Octopus, London, 1973)

Cameron, Elizabeth and Lewis Phillips, *Potters on Pottery* (Evans, London, 1976)

Cardew, Michael, *Pioneer Pottery* (Longman, Harlow, Essex. 1969; St Martin's Press, New York, 1971)

Casson, Michael, *The Craft of the Potter* (BBC Publications, London, 1977)

Ceramic Review Book of Glaze Recipes (Craftsmen Potters' Association of Great Britain)

Chandler, Maurice, *Ceramics in the Modern World* (Aldus Books, London, 1967)

Charleston, R.J. (Ed.), *World Ceramics* (Hamlyn, London, 1968)

Colson, Frank A., *Kiln Building with Space-Age Materials* (Van Nostrand, London & New York, 1975)

Cooper, Emmanuel and Royle, Derek, *Glazes for the Studio Potter* (Batsford, London, 1979)

Cowley, David, *Moulded and Slip-Cast Pottery and Ceramics* (Batsford, London, 1978)

Cushion, John, *Porcelain* (Orbis, London, 1975)

Dickerson, John, *Pottery Making: A Complete Guide* (Viking, New York, 1974)

Fisher, Stanley, *English Ceramics* (Ward Lock, London, 1966)

Fournier, Robert, *Illustrated Dictionary of Practical Pottery* (Van Nostrand, London & New York, 1973)

David Leach: A Potters Life with Workshop Notes (Fournier Pottery, Lacock, 1977)

Fraser, Harry, *Glazes for the Craft Potter* (Pitman, London, 1973; Watson-Guptill, New York, 1974)

French, Neal, *Industrial Ceramics: Tableware* (Oxford University Press, 1972)

Godden, Geoffrey A., *British Porcelain* (Barrie and Jenkins, London, 1974)

Gompertz G. St G. M., *Chinese Celadon Wares* (Faber and Faber, London, 1968)

Korean Pottery and Porcelain of the Yi Period (Faber and Faber, London, 1968)

Grebanier, Joseph, *Chinese Stoneware Glazes* (Pitman, London, 1975; Watson-Guptill, New York, 1975)

Green, David, *Understanding Pottery Glazes* (Faber and Faber, London, 1963)

A Handbook of Pottery Glazes (Faber and Faber, London, 1978)

Griffin, F., *Pottery and Porcelain* (Frederick Muller, London, 1967)

Hamer, Frank, *The Potter's Dictionary of Materials and Techniques* (Pitman, London, 1975; Watson-Guptill, New York, 1975)

Hamilton, David, *Manual of Pottery and Ceramics* (Thames and Hudson, London, 1974)

Haslam, Malcolm, *English Art Pottery 1865–1915* (Antique Collectors Club, London, 1975)

Honey, William B., *The Art of the Potter* (Faber and Faber, London, 1946)

Hughes, B. and T., *English Porcelain and Bone China* (Lutterworth Press, London, 1968)

Lane, Arthur, *Style in Pottery* (Faber and Faber, London, 1973)

Leach, Bernard, *A Potter's Book* (Faber and Faber, London, 1945; Transatlantic Arts, New York, 1973)

A Potter's Work (Adams and Dart, Bradford-on-Avon, Wiltshire, 1967)

Beyond East and West (Faber and Faber, London, 1978)

Medley, Margaret, *The Chinese Potter* (Phaidon, Oxford, 1976; Scribners, New York, 1976)

Neave-Hill, W.B.R., *Chinese Ceramics* (John Bartholomew, Edinburgh & London, 1975)

Nelson, Glenn C., *Ceramics* (Holt, Rinehart & Winston, New York, 1966)

Parmalee, Cullen W., *Ceramic Glazes* (Industrial Publications, Chicago, 1951)

Rhodes, Daniel, *Clay and Glazes for the Potter* (Chilton, Philadelphia, 1973; Pitman, London, 1973)

Stoneware and Porcelain (Chilton, Philadelphia, 1960; Pitman, London, 1960)

Kilns: Design, Construction and Operation (Chilton, Philadelphia, 1969; Pitman, London, 1969)

Pottery Form (Chilton, Philadelphia, 1977; Pitman, London, 1978)

Rose, Muriel, *Artist Potters in England* (Faber and Faber, London, 1970)

Rosenthal, Ernst, *Pottery and Ceramics* (Penguin, London, 1954)

Sandeman, Alison, *Working with Porcelain* (Pitman, London, 1979; Watson-Guptill, New York, 1979)

Sanders, Herbert, *The World of Japanese Ceramics* (Kodansha International, New York & Tokyo, 1978)

Savage, George, *Porcelain Through the Ages* (Penguin, London, 1954)

Shafer, Tom, *Pottery Decoration* (Watson-Guptill, New York, 1976; Pitman, London, 1976)

Staehelin, Walter A., *The Book of Porcelain* (Benteli Verlag, Berne, 1965; Lund Humphries, London, 1966)

Tait, Hugh, *Porcelain* (Hamlyn, London, 1962)

Wildenhain, Marguerite, *Pottery Form and Expression* (Van Nostrand Reinhold, New York, 1968)

Wood, Nigel, *Oriental Glazes* (Pitman, London, 1978; Watson-Guptill, New York, 1978)

Periodicals

Ceramic Review, London (Published by the Craftsman Potters' Association of Great Britain)

Ceramics Monthly, Ohio, USA

American Craft (formerly) *Craft Horizons* (Published by the American Crafts Council, New York)

Crafts (Published by the Crafts Council, London)

Pottery Quarterly (Published by Murray Fieldhouse, Northfields, Tring, Herts, England)

INDEX

Page numbers in *italics* refer to the illustrations